# SAVIOUR SIBLINGS AND THE REGULATION OF ASSISTED REPRODUCTIVE TECHNOLOGY

W0081296

# Saviour Siblings and the Regulation of Assisted Reproductive Technology

## Harm, Ethics and Law

MALCOLM K. SMITH
*Australian Centre for Health Law Research,*
*Queensland University of Technology, Australia*

**Routledge**
Taylor & Francis Group

LONDON AND NEW YORK

First published 2015 by Ashgate Publishing

2 Park Square, Milton Park, Abingdon, Oxfordshire OX14 4RN
711 Third Avenue, New York, NY 10017

*Routledge is an imprint of the Taylor & Francis Group, an informa business*

First issued in paperback 2018

Copyright © 2015 Malcolm K. Smith

Malcolm K. Smith has asserted his right under the Copyright, Designs and Patents Act, 1988, to be identified as the author of this work.

All rights reserved. No part of this book may be reprinted or reproduced or utilised in any form or by any electronic, mechanical, or other means, now known or hereafter invented, including photocopying and recording, or in any information storage or retrieval system, without permission in writing from the publishers.

Notice:
Product or corporate names may be trademarks or registered trademarks, and are used only for identification and explanation without intent to infringe.

**British Library Cataloguing in Publication Data**
A catalogue record for this book is available from the British Library.

**The Library of Congress has cataloged the printed edition as follows:**
Smith, Malcolm K., author.
  Saviour siblings and the regulation of assisted reproductive technology : harm, ethics and law / by Malcolm K. Smith.
      pages cm
  Includes bibliographical references and index.
  ISBN 978-1-4094-6096-1 (hardback) 1. Savior siblings--Legal status, laws, etc.--Great Britain. 2. Savior siblings--Legal status, laws, etc.--Australia. 3. Procurement of organs, tissues, etc. --Law and legislation--Great Britain. 4. Procurement of organs, tissues, etc.--Law and legislation --Australia. 5. Fertilization in vitro, Human--Law and legislation--Great Britain. 6. Fertilization in vitro, Human--Law and legislation--Australia. 7. Medical ethics. I. Title.
  K3611.A77S65 2015
  344.4104'19--dc23

                                                                            2015004754

ISBN 978-1-4094-6096-1 (hbk)
ISBN 978-1-138-37988-6 (pbk)

# Contents

# List of Abbreviations

| | |
|---|---|
| ACT | Australian Capital Territory |
| AHEC | Australian Health Ethics Committee |
| ART | Assisted reproductive technology |
| Cth | Commonwealth of Australia |
| EUTCD | European Union Tissues and Cells Directive |
| FSA | Fertility Society of Australia |
| HFEA | Human Fertilisation and Embryology Authority |
| HLA | Human leukocyte antigen |
| HSCT | Hematopoietic stem cell transplantation |
| HTA | Human Tissue Authority |
| ITA | Infertility Treatment Authority |
| IVF | In vitro fertilisation |
| NBCC | National Bioethics Consultative Committee |
| NHMRC | National Health and Medical Research Council |
| NSW | New South Wales |
| NT | Northern Territory |
| PGD | Pre-implantation genetic diagnosis |
| Qld | Queensland |
| RATE | Regulatory Authority for Tissue and Embryos |
| RTC | Reproductive Technology Council |
| RTAC | Reproductive Technology Accreditation Committee |
| SA | South Australia |
| SACRT | South Australian Council on Reproductive Technology |
| Tas | Tasmania |
| UK | United Kingdom |
| USA | United States of America |
| VARTA | Victorian Assisted Reproductive Treatment Authority |
| Vic | Victoria |
| VLRC | Victorian Law Reform Commission |
| WA | Western Australia |

# Preface

My interest in the topic of this book was sparked by an assignment that was set in 2004 as part of my Master of Laws course in health law. At that time, the debate in the United Kingdom (UK) concerning the creation of so-called 'saviour siblings' was very much in the public sphere, as the issue was covered in the media; the impact of regulatory policy on this topic was publicly conveyed through the personal stories of a number of families who shared their experiences publicly. These families were struggling in their attempts to access assisted reproductive technology (ART) services, so that they could purposely conceive children as tissue donors for the benefit of their sick children. Barriers were imposed on access by the UK's ART regulatory body – the Human Fertilisation and Embryology Authority (HFEA). Under this policy, some families were denied access to the technology, while others were not. The thought that the ethical and moral views of other people – who had no direct involvement with the issues facing these families – were being relied upon to justify the imposition of restrictive policies, encouraged me to research this topic further. At that time, it was not clear to me why illogical distinctions were being drawn between families who were seeking to pursue the same end – which might ultimately result in them saving the lives of their children. Although I now have a deep understanding of the reasoning that underpinned this distinction, I am perhaps no closer to accepting it as a valid justification for denying one family's request, but not the other's. It might be said that this concern is now merely a hypothetical one, as the UK regulator reversed its restrictive approach on this issue. However, as I discuss in this book, this distinction is still drawn in some Australian states, albeit indirectly. Furthermore, the regulation of this issue has progressed in a precautious way, despite the fact that there is no evidence to suggest that those children who have been conceived as 'saviours' are harmed.

In researching and writing this book, I have had the opportunity to reflect upon why it is that certain ethical and moral objections seem to be more compelling than others, at least from a regulatory point of view. As is clear from the focus that I adopt for analysing the issue of conceiving saviour children, this has led me to conclude that some of the wider ethical and moral concerns might not always be relevant to determining whether or not a particular type of conduct can be justifiably restricted by the state. Nevertheless, these ethical principles and theories are valuable as they help us to reflect upon how our actions might, and do, affect others and whether we are acting ethically.

Naturally, not everyone will agree with all of my views and the arguments that I pursue here.

I am indebted to Lindy Willmott and Ben White for helping me to raise the standard and quality of my scholarship in this area. They have challenged me to develop the reasoning and arguments that are set out in the chapters that follow and they have provided an exceptional level of support. I am also very grateful to others who have helped me to develop and strengthen the arguments that I have set out in this book, particularly Christine Knight, who encouraged me to spend time at the Economic and Social Research Council's Genomics Forum in 2011, at the University of Edinburgh. During this time, I developed my arguments concerning the statutory reforms enacted in the UK in 2008, which as discussed in the book, impact heavily on the accessibility of ART services for those wishing to conceive a saviour child. Thank you also to those at the Faculty of Law at the Queensland University of Technology, who have provided support over the years, particularly members of the Australian Centre for Health Law Research. I am lucky to be part of such a supportive and collegial group of academics. I am especially grateful to Louise Scahill for her work in editing the manuscript. Lastly, I would like to thank my friends and family for their support and for encouraging me to finish this book.

Malcolm Smith
Brisbane

# Chapter 1

# Conceiving Saviour Children: Technological Advances, Ethical Concern and Legitimate Regulatory Oversight?

## Introduction

Advances in the field of assisted reproductive technology (ART) have been revolutionary. The developments in these technologies have inevitably impacted on the nature of reproduction in modern society. Although such techniques were first developed to overcome infertility, they have more recently adopted a new focus, encompassing much wider potential.[1] These developments have occurred alongside advances in genetics and the mapping of the human genome. Reproductive techniques have progressed from their initial focus of alleviating the symptoms of infertility, towards a new direction of genetic determination and selection, and even potentially towards genetic enhancement.[2] These changes have resulted in regulatory oversight and have raised significant social and ethical concern.

Scientists can now screen human embryos to determine the genetics of an embryo before it is implanted during an in vitro fertilisation (IVF) cycle. This potentially enables prospective parents to select certain genetic characteristics or traits in their future children. Some families have used this technology to purposely conceive children as tissue donors for sick relatives (usually siblings of the donor). Such children have been referred to as 'saviour siblings' in the bioethical literature. However, I adopt the term 'saviour children' based on the view that the intended recipient of tissue does not necessarily have to be limited to a sibling. In this book I focus on the legal and regulatory frameworks that impact on the accessibility of this technology in Australia and the United

---

1  Ruth Deech and Anna Smajdor, *From IVF to Immortality: Controversy in the Era of Reproductive Technology* (OUP 2007) 1–6.

2  Colin Gavaghan, *Defending the Genetic Supermarket: The Law and Ethics of Selecting the Next Generation* (Routledge-Cavendish 2007) 217–22.

Kingdom (UK) and analyse the ethical and moral issues that arise from the use of the technology for this specific purpose.

My analysis of the regulatory framework on this topic focuses on whether the state has a legitimate role to play in regulating the use of ART techniques for the creation of saviour children. Despite the potential benefits that might flow from allowing parents to conceive saviour children, there are a number of concerns outlined in the bioethical literature. Most frequently, these concerns centre on whether children who are purposely conceived as tissue donors might be negatively affected by the fate that is pre-determined for them by their parents. Questions arise as to whether such children might suffer psychological harm as a result of the circumstances surrounding their conception or whether the use of ART services for this purpose is unethical or contrary to public morality. I examine these concerns in terms of their relevance to the regulatory position and consider whether there is any justification for interfering with a family's decision in such circumstances. My analysis in this regard is underpinned by liberal reasoning.

## Embryo Selection Techniques and the Selection of Saviours

Pre-implantation genetic diagnosis (PGD) was introduced in 1990 as an experimental procedure so that it was possible to determine – from a number of embryos created in an IVF cycle – which contain the genetic identifiers for certain hereditary conditions or disorders.[3] This allows ART service providers to identify 'unaffected' embryos, so that the transmission of a genetic condition or disease to a child is avoided. The process is undertaken as a step during IVF treatment, once the embryos are created. When the cells of the embryo begin to divide, one or two cells can be removed for genetic analysis.

When PGD was first developed its application was limited and there were problems with misdiagnosis. Initially, the technology could only be used to test for and prevent transmission of certain Mendelian diseases, such as cystic fibrosis and X-linked disorders.[4] By the late 1990s the technology advanced further.[5] In addition to screening embryos for specific genetic conditions, PGD techniques can also be used to positively select in favour of certain genetic characteristics.

As mentioned above, embryo selection technologies have been used in a number of cases for the purpose of selecting and implanting embryos on

---

3 Yury Verlinsky and others, 'Over a Decade of Experience With Preimplantation Genetic Diagnosis: a Multicenter Report' 82 Fertility and Sterility 292, 292.

  4 ibid.

  5 ibid.

the basis of their tissue type with the aim of conceiving a tissue donor for a sick child. One of the reasons that families have opted to use this technology is that the success rate of a tissue transplantation procedure (referred to as hematopoietic stem cell transplantation (HSCT) procedures) is improved when the donor and recipient are siblings and of a matching tissue type.[6] The tissue type of an individual is referred to as the human leukocyte antigen (HLA) type and is inherited from the genetics of both parents. As HLA type is inherited in this way, it is extremely unlikely that a parent or other relative will be an exact match to a child. Anasetti notes that each HLA mismatch (in basic terms, that is, each step away from an HLA identical donor) decreases the chance of disease-free survival for the recipient by 10 per cent.[7] Therefore, without an identical HLA matched sibling donor, the chances of the transplant succeeding are diminished.

In 2000, Adam Nash was the first child in the world to be purposely conceived as a saviour with IVF and PGD.[8] The Nash family gained access to the technology in a Chicago clinic in the United States of America (USA). The family intended to use the umbilical cord blood stem cells from the saviour, to treat their child Molly, who was born with Fanconi's anaemia. This condition is a recessive disorder, meaning that it is transmitted when inherited from the relevant genes of both parents. The use of PGD in this case had two purposes: the first was to ensure that any child the couple conceived was born free from the genetic condition that Molly was born with, and the second was to ensure that the new child was of a matching tissue type to Molly.[9]

The technology has also been used in the UK. In 2001, the Hashmi family sought access to ART services to create a saviour child as a potential cure for their child Zain, who was born with the condition beta thalassaemia. This blood disorder impacts on the body's ability to produce haemoglobin and red blood cells. It is genetically transmitted and 'causes such severe physical symptoms that, without life-long medical care, life expectancy would be only a few years'.[10] As a result, Zain required regular blood transfusions and repeated drug infusions.[11] It was hoped that the blood stem cells from the umbilical cord of

---

6 Claudio Anasseti, 'What are the Most Important Donor and Recipient Factors Affecting the Outcome of Related and Unrelated Allogeneic Transplantation?' 21 Best Practice & Research Clinical Haematology 691, 694–5.

7 ibid. 695.

8 Robert Boyle and Julian Savulescu, 'Ethics of Using Preimplantation Genetic Diagnosis to Select a Stem Cell Donor for an Existing Person' 32 British Medical Journal 1240.

9 ibid. 1240.

10 Deech and Smajdor (n 1) 65.

11 ibid. 65–6.

a tissue-matched sibling could be used to cure Zain. As with the Nash family, the Hashmi family were motivated by the same two factors – to conceive a child who would be free from beta thalassaemia and to ensure that he or she would be a matching tissue donor to their child.[12] The ART centre in this case was required to gain permission from the UK regulatory body for authorisation to provide the requested services.[13] The Human Fertilisation and Embryology Authority (HFEA) granted approval, commenting:

> We have considered the ethical, medical and technical implications of this treatment very carefully indeed. Where PGD is already being undertaken we can see how the use of tissue typing to save the life of a sibling could be justified. We would see this happening only in very rare circumstances and under strict controls.[14]

The HFEA was subsequently faced with a further request to approve pre-implantation tissue-typing services in relation to the Whitaker family, who sought to conceive a tissue-matched child for their son, Charlie, who was suffering from the condition Diamond Blackfan anaemia. The condition is rare and results in a deficit of red blood cells.[15] The symptoms are similar to other forms of anaemia,[16] and treatment requires the performance of repeated transfusion procedures.[17] The best chance of curing the condition is to perform a bone marrow transplant from a matched donor.[18]

The circumstances of the Whitakers were different to those of the Nash and Hashmi families as the condition affecting Charlie was not genetic. Diamond Blackfan anaemia is sporadic and onsets after birth. The chances of the Whitakers having another child with the same condition were no greater than the risk to the general population: 'five to seven per million live births'.[19] The use of PGD services was therefore intended only for the purpose of identifying and implanting an embryo of a matching tissue type to Charlie. This was one of

---

12 Sally Sheldon and Stephen Wilkinson, 'Hashmi and Whitaker: An Unjustifiable and Misguided Distinction?' 12 Medical Law Review 137, 138.

13 ibid.

14 Human Fertilisation and Embryology Authority, *HFEA to Allow Tissue Typing in Conjunction with Preimplantation Genetic Diagnosis* (2001) <http://www.hfea.gov.uk/961.html> accessed 10 August 2014.

15 Deech and Smajdor (n 1) 71.

16 Sheldon and Wilkinson (n 12) 140.

17 Deech and Smajdor (n 1) 71.

18 Sheldon and Wilkinson (n 12) 140.

19 ibid.

the key reasons why the HFEA refused the ART centre permission to provide the requested services to the Whitaker family.[20]

The HFEA was heavily criticised for its initial policy on this issue.[21] As discussed throughout this book, the HFEA put forward a number of justifications to support the distinctions that were drawn in relation to its tissue-typing policy. Notably, the HFEA subsequently changed its policy to allow access to the technology in cases where it is required solely to establish tissue type.[22] This restriction is therefore no longer imposed under the UK regulatory framework. However, as discussed in Chapters 2 and 3, access to the technology is restricted in such a way in some Australian jurisdictions, as ART services can only be provided to those who are infertile or at risk of transmitting a genetic condition when conceiving naturally. Therefore, the criticisms levelled at the HFEA's reasoning on this topic are of relevance to the Australian approach on this issue.

## Ethical and Moral Concerns

The use of PGD in this context demonstrates the shift in purpose of genetic testing, which has moved from disease prevention, towards positive selection of embryos on the basis of desired genetic characteristics.[23] The use of ART services for the creation of saviour children raises a number of concerns focused on the possibility that the saviour may be harmed by the circumstances surrounding his or her conception. For example, will the child suffer psychological harm by discovering that he or she was 'selected' for his or her potential to cure a relative? Will the child suffer harm by being born into a family setting with an existing health crisis, particularly if he or she is subjected to tissue harvesting procedures that are intended to benefit someone else? Does the creation of saviour children pose a threat of harm to society based on the view that children might be perceived as mere objects, who exist simply to serve the interests of their parents or sick

---

20 Human Fertilisation and Embryology Authority, *HFEA Confirms That HLA Tissue Typing May Only Take Place When PGD is Required to Avoid a Serious Genetic Disorder* (2002) <http://www.hfea.gov.uk/935.html> accessed 10 August 2014. This press release stated that '[o]ne of the criteria is that the embryos conceived in the course of this treatment should themselves be at risk from the condition by which the existing child is affected'.

21 Sheldon and Wilkinson (n 12); Gavaghan (n 2); House of Commons Science and Technology Committee, *Human Reproductive Technologies and the Law* (2005).

22 Human Fertilisation and Embryology Authority, *HFEA Agrees to Extend Policy on Tissue Typing* (2004) <http://www.hfea.gov.uk/763.html> accessed 10 August 2014.

23 For an excellent analysis of the ethical issues relating to the wider context of embryo selection technologies, see Gavaghan (n 2).

relatives? And does the use of the technology for this purpose signify a step on a slippery slope that will eventually result in acceptance of these techniques for the selection of 'less desirable' genetic characteristics? These are some of the questions that I address in this book.

Importantly, many of the ethical arguments in this context have competing views. For example, in the context of IVF and PGD more generally, the question arises as to whether it is acceptable to create multiple embryos – which to some members of society are viewed as tantamount to human life – so that some of the embryos can be discarded once the prospective parents establish that they are not 'suitable' for implantation.[24] As summarised by Gavaghan, for some members of society these issues are viewed as 'inherently hubristic, sacrilegious or dehumanising of a technology that allows the present generation to choose their successors',[25] and that for others, 'the concerns are more concrete, deriving from concern that people will be harmed, devalued or treated unjustly'.[26] The use of the technology cuts across a wide range of perspectives including religious viewpoints, philosophical and ethical principles, and concerns based on harm to the child. These wider moral and ethical concerns are relevant to the debate and have heavily influenced debate on this topic. Such concerns have also arguably swayed the direction of regulatory policy.

## The Regulatory Approach

One of the difficulties of regulating in this field is the extent to which competing viewpoints and perspectives should be reflected in regulatory policy. Deech and Smajdor summarise:

> This is part of the perennial problem for the regulator. It seems inevitable that for any decision, a vocal cohort of dissenters will emerge, while those who might have agreed, or are indifferent, may remain silent. This means that media attention and public perceptions are nearly always polarized in a way which makes dialogue fraught.[27]

Whilst the competing views may prove a challenge for regulators and policy makers, according to Black, the regulatory process is central to considering such differing viewpoints:

---

24 See Human Genome Research Project, *Choosing Genes For Future Children: Regulating Preimplantation Genetic Diagnosis* (2006 Dunedin) 193.

25 Gavaghan (n 2) 2.

26 ibid.

27 Deech and Smajdor (n 1) 74.

> Regulation has an important role to play in connecting the arguments of participants, in facilitating the integration of the wide range of views as to the appropriate course that technology and its regulation should take.[28]

Regulation on the topic of conceiving saviour children incorporates a range of ethical perspectives from the bioethical literature. However, many of the ethical and moral debates in this field have arguably illegitimately influenced dialogue on this topic.[29] It is questionable whether the ethical and moral viewpoints provide us with a sufficient basis for justifying a restrictive regulatory approach. This is because it is generally accepted that people should be at liberty to pursue their own life choices.[30] This way of thinking has been described as the dominant approach of legislatures in Western democratic society. Sheila McLean comments that:

> This approach owes much to the work of John Stuart Mill whose libertarian approach to the relationship between the state and the individual has underpinned the philosophy of many western democracies.[31]

This approach to decision-making holds that liberty can be restricted in cases where harm is likely to result to others.[32] There is a significant body of literature that addresses liberal theory and its relevance to regulation, particularly as a basis for state interference with individual decision-making. Central to this approach is the view that liberty can be restricted in cases where the conduct of individuals or a group of people, is likely to result in harm to others. In this book, I argue that this harm-based approach to justifying regulatory intervention is relevant in the context of ART, and most importantly, that it is currently adopted within ART regulatory policy by virtue of the need to prioritise the welfare of children who are conceived using ART services. I therefore analyse the current regulatory frameworks in place in Australia and the UK using a harm-based approach, and consider the relevance of the wider ethical and moral views to the regulatory approach concerning the creation of saviour children.

---

28 Julia Black, 'Regulation as Facilitation: Negotiating the Genetic Revolution' 61 Modern Law Review 621, 621.

29 Kimberly A Strong and others, 'It's Time to Reframe the Saviour Sibling Debate' 2 AJOB Primary Research 13.

30 Deech and Smajdor (n 1) 68.

31 Shelia McLean, *Modern Dilemmas: Choosing Children* (Capercaillie Books 2006) 9.

32 ibid. 9.

## Conclusion

ART techniques have advanced significantly since they were first developed and this has opened up the possibility of using embryo selection technologies to select in favour of desired genetic characteristics or other factors (such as HLA type). The use of these technologies for the creation of saviour children is not radically new; the first child conceived in this way was born in October 2000. However, regulatory policy on this specific topic requires review. ART regulation now generally adopts a more 'hands off' approach, leaving these techniques to be regulated by professional bodies (particularly in Australia). In this book, I argue that there is a need to move away from policies that are underpinned by wider ethical and moral arguments, and instead focus on whether there is justification for restricting reproductive decision-making based on evidence of harm to the child who may be born, or to others. I build these arguments as follows.

In Chapter 2 of this book, I outline the regulatory frameworks that determine the delivery of ART services in Australia and the UK. This overview of the regulatory position provides the key foundations for understanding how the more specific issue of creating saviour children is regulated, which is an issue examined in Chapter 3. I then consider the notion of liberty in Chapter 4 and determine how this principle is relevant to the provision of ART services, particularly in circumstances where a family wish to conceive a saviour child. This is where my argument in favour of reproductive liberty is crafted. In Chapter 5 I then consider the circumstances in which interference with reproductive liberty is justified, by reference to the Harm Principle. In Chapter 6 I apply this harm-focused approach to the issue of conceiving saviour children. The wider ethical and moral arguments are then explored in Chapter 7, to determine the relevance of these principles to the regulatory position. Lastly, in Chapter 8, I analyse the current regulatory landscape based on my normative analysis, and conclude by suggesting a way forward for regulation on this topic.

# Chapter 2
# The Regulatory Landscape Relevant to Assisted Reproductive Technology

## Introduction

In vitro fertilisation (IVF) and other assisted conception techniques can often prove burdensome and stressful for participants who attempt to conceive a child in this way. Due to the fact that such procedures are provided with the intention to create human life, they carry profound consequences for those involved, including the children who may be born following the provision of such techniques. It is therefore not surprising that assisted reproductive technology (ART) services are regulated in many jurisdictions. Regulation is often intended to protect the welfare of those who undergo treatment, the welfare of any children who may be conceived following the provision of such services, and to address the ethical concerns that arise from specific uses of the technology.

As outlined in Chapter 1, in circumstances where embryo selection technologies are utilised for the purpose of establishing the tissue type of the embryo so that a saviour child can be conceived, this is ethically problematic. It is therefore not surprising that this specific use of the technology is subject to regulatory control. However, before considering whether the ethical concerns are significant enough to warrant regulatory oversight, it is necessary to consider the regulatory landscape relevant to ART services more generally. This is important because the accessibility and utilisation of ART services for the specific purpose of creating a tissue-matched child is determined, to a large extent, by the general approach to ART regulation within a specific jurisdiction. This chapter therefore provides an outline of the regulatory frameworks relevant to the provision of ART services in Australia and the United Kingdom (UK). There are some key differences between the different jurisdictions and as discussed in Chapter 3, these differences impact on the accessibility and utilisation of embryo selection techniques for the purpose of selecting embryos on the basis of their tissue type.

One specific aspect of ART regulation that impacts on whether families are able to access ART services for the purpose of conceiving a saviour

child is the approach to determining who should be granted access to ART
services more generally. When a restrictive approach is adopted on the issue
of who should be able to access ART services, this indirectly impacts on the
accessibility of services for those seeking to create a saviour child. In other
circumstances, if there are no general restrictions that preclude access to ART
services for the purpose of selecting embryos on the basis of their tissue type,
it may be that in some circumstances, the regulatory approach concerning pre-
implantation genetic diagnosis (PGD) precludes families from accessing ART
services if the sole reason for seeking access is to determine the tissue type of
their embryos. A broad understanding of the applicable regulatory frameworks
is also important so that any proposals for changing the regulatory position
concerning pre-implantation tissue-typing can be considered within the context
of the existing regulatory frameworks currently in place in Australia and the
UK. The proposed changes to the current position are outlined in Chapter 8.


## The Australian Regulatory Landscape

The Australian regulatory regime is a complex mix of state legislation,
professional standards and ethical guidelines, and the regulatory approach can
vary significantly across jurisdictions. As Helen Szoke observes, 'Australia may
be described variously as a rich tapestry of diversity in terms of the regulatory
structure, or a patchwork of regulatory stitching lacking cohesion and order'.[1]
And as Belinda Bennett has noted, the 'regulatory framework for assisted
conception is complicated by Australia's federal legal structure'.[2] Although
there is no legislation at a federal level governing the provision of ART services,
Commonwealth legislation relating to human embryo research and cloning
impacts on the regulatory requirements for ART providers.[3] Consequently, all
ART providers in Australia must receive accreditation from the Reproductive

---

1 Helen Szoke, 'Australia – A Federated Structure of Statutory Regulation of
ART' in Jennifer Gunning and Helen Szoke (eds), *The Regulation of Assisted Reproductive
Technology* (Ashgate 2003) 75.

2 Belinda Bennett, 'Symbiotic Relationships: Saviour Siblings, Family Rights and
Biomedicine' 19 Australian Journal of Family Law 195.

3 Prohibition of Human Cloning Act 2002 (Cth); Research Involving Human
Embryos Act 2002 (Cth). Both Acts were reviewed by a Legislation Review Committee
in 2005 (Australian Government, *Legislation Review: Prohibition of Human Cloning Act
2002 and the Research Involving Human Embryos Act 2002* (Lockhart Review, 2005)) and
subsequently reformed: see Prohibition of Human Cloning for Reproduction and the
Regulation of Human Embryo Research Amendment Act 2006 (Cth). For an overview
of the issues arising from the review, see Donna Cooper, 'The Lockhart Review: Where
Now for Australia?' (2006) 14 Journal of Law and Medicine 27.

Technology Accreditation Committee (RTAC), a committee of the Fertility Society of Australia (FSA). The terms of the accreditation process require clinics to adhere to all relevant legislation and applicable guidelines,[4] and the RTAC Code of Practice[5] also requires clinics to adhere to the National Health and Medical Research Council (NHMRC) guidelines.[6] Specific ART statutes exist in New South Wales, South Australia, Victoria and Western Australia.[7] In these jurisdictions, legislation prevails over both the RTAC Code of Practice and the NHMRC guidelines,[8] although for the most part legislation on the topic is consistent with the guidelines. In those jurisdictions where no ART legislation exists, the system of professional and ethical guidelines is the only form of regulation in place.

The RTAC Code of Practice primarily addresses issues of clinical practice concerning ART services and imposes standards that apply to all ART providers. The Code was drafted so that it aligns with existing legislation and regulatory policies. However, due to the multi-layered regulatory approach that exists in Australia, there may be some slight variances between the provisions in the Code and other relevant regulation. If this is the case then federal legislation (such as that relating to embryo research, which is not considered in this context) overrides state legislation, and all legislation overrides regulatory guidelines (if both legislation and the guidelines address the same issue).[9] Where legislation does not address a particular aspect of ART services but the issue is addressed by the NHMRC guidelines, those aspects of the guidelines will continue to apply in the relevant statutory jurisdiction.

---

4 This is a requirement under the RTAC Code of Practice, which is discussed below.

5 Reproductive Technology Accreditation Committee, *Code of Practice for Assisted Reproductive Technology Units* (Fertility Society of Australia, revised May 2008).

6 National Health and Medical Research Council, *Ethical Guidelines on the Use of Assisted Reproductive Technology in Clinical Practice and Research* (2007).

7 Assisted Reproductive Technology Act 2007 (NSW); Assisted Reproductive Treatment Act 1988 (SA); Assisted Reproductive Treatment Act 2008 (Vic); Human Reproductive Technology Act 1991 (WA).

8 In Victoria for example, 'where the requirements of the Act are different to those of the RTAC *Code of Practice for Assisted Reproductive Technology Units* (2005), then the requirements of the Act take precedence and will be enforced' and similarly, 'where NHMRC Guidelines are inconsistent with the Victorian legislation, the Act takes precedence and over-rides the NHMRC Guidelines'. Infertility Treatment Authority, *Conditions for Licence: Clinics, Hospitals and Day Procedure Centres* (8th edn, Victoria Parliament 2008) 9.

9 Reproductive Technology Accreditation Committee, *Code of Practice for Assisted Reproductive Technology Units 2005* (Fertility Society of Australia, 4th revision, February 2005) 9.

At first glance, it may seem as though there is no direct mechanism for enforcing compliance with the national guidelines that impact on ART services, as infringement of the applicable guidelines is not a criminal offence (although it will normally lead to a loss of funds from the NHMRC for the purpose of research, or publication of infringement in Parliament).[10] However, the federal legislation overseeing human embryo research imposes criminal sanctions on ART service providers for providing any reproductive treatments involving human embryos without RTAC accreditation.[11] Therefore, the requirement that *all* clinics are accredited and adhere to the professional and NHMRC guidelines is indirectly enforced as a result of the federal legislation. For this reason it has been noted that together with the statutory frameworks, the NHMRC guidelines in conjunction with the RTAC accreditation process provide an example of a system of 'soft' regulation.[12]

Legislation has been passed in New South Wales, South Australia, Victoria and Western Australia, to deal specifically with the issues that arise from the provision of ART services. Each jurisdiction adopts a slightly different approach; the statutory frameworks are outlined below. First, however, the relevant ethical guidelines that apply at a national level are considered.

### The National Health and Medical Research Council Guidelines

The NHMRC guidelines play an important role in the Australian regulatory landscape as they have applicability in all states and territories, even where specific ART legislation is in place. The NHMRC guidelines aim to address a number of social and ethical concerns relating to ART practices and have been

---

10 ibid.

11 The FSA considers the meaning of s 11 of the Research Involving Human Embryos Act 2002 (Cth) to encompass the use of human embryos in *any* way without RTAC accreditation to amount to a criminal offence under federal law. See Fertility Society of Australia (n 5) 4. That section states that a person who 'intentionally uses, outside the body of a woman, a human embryo that is not an excess ART embryo; and the use is not for a purpose relating to the assisted reproductive technology treatment of a woman carried out by an accredited ART centre', commits an offence. Section 8 of the Research Involving Human Embryos Act 2002 (Cth) defines an 'accredited ART Centre' as a 'person or body accredited to carry out assisted reproductive technology by the Reproductive Technology Accreditation Committee of the Fertility Society of Australia'.

12 Kerry Petersen and Martin H. Johnson, 'SmARTest regulation? Comparing the regulatory structures for ART in the UK and Australia' 15 Reproductive BioMedicine Online 236.

described by some commentators as national standards of acceptable practice.[13]
The provisions address:

- the use and storage of gametes and embryos (including donated gametes and embryos);[14]
- the level of information that clinics must give to those seeking treatments;[15]
- the counselling and consent requirements for participants undergoing treatments;[16]
- the requirement for the keeping of records and data by clinics.[17]

The original guidelines, which were released in 1996, did not address a number of more controversial ART practices such as sex selection, PGD and surrogacy; these were considered to be beyond the remit of the Australian Health Ethics Committee (AHEC) – the major committee of the NHMRC responsible for developing the guidelines.[18] Consequently, the NHMRC issued a call to all states and territories to adopt a uniform and comprehensive framework of legislation to address the social and ethical issues arising from the more controversial aspects of ART.[19] Despite this, the large majority of Australian jurisdictions did not address those additional issues and when the NHMRC re-issued the guidelines in 2004, they specifically addressed issues such as sex selection, PGD and surrogacy. (The guidelines were again updated in 2007 to incorporate changes in federal legislation relating to human embryo research and cloning.) It has been noted by Szoke, Neame and Johnson that these 'changes may well be because the NHMRC's advice in the 1996 guidelines ... went unheeded'.[20] Some of the particular aspects of the guidelines are considered below.

---

13 Don Chalmers, 'Professional Self-regulation and Guidelines in Assisted Reproduction' 9 Journal of Law and Medicine 414.

14 National Health and Medical Research Council (n 6) 25–40.

15 ibid. 41–7.

16 ibid.

17 ibid. 49–52.

18 See National Health and Medical Research Council, *Ethical Guidelines on Assisted Reproductive Technology* (NHMRC 1996) v.

19 ibid. 2.

20 Helen Szoke, Lexi Neame and Louise Johnson, 'Old Technologies and New Challenges: Assisted Reproduction and its Regulation' in Ian Freckelton and Kerry Petersen (eds), *Disputes and Dilemmas in Health Law* (Federation Press 2006).

## A National Approach for Australian Assisted Reproductive Technology Regulation?

There have been a number of recommendations arguing in favour of a national approach to ART regulation in Australia.[21] As already mentioned, federal legislation has been passed to regulate human cloning and the practice of medical research involving human embryos (including the use of excess embryos from ART procedures that are no longer needed by the participants).[22] Many jurisdictions have also passed legislation to regulate the practice of surrogacy.[23] However, there has been no uniform approach to legislation across jurisdictions to address the issues arising from the delivery of ART services. This seems surprising as nearly all Australian jurisdictions have considered the issues arising from the use of ART in some detail. At some point in time, most jurisdictions have instructed specialist committees to review the issues raised by the technologies and make recommendations for how regulation should progress.[24] Moreover, there was also the potential for a consistent

---

21 The Family Law Council of Australia report on reproductive technology recommended that a multi-disciplinary body oversee matters relating to reproductive technology at a national level (Family Law Council of Australia, *Creating Children: A Uniform Approach to the Law and Practice of Reproductive Technology in Australia* (AGPS 1985). The functions of the body were suggested to include advising federal and state governments; monitoring medical research; analysing the implications of ART for society; providing information for the community; developing clear guidelines for ethics, practice records, providing access to information and counselling; recommending research on the ongoing effects of reproductive technology; and presenting an annual report. The plans to implement such a body were not followed through fully, but the National Bioethics Consultative Committee (NBCC) was created, which, according to Chalmers, had success in focusing debate and preparing reports, but not in changing public policy. For a detailed review of the development of such issues, see Chalmers (n 13).

22 Prohibition of Human Cloning Act 2002 (Cth); Research Involving Human Embryos Act 2002 (Cth). Both pieces of legislation have recently been reviewed by a Legislation Review Committee: Australian Government, *Legislation Review: Prohibition of Human Cloning Act 2002 and the Research Involving Human Embryos Act 2002* (2005) and subsequently reformed: Prohibition of Human Cloning for Reproduction and the Regulation of Human Embryo Research Amendment Act 2006 (Cth). For an overview of some of the issues arising from the review, see Donna Cooper (n 3).

23 Parentage Act 2004 (ACT); Surrogacy Act 2010 (NSW); Surrogacy Act 2010 (Qld); Family Relationships Act 1975 (SA); Surrogacy Act 2012 (Tas); Assisted Reproductive Treatment Act 2008 (Vic); Surrogacy Act 2008 (WA).

24 Alan Demack, *Report of the Special Committee Appointed by the Queensland Government to Enquire into the Laws Relating to Artificial Insemination, In Vitro Fertilisation and Other Related Matters* (Queensland Parliament 1984); New South Wales Law Reform Commission,

national approach to be developed following the enactment of the legislation that created the AHEC.[25] This committee could have been granted authority to oversee the national standards that had been formulated by the AHEC in the NHMRC guidelines. However, this did not happen for a number of reasons, which 'primarily included the fact that regulation was simultaneously being developed through legislation at the State level and ... self-regulation was seen to be achieving a measure of success'.[26] It is to the state level legislation that the discussion will now turn.

## Statutory Regulation of Assisted Reproductive Technology in Australia

The discussion below outlines the approach of each of the statutory regimes and considers the role played by each of the statutory bodies, which are vested with the responsibility of overseeing the statutory frameworks in place (where relevant). Those Australian states and territories that are not mentioned in this section rely solely on the national guidelines, which were outlined above.

### New South Wales
The issue of ART has been the subject of review in New South Wales since the 1980s. The New South Wales Law Reform Commission produced a number of reports on the topic,[27] but no action was taken to implement the recommendations that were made.[28] In 1997, the New South Wales Department of Health conducted a review of the human tissue legislation, which also considered whether legislation was needed on the topic of ART.[29] The outcome of the process resulted in the production of a consultation draft Bill, the Assisted Reproductive Technology Bill 2003. The Bill was presented to Parliament in 2003 and was then subject to ongoing consultation. In November 2007, the Bill was re-introduced to Parliament and passed as the Assisted Reproductive

---

*Artificial Conception – Human Artificial Insemination*, Report No 49 (1986); New South Wales Law Reform Commission, *Artificial Conception – In Vitro Fertilisation*, Report No 58 (1988); New South Wales Law Reform Commission, *Artificial Conception – Surrogate Motherhood*, Report No 60 (1988); Don Chalmers, *Committee to Investigate Artificial Conception and Related Matters* (Tasmania Parliament 1985).

25  National Health and Medical Research Council Act 1992 (Cth).

26  Chalmers (n 13) 418.

27  See New South Wales Law Reform Commission (n 24).

28  Szoke, Neame and Johnson (n 20) 250.

29  New South Wales Department of Health, *Review of the Human Tissue Act 1983*, Discussion Paper: Assisted Reproductive Technologies (1997).

Technology Act 2007 (NSW).[30] At the time of writing, the current framework
in New South Wales is under review as required under s 74 of the Act.[31]

It is stated that the Act's main purpose is to prevent the commercialisation
of human reproduction and to protect the interests of those involved in the
provision of ART services.[32] The New South Wales legislative framework does
not establish a statutory body to oversee the legislative provisions.[33] The aim
of the regulatory framework is intended to complement the current system of
regulation under the national guidelines (as outlined above). At the time the
legislation was being debated, the Minister for Health noted:

> The [legislation] does not duplicate the existing regulatory framework that
> applies to the clinical aspects of assisted reproductive technology practice.
> Rather, it complements and enhances the current system to clarify and
> protect the rights and obligations of people involved in assisted reproductive
> technology treatment.[34]

On this basis, it can be stated that the New South Wales legislation is intended
to focus on aspects of ART which are left unregulated or where there is 'real
potential for individual or social harm'.[35] There is clear evidence that the
underlying regulatory objective in New South Wales is focused on protecting
those undergoing ART services and children born following such procedures,
from harm. This underlying objective is particularly worthy of note and is a
matter to which I shall return in Chapter 6. The legislation seeks to:

- provide access to information for donor offspring in relation to
  genetic parentage;
- ensure that gametes and embryos are used only in ways that are consistent
  with the consent of the gamete provider;

---

30 New South Wales, Legislative Assembly, *Parliamentary Debates* 7 November 2007,
1 (Reba Meagher).

31 New South Wales Health, *Assisted Reproductive Technology Act 2007: Statutory
Review*, Discussion Paper (2013) <www.health.nsw.gov.au/legislation/Documents/art-
act-2007-statutory-review.pdf> accessed 25 July 2014.

32 Assisted Reproductive Technology Act 2007 (NSW), s 3.

33 See Malcolm K Smith, 'Reviewing Regulation of Assisted Reproductive
Technology in New South Wales: The Assisted Reproductive Technology Act 2007
(NSW)' 16 Journal of Law and Medicine 120

34 New South Wales, Legislative Assembly, *Parliamentary Debates* 7 November 2007,
1 (Reba Meagher).

35 New South Wales Department of Health, *Consultation Draft, Assisted Reproductive
Technology Bill 2003*, Information Guide (November 2003) [3.1].

- regulate ART in order to protect potential harm to society from the devaluation of human life and dignity through the introduction of commercialism.[36]

The legislation also seeks to regulate a number of further issues, including the implementation of infection control standards for clinics[37] and the implementation of a central ART donor register.[38]

ART providers in New South Wales must be registered under the legislation.[39] Registration does not require compliance with a list of conditions, but is instead concerned with identifying 'the providers of ART services in order to facilitate appropriate compliance and enforcement activity in respect of the provisions of the [legislation]'.[40] It is questionable whether the legislative provisions address some areas that are of individual or social harm, as the Act does not address some ethically problematic issues, such as PGD. Furthermore, many of the provisions set out in the legislation do in fact duplicate the existing framework imposed under the national guidelines.[41]

### South Australia

In South Australia, the legislative framework was first established by the Reproductive Technology (Clinical Practices) Act 1988 (SA). However, the legislation was reformed in 2009 as a result of the enactment of the Reproductive Technology (Clinical Practices) (Miscellaneous) Amendment Act 2009 (SA); the legislation was renamed the Assisted Reproductive Treatment Act 1988 (SA). The pre-reformed framework had imposed a licence-based system, which was overseen by the South Australian Council on Reproductive Technology (SACRT). However, following reform, a system of registration is now in place which instead requires ART providers to be registered in compliance with the Assisted Reproductive Treatment Regulations 2010 (SA).[42] The SACRT

---

36 ibid. The same sentiment was echoed in the Legislative Council's second reading of the Bill as it was progressing through Parliament: New South Wales, Legislative Council, *Parliamentary Debates* 27 November 2007, 4382 (Tony Kelly).

37 Assisted Reproductive Technology Act 2007 (NSW), s 10.

38 Assisted Reproductive Technology Act 2007 (NSW), pt 3.

39 Assisted Reproductive Technology Act 2007 (NSW), s 6.

40 New South Wales Department of Health (n 35) [3.2].

41 For further discussion, see Smith (n 33).

42 This requirement does not apply to those providing assisted insemination in circumstances where such services are carried out gratuitously or where the person is approved by the Minister to provide such services (Assisted Reproductive Treatment Act 1988 (SA), s 5(2)).

no longer exists;[43] the Minister for Health is responsible for overseeing the legislative scheme.

The Assisted Reproductive Treatment Regulations 2010 detail further conditions of registration that ART providers must comply with. The legislation imposes eligibility criteria that must be satisfied by prospective ART participants,[44] and also requires that the welfare of any child born as a result of an ART procedure is placed as the principle of paramount importance in relation to the operation of the legislation.[45]

## Victoria

Victoria was the first common law jurisdiction in the world to regulate ART by statute.[46] Since then, the statutory framework has been updated a number of times. The current legislative framework was enacted following an extensive review of the law, which was undertaken by the Victorian Law Reform Commission (VLRC). The Commission published its proposals for reform in its final report in 2007.[47] The Assisted Reproductive Treatment Act 2008 (Vic) incorporates many of the Commission's proposals for reform.[48]

The Victorian statutory framework is the most prescriptive of all of the approaches in Australia.[49] However, the reformed framework is far less prescriptive than the previous legislative scheme set out under the Infertility Treatment Act 1995 (Vic). The legislation in Victoria similarly imposes a system of registration.[50] Applications for registration must be made to the statutory body established under the legislation, the Victorian Assisted Reproductive Treatment Authority (VARTA).[51] This system of registration works alongside the national accreditation requirements set out by the FSA. For example, once RTAC accreditation expires, registration under the Victorian legislation also

---

43 Reproductive Technology (Clinical Practices) (Miscellaneous) Amendment Act 2009 (SA), s 8.

44 Assisted Reproductive Treatment Act 1988 (SA), s 9(1)(c).

45 Assisted Reproductive Treatment Act 1988 (SA), s 4A.

46 Szoke (n 1) 75.

47 Victorian Law Reform Commission, *Assisted Reproductive Technology & Adoption: Final Report* (2007).

48 For a discussion of the Victorian legislative framework, see Malcolm Smith, 'Regulating Assisted Reproductive Technologies in Victoria: The Impact of Changing Policy Concerning the Accessibility of In Vitro Fertilisation for Preimplantation Tissue-typing' (2012) 19 Journal of Law and Medicine 820.

49 See Kerry Petersen, 'The Regulation of Assisted Reproductive Technology: A Comparative Study of Permissive and Prescriptive Laws and Policies' (2002) 9 Journal of Law and Medicine 483.

50 Assisted Reproductive Treatment Act 2008 (Vic), s 74.

51 Assisted Reproductive Treatment Act 2008 (Vic), s 99.

expires. As with the previous system of licensing, the statutory body can impose a number of conditions on registered providers.[52] Non-compliance with the statutory provisions may lead to criminal sanction.[53]

It has been stated that the changes to the legislative framework represent 'a change in focus from treatment of infertility to a broader purpose of regulating assisted human fertilisation procedures'.[54] This is immediately obvious from the change in the legislation's title.[55] The current legislation imposes wider eligibility criteria (discussed below) and establishes a Patient Review Panel to determine whether an individual or a couple should be granted access to ART services in certain circumstances, or to determine whether access should be granted in circumstances where there is a presumption against treatment.[56] The legislation also attempts to further entrench the rights of donor-conceived children to access information about their genetic origins and implements detailed provisions relating to the practice of surrogacy.[57]

The VARTA has a wide scope of authority according to its duties and responsibilities outlined under the legislation, which includes:

- administering the system of registration for ART providers;
- undertaking public education about treatment procedures and the best interests of children born as a result of treatment procedures;
- consulting with the community about matters relevant to the legislation;
- monitoring the programs and activities relating to the Act, the causes and preventions of infertility, and treatment outside Victoria;
- keeping the body's functions, operation and composition under review;

---

52 Assisted Reproductive Treatment Act 2008 (Vic), s 75.

53 See for example, Assisted Reproductive Treatment Act 2008 (Vic), ss 35–38.

54 Victoria, Legislative Assembly, *Parliamentary Debates* 10 September 2008, 3442 (Rob Hulls). Another MP notes that the 'bill abandons the long-held principle of Victorian legislation that reproductive treatment is to help infertile couples to have children and replaces it with the concept that any person who is unable or unwilling to have children by natural means can have children produced for them': Victoria, Legislative Assembly, *Parliamentary Debates* 7 October 2008, 3759 (Robert William Clark).

55 The legislation previously in force was the Infertility Treatment Act 1995 (Vic). As one MP acknowledged when the Bill was passing through the Legislative Assembly, '[t]he change is explicit even in the name of the bill': Victoria, Legislative Assembly, *Parliamentary Debates* 7 October 2008, 3783 (David Morris).

56 The Patient Review Panel has responsibility for approving certain uses of ART, such as surrogacy and posthumous conception, and extending permitted storage periods of gametes and embryos under the legislation: Assisted Reproductive Treatment Act 2008 (Vic), s 85.

57 See for example, pts 4 and 6 of the Assisted Reproductive Treatment Act 2008 (Vic).

- promoting research into the causes and prevention of infertility;
- approving the import and export of gametes and embryos;
- other functions required by the Act or any other Act.[58]

The legislative scheme (and its administration) is informed by the five guiding principles outlined in the legislation, which are:[59]

- that the welfare and interests of persons born or to be born as a result of treatment procedures are to be paramount;
- that at no time should the use of treatment procedures be for the purposes of exploiting the reproductive capabilities of men and women, or children born as a result of treatment procedures;
- that children born as a result of the use of donated gametes have a right to information about their genetic origins;
- that the health and wellbeing of persons undergoing treatment procedures must be protected at all times;
- that persons seeking to undergo treatment procedures must not be discriminated against on the basis of their sexual orientation, marital status or religion.

The relevance of these principles – particularly the requirement to place the welfare of children born following ART procedures as paramount – will be considered further in Chapter 3.

The Victorian legislation does not specifically delegate responsibility to the statutory body to formulate a Code of Practice relating to the delivery of ART procedures. However, the legislation does provide for the Governor in Council to make regulations on a number of issues under the scope of the Act.[60]

## Western Australia

ART legislation also exists in Western Australia, which is the only Australian jurisdiction that still maintains a system of licensing for the provision of ART services. The regulatory framework in Western Australia is outlined in the Human Reproductive Technology Act 1991 (WA).[61] Under this framework, the

---

58 Assisted Reproductive Treatment Act 2008 (Vic), s 100.

59 Assisted Reproductive Treatment Act 2008 (Vic), s 5.

60 See Assisted Reproductive Treatment Act 2008 (Vic), ss 124, 125.

61 The preamble to the Human Reproductive Technology Act 1991 (WA) describes the Act as 'an Act to establish the Western Australian Reproductive Technology Council; to require the compilation of a Code relating to the practice of, the procedures used in, and the ethics governing, human reproductive technology; to make provision

Commissioner of Health acts as the Licensing Authority and administers the legislation subject to the Minister for Health.[62] The Reproductive Technology Council (RTC) is required to advise the Commissioner of Health on issues relating to the provision of ART services.[63] The RTC is also specifically required to develop, review and amend a Code of Practice under the legislation.[64] The Code of Practice is required to set out rules, guidelines and other relevant information, establish ethical standards required of licensees and give effect to the principles stipulated under the legislation.[65]

---

with respect to the use of that technology in relation to artificially assisted human conception and for the regulation of certain research; and for related purposes'.

62 When seeking a licence, applications must be made directly to the Commissioner of Health, who in turn seeks advice from the RTC (Human Reproductive Technology Act 1991 (WA), s 29). The RTC also has reporting requirements under the legislation, which lead to the Minister of Health reporting to Parliament: Human Reproductive Technology Act 1991 (WA), s 5(6) and cl 11 of the schedule. The RTC makes a recommendation based upon the suitability of the applicant and this can be formulated on the basis of a centre's RTAC accreditation visit and other investigations required (Parliament of Western Australia, Legislative Assembly, *Select Committee on the Human Reproductive Technology Act 1991* (1999) 167). The Commissioner of Health on advice from the RTC is able to grant a storage licence, a practice licence, or both. It is also possible for the Commissioner of Health to grant an exemption relating to artificial insemination: Human Reproductive Technology Act 1991 (WA), s 28. This exemption enables a currently registered medical practitioner to carry out artificial insemination without a licence. The practitioner is however required to notify the Commissioner of Health of the procedures to be carried out, and under s 28(2)(a) a person holding exemption is subject to 'the like disciplinary procedures in relation to that exemption as would have been applicable had the exemption been a licence under [the Human Reproductive Technology Act 1991 (WA)]'. Licensees are expected to maintain records of all artificial fertilisation procedures including the keeping and use of all gametes and eggs, and records must be maintained for a period of 25 years (Directions, *Western Australian Government Gazette* 30 November 2004, No 201, pt 2). Further detailed reporting requirements are stipulated under s 2 of the Directions.

63 Other responsibilities of the RTC include advising the Minister of Health on matters relating to ART, encouraging and facilitating research into the cause and prevention of human infertility, considering the social and public health implications of ART and also promoting informed public debate and education on such issues: Reproductive Technology Council, *Western Australia's Human Reproductive Technology Act 1991 and Human Reproductive Technology Amendment Act 1996: Summary* (April 1996) 5.

64 Human Reproductive Technology Act 1991 (WA), s 14(1)(c).

65 The Code of Practice must also provide for any other matters as instructed by the Minister, or as the Council may determine in accordance with the main provisions of the Act: Human Reproductive Technology Act 1991 (WA), s 14(1)(c).

The main object of the legislation, in accordance with the administration of such issues by the RTC, is:

- to regulate and guide the use of reproductive technology, by making sure that standards set by and under the Act are adhered to by licensees;
- to ensure that artificial fertilisation procedures are used only on participants eligible under the Act itself, with consideration of their welfare and the welfare of any child likely to be born as a result, and after participants have been adequately assessed medically as to the need for these procedures and informed and counselled as to their implications;
- to require that equity, welfare and general community standards are considered in any decisions about reproductive technology;
- to promote public debate on reproductive technology on an informed basis;
- to allow beneficial developments in reproductive technology to take place.[66]

Despite the requirement to implement a Code of Practice under the legislation, no such Code has been developed. In effect, the Code of Practice has been substituted by the Directions and Guidelines developed by the RTC. The Directions published in the Western Australian Government Gazette[67] have the status of subsidiary legislation.[68] This makes the provisions contained in the Directions equal to the status of a Code of Practice if it had been produced, and for this reason, the Select Committee on the Human Reproductive Act advised that the creation of a Code of Practice would be too inflexible.[69] It was therefore suggested that the Directions should remain in place of the Code of Practice.[70]

As with the guiding principles in Victoria, there are a number of factors that should guide the delivery of ART services in Western Australia, including:

- that respect should be given to human life at all stages of its development;
- that help and encouragement should be given to couples who are unable to conceive children naturally or whose children may be affected by a genetic disease;

---

66  See Reproductive Technology Council (n 63) 5.

67  See Directions (n 62).

68  Under the legislation, the Commissioner of Health may issue Directions (or Directions varying or revoking such) for any matter authorised under the legislation or in accordance with the Code of Practice: Human Reproductive Technology Act 1991 (WA), s 31.

69  Select Committee, Parliament of Western Australia (n 62) 137.

70  ibid.

- the welfare of any children who may be born as a result of treatment;
- that ART services providers should recognise that the responsible pursuit of medicine and science may lead to benefits for individuals and for society.[71]

Unlike the guiding principles set out under the Victorian framework, arguably, these factors demonstrate a mixed underlying regulatory approach. Thus, the requirement to respect human life at *all* stages of development arguably translates into a requirement to value the embryo for its intrinsic worth whereas the requirement to consider the welfare of any child who may be born following ART procedures is a requirement to consider whether children will, or may, be harmed. Similarly, the need to recognise that the responsible pursuit of medicine and science may lead to *benefits* for the individual or society, displays an element of utilitarian reasoning. Despite this mixed reasoning, there is no guidance as to how the principles should be applied.

## Comment

There are some key differences between the statutory approaches. Although an analysis and evaluation of the different regulatory frameworks at a general level falls outside the focus of this book, it is worth noting that there appears to be a trend in the Australian ART legislation as recently reformed (or, as in New South Wales, where legislation on ART is relatively new) frameworks appear to be adopting a less prescriptive approach to regulation than traditionally adopted in Australia. For example, in New South Wales, South Australia and Victoria, the legislation now adopts a system of registration instead of the more onerous system of licensing that existed in some jurisdictions. The system of registration works alongside the national accreditation process administered by the FSA. As outlined below, this less prescriptive approach is most evident in the context of PGD, where regulation of embryo selection technologies occurs predominantly by way of the national professional standards and ethical guidelines. For some jurisdictions, such as Victoria, this is a far less prescriptive approach to PGD regulation than was previously in place.

Another important factor to note is that there are a number of key underlying principles that guide the different Australian statutory frameworks relevant to ART services. Of most significance is the requirement in all Australian jurisdictions that ART providers prioritise the welfare of any child who may be born as a result of providing ART services (a requirement that is similarly reflected in the national ethical guidelines relating to ART). This is an issue that is considered further in Chapter 3.

---

71 The Select Committee reported that the Directions first issued in 1997 were framed under the principles listed: see Parliament of Western Australia (n 62) 140.

Importantly, the statutory reforms in some jurisdictions have also resulted in a more permissive approach in terms of widening access to ART services. As discussed below, there are some key differences between the statutory approaches concerning eligibility for ART services. In some jurisdictions, restrictions were previously imposed based on the view that certain classes of people should be prevented from conceiving children by way of ART services, as this was intended to protect the welfare of children who may be born as a result of such services. However, the view that certain classes of people should be prohibited from accessing ART services has shifted quite significantly in recent times. Consequently, some Australian jurisdictions now adopt a more liberal approach in determining who should be deemed eligible for ART services. As discussed in the following chapter, this also consequently impacts on the accessibility of ART services for families seeking to create a saviour child.

Western Australia is the only jurisdiction to maintain the more onerous system of licensing, which is administered by the state's Health Department and the statutory regulatory body. In comparison to the other statutory jurisdictions in Australia, the approach in Western Australia is restrictive, particularly in relation to PGD. At the time of writing, it is anticipated that the regulatory framework in Western Australia will be subject to legislative reform to bring it into line with the other Australian jurisdictions, although plans for reform in this regard are not forthcoming.

## Key Aspects of ART Regulation in Australia

The regulatory approaches outlined above address a wide range of issues that fall within the ambit of ART services. Although there are some differences between each of the approaches, they each generally address issues such as the need for clinics to provide adequate information to participants[72] and the requirements

---

72 The National Health and Medical Research Council guidelines are comprehensive on this issue and outline a number of factors that must be explained to all participants so that they are able to 'develop an accurate understanding' of some of the following issues: the likelihood of the woman becoming pregnant other than through ART; recent success and failure rates relevant to the particular participants; any significant risks involved in the proposed procedures; the likelihood and significance of potential short-term or long-term physical and psychosocial implications for the person born and the participants; the currently available published data on morbidity, and both long-term and short-term outcomes, for persons born through ART; whether the proposed procedure is accepted practice or an innovative procedure; options for use, storage, donation and disposal of gametes and embryos; an explanation of all costs involved; the clinic's privacy policy; and any planned or possible follow-up studies and/or the possibility of later contact and request to take part in such studies: National Health and Medical Research Council (n 6) [9.1].

relating to consent[73] (which include a requirement that the consent is made in writing or is documented);[74] the permitted length of storage for gametes and embryos;[75] the requirement for participants to be offered or undergo counselling;[76] and the requirement for clinics (or other state bodies) to maintain records concerning donated gametes and/or embryos created from donated gametes, so that adequate information is maintained in relation to donors and donor-conceived children.[77] One particular issue that is regulated inconsistently between jurisdictions concerns the imposition of eligibility criteria for ART services. In some jurisdictions, restrictions are imposed by the state that have the effect of limiting services so that only those who have a medical need can access them. It is important to outline these general restrictions as they indirectly

---

73 National Health and Medical Research Council, (n 6) [9.4] (the National Health and Medical Research Council guidelines apply in those jurisdictions where legislation does not address this specific issue); Reproductive Technology Accreditation Committee (n 5) 14; Assisted Reproductive Technology Act 2007 (NSW), ss 17–18; Assisted Reproductive Treatment Act 2008 (Vic), s 10(1); and Human Reproductive Technology Act 1991 (WA), s 22(1).

74 National Health and Medical Research Council (n 6) [9.4]; Reproductive Technology Accreditation Committee (n 5) 14; Assisted Reproductive Technology Act 2007 (NSW), s 17; Assisted Reproductive Treatment Act 2008 (Vic), s 11; Human Reproductive Technology Act 1991 (WA), s 22(8)(a).

75 National Health and Medical Research Council (n 6) [8.3], [8.8.1]; Assisted Reproductive Technology Act 2007 (NSW), ss 25–26; Assisted Reproductive Treatment Act 2008 (Vic) ss 31–34A; Directions, *Western Australian Government Gazette* (n 62) ss 3.1, 6.8–6.9; Human Reproductive Technology Act 1991 (WA), s 24.

76 The Victorian legislation requires all women (and where applicable, their partners) to *receive* counselling from an approved counsellor prior to treatment (Assisted Reproductive Treatment Act 2008 (Vic), s 13). However, in the remaining jurisdictions, counselling is not mandatory. Thus, in Western Australia, clinics providing services must also ensure that each participant is provided with a suitable *opportunity* to receive counselling about the implications of the proposed treatment and any further information as is 'proper or as may be specifically required by the Code or directions' (Human Reproductive Technology Act 1991 (WA), s 22(7)). Similarly, in New South Wales, counselling must be made available by ART providers (Assisted Reproductive Technology Act 2007 (NSW), s 12), and under the National Health and Medical Research Council guidelines, clinics are required to provide 'readily accessible services from accredited counsellors to support participants in making decisions about their treatment', but this does not stipulate that counselling is mandatory (National Health and Medical Research Council (n 6) [9.3]).

77 For an overview of the Australian regulatory landscape and the way in which these issues (and others) are regulated, see Belinda Bennett and Malcolm Smith, 'Assisted Reproductive Technology' in Ben White, Fiona McDonald and Lindy Willmott (eds), *Health Law in Australia* (2nd edn, Thomson Reuters 2014).

impact on the accessibility of ART services for families seeking to utilise IVF
and pre-implantation tissue-typing for the creation of a saviour child.

## Limitations on access

The availability of ART services will be dependent upon a number of factors,
including but not limited to the personal circumstances of those seeking
treatments; the financial costs of such treatments; the geographical proximity
of treatment services; and the statutory or other legal limits (if any) imposed
on those seeking to gain access to treatments. While the factors in this list
may be significant in the debate surrounding access to ART services generally
(particularly in relation to the issue of public funding for ART services), it is the
issue of state-imposed limits on access that will be considered in the context of
the legal regime.

## Limits imposed by legislation

When assisted reproductive techniques were first developed, access to the
technology was limited based on the view that it is better for children to be
conceived into two-parent heterosexual families. This position was adopted
in the UK legislation following the recommendations of the Warnock
Committee in the early 1980s.[78] A similar view was also adopted in a number of
Australian jurisdictions.

Although the New South Wales legislation does not address the issue of
eligibility for ART services, the legislation in Victoria, Western Australian and
South Australia imposes requirements that must be met by prospective ART
participants. These Australian jurisdictions originally required ART participants
to be married or in an established heterosexual de facto relationship.[79] However,
the marriage requirement was challenged in both Victoria and South Australia,
as federal legislation – the Sex Discrimination Act 1984 (Cth) – prohibits service
providers from discriminating on the basis of marital status. In *McBain v The
State of Victoria*,[80] a single woman was not eligible for ART services under the
Victorian legislation. It was therefore argued that a refusal to provide services to
the woman contravened provisions of the Sex Discrimination Act 1984 (Cth).
The Federal Court of Australia held that this specific aspect of the former
Victorian legislation was discriminatory and that the marriage requirement was
inconsistent with the Commonwealth legislation under s 109 of the Australian

---

78 Mary Warnock, *Report of the Committee of Inquiry into Human Fertilisation and
Embryology*, The Warnock Report (Cmnd 9314, HMSO 1984) [2.11].

79 Reproductive Technology (Clinical Practices) Act 1988 (SA) (pre-amended),
s 13(3); Infertility Treatment Act 1995 (Vic) (repealed), s 8(1); Human Reproductive
Technology Act 1991 (WA), s 23(1)(c).

80 [2000] 99 FCR 116.

Constitution thus rendering the provision void to that effect.[81] Similarly, in *Pearce v South Australian Health Commission*,[82] the Supreme Court of South Australia declared that the marriage requirement under s 13(3) of the Reproductive Technology (Clinical Practices) Act 1988 (SA) (pre-amended) was inconsistent with the Sex Discrimination Act 1984 (Cth). Based on these challenges and changes in social attitudes concerning parenting and modern family structures, the restrictions based on the relationship status of prospective participants have been removed from the legislation in Victoria and South Australia.[83]

The legislation in Western Australia still stipulates that prospective ART participants must either be married or in a heterosexual de facto relationship.[84] However, these terms are modified by the Acts Amendment (Lesbian and Gay Law Reform) Act 2002 (WA). The reforms effectively mean that the definitions of de facto relationship and de facto partner include same-sex relationships as well as heterosexual relationships.[85]

Despite the fact that Australian ART legislation no longer restricts services to married and heterosexual de facto couples, there are additional requirements that must be satisfied under the legislation in South Australia, Victoria and Western Australia before services can be provided. To be eligible for services, prospective participants in these jurisdictions must be either medically infertile or at risk of passing on a genetic condition when conceiving naturally (although, as outlined below, the law in Victoria has been reformed and adopts a more liberal approach than the legislation in South Australia and Western Australia).[86] The infertility requirement outlined under the legislation in South Australia and Western Australia requires that a woman's inability to conceive is based on a *medical* reason that has rendered the woman or her partner infertile. For example, in South Australia the definition of 'infertility' has been interpreted

---

81  Section 9 of the Commonwealth of Australia Constitution Act states that 'when a law of a State is inconsistent with a law of the Commonwealth, the latter shall prevail, and the former shall, to the extent of the inconsistency, be invalid'.

82  [1996] 66 SASR 486.

83  The new legislation is based on many of the recommendations made by the Victorian Law Reform Commission and the final report concluded 'that the marital status requirement is not only inconsistent with the principle of non-discrimination, but it also bears no relationship to the health and wellbeing of children, which must be the paramount concern of the law governing ART': Victorian Law Reform Commission, *Assisted Reproductive Technology & Adoption: Final Report* (2007) 67.

84  Human Reproductive Technology Act 1991 (WA), s 23(1)(c).

85  Acts Amendment (Lesbian and Gay Law Reform) Act 2002 (WA), ss 73–76.

86  Assisted Reproductive Treatment Act 1988 (SA), s 9(1)(c); Assisted Reproductive Treatment Act 2008 (Vic), s 10; Human Reproductive Treatment Act 1991 (WA), s 23(1).

to refer to *clinical* infertility,[87] and in Western Australia the Select Committee expressed the view that infertility should be one of the main reasons for accessing ART procedures.[88]

The infertility requirement has created a barrier for single and lesbian women seeking access to ART services, as these women are not generally regarded as *clinically* infertile. The inability to conceive in such circumstances arises because the woman is not engaging in heterosexual intercourse, and not because of a medical issue that affects the woman's fertility (or her partner's fertility). The term 'social infertility' has been adopted in such circumstances. Notably, however, if a single or lesbian woman is able to establish a medical basis for her inability to conceive, she will satisfy the statutory eligibility criteria in the applicable jurisdictions. As part of the review of the law in Victoria, the VLRC highlighted the way that the pre-reformed eligibility criteria in Victoria (which was the same as the current approach in South Australia and Western Australia) applied unequally to different women. One submission to the VLRC's review poignantly observed: 'it is a sad indictment upon Australian law that a lesbian celebrates a diagnosis of an undesirable gynaecological condition just so that she can fulfil the legal criteria of 'medical infertility' and gain access to safe, identity traceable donor sperm'.[89]

In Victoria, the legislation now adopts a more liberal view on the issue of who should be permitted to access ART services, which can be provided in cases where a doctor is satisfied on reasonable grounds that:

- the woman is unlikely to become pregnant other than by a treatment procedure; or
- the woman is unlikely to be able to carry a pregnancy or give birth to a child without a treatment procedure; or
- the woman is at risk of transmitting a genetic abnormality or genetic disease as a result of a pregnancy conceived other than by a treatment procedure, including a genetic abnormality or genetic disease for which the woman's partner is the carrier.[90]

---

87 'Infertility refers to the inability or significantly reduced capacity of a person to conceive or otherwise bear or father a child, evidenced by: (i) a reasonable period of unprotected intercourse with no resulting pregnancy; or (ii) a proven medical condition resulting in reduced fertility; or (iii) other evidence presented to the treating medical practitioner ... Further as a guide: a man may be considered infertile if his female partner has been unable to conceive a child naturally; a woman may be considered infertile if, with a male partner, she has been unable to conceive a child naturally'. (SACRT, 'Eligibility for Assisted Reproductive Technology' Memorandum 1, reported in South Australian Council on Reproductive Technology, *Annual Report* (2004) 21).

88 Parliament of Western Australia (n 62) 46.

89 Victorian Law Reform Commission (n 83) 55.

90 Assisted Reproductive Treatment Act 2008 (Vic), s 10(2).

In line with this progressive approach, one of the guiding principles in the current legislation is centred on the notion of non-discrimination.[91]

The changes to the law in Victoria permit access to services in a wider range of circumstances than under the previous statutory framework. Not only is the wording of the reformed legislation broad enough to encompass the provision of services to single and lesbian women (as these women are 'unlikely to become pregnant other than by a treatment procedure'), in cases where prospective participants do not meet the statutory eligibility criteria, the Patient Review Panel is able to make a decision to determine whether access should be permitted.[92] As discussed in Chapter 3, this may provide an avenue for some families to access ART services for the purpose of utilising embryo selection technologies for the creation of a saviour child. In cases where the Patient Review Panel is asked to determine whether access to services should be granted in a given case, it is required to make a decision in accordance with the guiding principles and whether the general or specific treatment is consistent with the best interests of a child born following the provision of services.[93] In certain circumstances, a presumption against treatment will also apply against participants if certain criminal convictions are discovered after a criminal record check.[94] In such cases, the Patient Review Panel is similarly able to review whether those seeking treatments should be provided with ART services.[95]

A proposal to widen the eligibility criteria has been put forward in South Australia (which would amend the eligibility criteria in a similar way to the Victorian legislation), but this is yet to be enacted.[96] In Western Australia, there have been no proposals announced to reform the statutory eligibility criteria, thus restricting the provision of services to those who have a 'medical' need for them.

---

91 Assisted Reproductive Treatment Act 2008 (Vic), s 5(e).

92 Assisted Reproductive Treatment Act 2008 (Vic), s 10(1)(b)(ii).

93 Assisted Reproductive Treatment Act 2008 (Vic), s 15(3).

94 Those seeking treatments are also required to undergo a criminal records check and where the woman or her partner (where relevant) has been convicted of particular sexual offences, or where there is a conviction in relation to a violent offence (or where a child protection check reveals that a child has been removed from the custody of the woman and/or her partner), a presumption against treatment will be imposed: Assisted Reproductive Treatment Act 2008 (Vic), s 14. These factors will be considered in further detail under the scope of the welfare principle.

95 Assisted Reproductive Treatment Act 2008 (Vic), s 15(1)(a). See *ABY & ABZ v Patient Review Panel (Health & Privacy)* [2011] VCAT 1382; *Patient Review Panel v ABY & ABZ* [2012] VSCA 264; *ABY & ABZ v Secretary to the Department of Health (Human Rights)* [2013] VCAT 625; *PQ v Patient Review Panel (Health & Privacy)* [2012] VCAT 291.

96 Assisted Reproductive Treatment (Equality of Access) Amendment Bill 2012 (SA), cl 4.

*Non-statutory limitations on access*

In the jurisdictions where no ART legislation exists, the NHMRC guidelines apply. The guidelines are silent on the issue of eligibility for services and therefore, access to ART services is not formally restricted in the remaining Australian jurisdictions (including New South Wales where the legislation is silent on the issue of eligibility for services). Therefore, the decision to provide (or refuse) ART services in these jurisdictions is determined by individual clinics. In this respect, as already established, clinics are required to prioritise the welfare of any child who may be born as a result of providing ART services, as this is stated to be a principle of paramount importance in the national guidelines.[97] This may provide a justification for limiting the provision of services in some circumstances; this issue is considered further in Chapter 3.

As the NHMRC guidelines do not address the issue of eligibility for services, it appears as though ART services are more widely accessible in the remaining Australian jurisdictions (at least in terms of there being no state-imposed barrier to access). However, as with the approach in some of the statutory jurisdictions, where there are no state-imposed restrictions on access, *clinics* may choose to limit their services to those who have a medical need for them. Arguably, if this occurs, those seeking services may choose to approach a different clinic that has a more liberal perspective concerning the issue of who should be able to access ART services. However, in those areas where there is a limited range of service providers, this may place an increased burden on those seeking to access ART services as they may be required to travel significant distances to access services. This could be particularly burdensome for a family that is caring for a sick child and is, for example, required to travel interstate to obtain access to IVF services in an attempt to conceive a tissue-matched child who will serve as a tissue donor for their existing sick child.

Interestingly, in New South Wales, the Department of Health (which was responsible for managing the consultation process and making recommendations for the implementation of ART legislation) recommended that the issue of eligibility for services should not be addressed on the face of the legislation, to encourage a more inclusive approach to the issue of access to services:

> The decision not to include eligibility criteria is based on the notion that it is not the role of legislation to screen out 'good' prospective parents from 'bad' prospective parents. The law does not impose restrictions upon individuals in the general community who wish to become parents. Indeed, it is generally considered a fundamental right of individuals to be able to have children and form families as they choose.

---

97  National Health and Medical Research Council (n 6) [2.5], [5.1].

… The role of the legislature has not been to make rules regarding classes of persons who may or may not become parents (as this is not a predictor of harm) but to make rules to safeguard the rights of individual children whose welfare has been compromised.[98]

Clearly, an underlying principle of relevance to the New South Wales legislative framework is focused on harm prevention, in terms of preventing patients and those who may be conceived following the provision of ART services from harm. However, while one of the key reasons for not implementing statutory eligibility criteria in New South Wales was to prevent discrimination against particular classes of people, the failure to outline a more inclusive approach to eligibility in legislation may permit individual clinics to adopt restrictive (and thereby discriminatory) practices. Some clinicians may refuse to provide services to those who do not have a *medical* need for them (such as single women, same-sex couples, and potentially, prospective parents who themselves have no medical need for accessing ART services other than to create a tissue donor for an existing sick child). The ability to challenge a refusal of services is affected by the presence of statutory eligibility criteria. As summarised by Kerry Petersen:

If an ART statute excludes women on the grounds of marital status, discrimination laws can be invoked to strike down these provisions. However, if gate-keeping is left to clinics, and medical practitioners, it can be difficult to obtain the evidence necessary to challenge medical decisions to refuse treatment on discrimination grounds.[99]

This distinction is highlighted by a discrimination claim that was commenced by a woman in Queensland. ART services in Queensland are regulated predominantly by the NHMRC guidelines. As established above, this means that there are no statutory criteria imposed to determine the issue of eligibility for services in that state. In *JM v QFG*,[100] the Queensland Supreme Court held that a clinic – which had denied a lesbian woman access to artificial insemination services – did not directly or indirectly discriminate against her under the Queensland anti-discrimination legislation, based on her sexual orientation.[101] It was held that the ART provider had chosen to confine services to those who were medically infertile; that being heterosexual couples who were unable to conceive naturally. The Court also held that the clinician's requirement for the consent form to be signed by the applicant's male partner did not amount to a

---

98 New South Wales Department of Health (n 35) [4.3].
99 Petersen (n 49) 484–5.
100 (Sup Ct, Qld, No 1877 of 1997, 24 October 1997, Ambrose J).
101 Anti-Discrimination Act 1991 (Qld), ss 10–11.

form of indirect discrimination as it was established that this was not a practice adopted specifically towards the applicant, but a practice adopted generally towards all prospective ART participants. The Queensland Court of Appeal, however, remitted the issue of whether there had been indirect discrimination to the Anti-Discrimination Tribunal on the question of reasonableness.[102] The Anti-Discrimination Tribunal held that the practice adopted by the clinician was reasonable as it was based on guidance issued by Queensland Health and also representations made to donors that their gametes would only be used by heterosexual couples seeking access to treatments.[103] The Tribunal stated:

> Given that the respondent was clearly conducting his practice in accordance with established medical and ethical guidelines (whether out-dated, soundly based, or whether legally binding upon him or not), and was requesting sperm donations as part of that practice, the use to which he was obliged to put the donated sperm cannot be overlooked. It would not be unreasonable to confine the use of the sperm to 'infertile couples' in accordance with his representations to the potential donors ... the donated sperm had been collected by reference to representations that it would be used for infertile heterosexual couples, and it is at that time and in those circumstances that the issue of reasonableness arises.[104]

This case demonstrates that when ART legislation does not address the issue of eligibility, clinics may choose to limit services in ways that appear to be discriminatory (and often, for reasons that are not fully supported by reliance on the welfare principle which is an overarching principle in Australian ART regulation). Interestingly, the acceptability of refusing services to women in such circumstances has been endorsed by legislation in Queensland. The Anti-Discrimination Act 1991 (Qld) was amended following the case to exclude ART providers from the scope of the legislation, so that services can be refused on the basis of relationship status or sexuality (s 45A).

Most importantly, the discussion above highlights the fact that when ART providers limit their services in a narrow sense (for example, on the basis of *medical* need), this results in an overly restrictive approach. As discussed in Chapter 3, when a narrow approach is adopted concerning the issue of access to services, this also impacts on the accessibility of IVF services for the use of embryo selection technologies, particularly in the context of pre-implantation tissue-typing. Moreover, even where there are no restrictions placed upon who may access services, the regulatory approach to PGD may nevertheless prohibit the use of embryo selection technologies for this specific purpose, in certain

---

102 *JM v QFG* [2000] 1 Qd R 373.
103 *Morgan v GK* [2001] QADT 10, 24.
104 ibid.

circumstances. Therefore, the regulatory approach concerning PGD is also of significance.

## Regulation of pre-implantation genetic diagnosis

As discussed in Chapter 1, ART techniques were originally developed with the primary aim of treating infertility. More recently, alongside scientific advancements, the technology is being used to determine the genetics of embryos prior to implantation so that certain genetic conditions or traits can be avoided, or in some circumstances, so that they can be positively selected.[105] It is likely that the technology has been closely monitored and regulated by some jurisdictions based on the ethical and social concerns arising from its use.[106]

At a national level, the NHMRC guidelines provide some regulatory oversight for PGD practices. The guidelines note that the technology can be used to detect serious genetic conditions in order to improve ART outcomes,[107] and in rare circumstances, for pre-implantation tissue-typing.[108] The guidelines also go on to state that pending further community discussion, PGD must not be used to detect conditions that will not be of serious harm to the person to be born. The guidelines prohibit the use of the technology for social sex selection or selection in favour of a defect or disability.[109] In terms of other potential uses of the technology, there is no requirement for clinics to seek permission prior to undertaking PGD except in the case of selection of an embryo with compatible tissue for a sibling.[110] In the latter circumstances, the matter must be put before an institutional ethics committee and the committee must address a number of points outlined in the guidelines. The guidelines also require that those seeking PGD must be given access to both a clinical geneticist and a genetic counsellor so that they understand how the technology works and how it is applied to

---

105 For an overview of the issues raised by PGD, see Human Genome Research Project, *Choosing Genes for Future Children: The Regulatory Implications of Preimplantation Genetic Diagnosis* (University of Otago, 2006).

106 See Kerry Petersen, 'Genetic Technologies and ART: Ethical Values, Legal Regulation and Informal Regulation' in Ian Freckelton and Kerry Petersen (eds), *Disputes and Dilemmas in Health Law* (Federation Press 2006).

107 Many women suffer from recurrent pregnancy loss (RPL) which can happen for a number of reasons. One cause is chromosomal abnormalities (aneuploidy) in embryos. PGD can be used to genetically analyse the embryos of women who suffer from RPL and those embryos that do not show abnormalities can be implanted in order to try and achieve a higher successful pregnancy rate. See Pasquale Patrizio and others, 'High Rate of Biological Loss in Assisted Reproduction: It is in the Seed, Not in the Soil' (2007) 14 Reproductive BioMedicine Online 92.

108 National Health and Medical Research Council (n 6) [12.1].

109 ibid. 12.2.

110 ibid. 12.

their embryos.[111] There are no notification or reporting requirements under the NHMRC guidelines concerning PGD practices, which means that there is no regulatory body overseeing the technology in the majority of Australian jurisdictions. Only one Australian jurisdiction – Western Australia – imposes more stringent requirements concerning PGD; those requirements are considered below.

It is worth noting that PGD regulation in Victoria has taken a different direction under the oversight of the new statutory body, compared to the way it was monitored by the former Infertility Treatment Authority (ITA). Under the former statutory framework, the ITA heavily regulated and monitored PGD techniques. Victoria's approach to PGD regulation was one of the most comprehensive and prescriptive of all the Australian states and territories. A three-tier system of regulation existed requiring clinics to gain permission prior to undertaking PGD for certain purposes,[112] including the detection and selection of embryos on the basis of tissue type.[113] It was initially expected that the VARTA would assume a similar responsibility for overseeing the regulation of PGD, as the new statutory body had updated the ITA's guidance concerning PGD and pre-implantation tissue-typing.[114] However, the statutory body has confirmed that it will not play a role in the future regulation of PGD

---

111 ibid. 12.4–12.5. Clinics are also required to give up-to-date, objective and accurate information in line with the 'information giving' section of the guidelines (9.1 and 9.2), and that those seeking the treatment should be encouraged to consider the following factors when deciding the appropriateness of PGD: information regarding the reliability of results; genetic and clinical information about the condition; the clinic's previous reproductive experience; information regarding the condition being tested for including the range of effects of the disease or abnormality; the experience of families living with the condition and how it can be managed; and the extent of social support available.

112 The three-tier system permitted the use of PGD under three categories: (i) cases for which no permission or notification is required to undertake preimplantation genetic diagnosis – this only applied to established uses as outlined in the preimplantation genetic diagnosis policy; (ii) cases that are not established did not require permission to be obtained, but the use of preimplantation genetic diagnosis was reportable to the ITA; and (iii) in cases where the use of the technology is novel, approval had to be obtained from the ITA (and clinics were also required to notify the Authority of such uses): Infertility Treatment Authority, *Genetic Testing and the Requirements of the Infertility Treatment Act 1995: Policy in Relation to the Use of Pre-implantation Genetic Diagnosis (PGD)* (2008) 5–6.

113 Infertility Treatment Authority, *Tissue Typing in Conjunction with Preimplantation Genetic Diagnosis: Interim Guidelines* (2007) 1.

114 Victorian Assisted Reproductive Treatment Authority, *Conditions for Use of Tissue Typing in Conjunction with Preimplantation Genetic Diagnosis (PGD)* (2010).

techniques.[115] Consequently, regulation is a matter to be determined by individual clinics. This significant change in regulatory approach seems to accord with the general spirit of the reformed statutory framework in Victoria, which is less prescriptive compared to the former framework.[116] This change in policy leaves the regulatory position in Victoria concerning PGD similar to the position in New South Wales; despite legislation addressing ART more generally, PGD is regulated by the NHMRC guidelines.[117]

PGD in Western Australia is permitted for the detection of genetic conditions.[118] All diagnostic procedures must have the prior approval of the RTC.[119] Approval must be sought by clinics and an application should be made

---

115  This information was provided by Tracey Petrillo, Senior Policy and Education Officer, Victorian Assisted Reproductive Treatment Authority: email communication from Tracey Petrillo to author (February 2011).

116  See Smith (n 48).

117  See Smith (n 33).

118  In Western Australia, PGD has been permitted since the enactment of the Human Reproductive Technology Amendment Act 2004 (WA) and the Acts Amendment (Prohibition of Human cloning and Other Practices) Act 2004 (WA). When the Human Reproductive Technology Act 1991 (WA) was first enacted, it was not clear whether PGD was permitted. Some of the wording in the legislation implied that PGD procedures may be used and that embryos could be selected on the basis of such, but also stated that genetic testing would not be permitted for therapeutic purposes. Section 21 states that:
'without limiting the generality of s 14(1)(c), the Code, or directions, may make provision as to    ... (b) the means of determining and evaluating the considerations which should or may be taken into account before an artificial fertilisation procedure is commenced, including the diagnostic procedures involved; ... (d) the practice and procedures to be carried out in relation to the collection, keeping, use and disposal of gametes, eggs in the process of fertilisation or embryos, or for securing that such eggs or embryos are in a suitable condition for implantation; ... (k) what, for the purposes of this Act, may constitute an authorised diagnostic procedure in relation to any egg in the process of fertilisation or an embryo or an approved project of research, or may be carried out or performed in any particular kind of research, and what shall not.'
Furthermore, under the initial legislation, the effect of s 14(2)(a) ruled out the application of any diagnostic procedures, including ones that would not directly harm the embryo, if it was not intended to be therapeutic for that egg or embryo. In the report, *Select Committee on the Human Reproductive Technology Act 1991*, it was noted that 'PGD would be prohibited where the result would be to terminate an embryo with a genetic or other defect': Parliament of Western Australia (n 62) 93.

119  Reproductive Technology Council, 'Policy on Approval of Diagnostic Procedures Involving Embryos' (2008) 1 http://www.rtc.org.au/clinics/docs/PGD_Policy_on_approval_of_diagnostic_procedures_involving_embryos.pdf> accessed 29 November 2014.

on the relevant form provided by the RTC.[120] If pre-implantation tissue-typing were to be undertaken in Western Australia, it would require authorisation by the RTC. There are different requirements for the approval of embryo diagnostic procedures depending on whether the procedure is to be carried out prior to implantation or on embryos that are not to be implanted.[121]

The RTC's policy concerning diagnostic procedures on embryos states that genetic analysis of embryos can occur as long as the procedure is 'unlikely to leave the embryo unfit for implantation' and there is 'a significant risk of a serious genetic abnormality or disease being present in the embryo'.[122] The advice goes on to state that for the most part, the purpose of genetic screening of embryos is to prevent the passing on of genetic disease, but it can also be used for patients thought to be at higher than average risk of conceiving abnormal embryos (also known as aneuploidy screening).[123] When deciding whether to approve PGD, the RTC will consider the risk and severity of the condition that is to be tested for and the safety and reliability of the procedure.[124] The RTC will also consider the severity of the condition being tested for in context of the environmental and personal factors of the participants seeking the testing.[125] The RTC has not provided a list of genetic diseases or abnormalities that will be approved for PGD testing, but will instead approve individual cases 'based on support of a clinical geneticist (accredited by the Human Genetics Society of Australasia (HGSA)) who has assessed the risk and seriousness of the condition to be tested for and discussed relevant issues with the participants requesting the testing'.[126] An application submitted by the clinic must include a report from the geneticist addressing an extensive list of questions outlined in the RTC's 'Policy on Approval of Diagnostic Procedures Involving Embryos'.[127] Consultation with a clinical geneticist is mandatory and in order to comply with the information and counselling provisions under the legislation, this may include a further consultation with a genetic counsellor.[128] Screening for aneuploidy is not dealt with on a case-by-case basis, but is instead permitted for certain categories of people who are considered to be at significant risk of producing an embryo that is chromosomally abnormal.[129]

---

120  ibid. 2.
121  ibid.
122  ibid. 2.
123  ibid.
124  ibid. 5.
125  ibid. 4.
126  ibid. 6.
127  ibid. 6–7.
128  ibid. 10.
129  ibid. 5.

## Regulation of Assisted Reproductive Technology in the United Kingdom

The UK regulatory framework is less complex than the Australian approach to ART regulation. This is largely because multi-jurisdictional issues and a federal legal structure do not complicate the UK framework.[130] The first child in the world to be born following an IVF procedure – Louise Brown – was born in 1978 in the UK.[131] In the early 1980s, the Committee of Enquiry into Human Fertilisation and Embryology was established to consider the issues in the UK and was chaired by the philosopher, Dame Mary Warnock (later to become Baroness Warnock). The Committee published a report in 1984 which suggested a relatively liberal regulatory regime for ART.[132] However, legislation was not immediately forthcoming as the Committee recommended that there should be some delay in implementing regulation as social attitudes were still forming on the subject at that time.[133] The Human Fertilisation and Embryology Act 1990 (UK) was passed six years after the report was published.

### A System of Licensing

The Human Fertilisation and Embryology Act 1990 (UK) implements a licence-based system. The UK statutory framework has been subject to significant review and has been updated as a result of the Human Fertilisation and Embryology Act 2008 (UK).[134] However, the framework implemented

---

130 Although, it should be noted that the scope of European Union law is beginning to impact on the provision of ART services in the UK. This is briefly considered below: see (n 154).

131 House of Commons Science and Technology Committee, *Human Reproductive Technologies and the Law* (2005) 3.

132 Warnock (n 78). The reaction to the report was mixed. When the report was issued, the use of IVF procedures was extremely controversial; Professor Brazier comments that the report 'fuelled rather than stilled controversy', and the publicity surrounding the report 'distorted debate on the Report as a whole'. There was vast opposition to the introduction of laws permitting embryo research and assisted reproduction on the basis that embryo destruction was facilitated. The anti-abortion and pro-life lobbying groups campaigned against the recommendations, and this had an impact on the debate surrounding the passing of the legislation. See Margaret Brazier, *Medicine, Patients and the Law* (3rd edn, Penguin 2003) 281.

133 Helen Szoke, 'Social Regulation, Reproductive Technology and the Social Interest. Policy and Process in Pioneering Jurisdictions' (PhD thesis, University of Melbourne 2004) 2.

134 For an overview of some of the changes to the legislative framework and a critique of the law reform process, see issue 32(2) of New Genetics and Society; a special issue of the journal on the topic of the Human Fertilisation and Embryology Act 2008 (UK).

by the original 1990 legislation was retained, based on the view that it has operated reasonably well.[135] The extensive review of the UK legislation that was undertaken is considered below.

The UK legislative scheme delegates a range of duties and responsibilities to the statutory body created by it – the Human Fertilisation and Embryology Authority (HFEA).[136] The HFEA is an independent body and is responsible for overseeing the regulatory framework. The UK framework is somewhat permissive as it has traditionally enabled the HFEA to exercise discretion in terms of regulatory control.[137] Thus, Petersen and Johnson describe the UK legislation as being 'relatively permissive, containing a limited number of express prohibitions, but is otherwise facilitative of a flexible regime administered by the Human Fertilisation and Embryology Authority'.[138] A number of duties are imposed upon the HFEA and its main functions are to:

- license treatment services, the storage of gametes and embryos and research on embryos;[139]
- monitor and inspect premises and activities carried out under statutory licence;[140]
- submit an annual report to the Secretary of State on its activities;[141]
- maintain a Code of Practice as guidance for the proper conduct of activities carried out under a licence.[142]

---

135 Department of Health (UK), *Review of the Human Fertilisation and Embryology Act* (2005) 13. Thus, at the time the reforms were being debated, Lord Darzi of Denham (the Parliamentary Under Secretary of State, Department of Health) stated '[w]e have not, however, proposed to abandon the basic foundations on which the existing law is based. We have not tried to fix what is not broken, nor have we thrown the baby out with the bathwater' (United Kingdom, House of Lords, *Parliamentary Debates* 19 November 2007, 665 (Lord Darzi of Denham)).

136 Human Fertilisation and Embryology Act 1990 (UK), s 5. Prior to the enactment of the UK legislation, the Royal College of Obstetricians and Gynaecologists and the Medical Research Council played a regulatory role, overseeing regulation as the Voluntary (and then Interim) Licensing Authority: Emily Jackson, *Medical Law: Text, Cases and Materials* (OUP 2006) 806.

137 Some commentators have noted that this is one of the very reasons as to why the legislative scheme requires updating: Rachel Anne Fenton and Fiona Dabell 'Time for change (1)' (2007) 157 *New Law Journal* 848.

138 Petersen and Johnson (n 12) 241.

139 Human Fertilisation and Embryology Act 1990 (UK), s 11.

140 Human Fertilisation and Embryology Act 1990 (UK), s 9.

141 Human Fertilisation and Embryology Act 1990 (UK), s 7.

142 Human Fertilisation and Embryology Act 1990 (UK), s 25. The Code of Practice is currently in its eighth edition: Human Fertilisation and Embryology

As a result of the reforms to the UK legislation, the HFEA is required to develop and maintain a set of general principles that should inform the practices and activities governed by the UK legislation.[143] The principles formulated by the HFEA are set out in the Code of Practice and relate to a wide range of issues applicable to licensed centres.[144] One of the key responsibilities of the HFEA is to produce and maintain the Code of Practice. The advice contained in the Code elaborates on the legislation, providing clinics with advice as to what constitutes good practice. The Code of Practice is not legally binding but if ART clinics fail to observe the guidance contained within it, this may be considered against an ART provider should there be any civil and/or criminal action.[145] Furthermore, the HFEA is empowered to vary, revoke or refuse to renew a licence based on deviations from the Code.[146]

The legislation enacted in the UK provides the HFEA with discretion in terms of its decision-making powers under the Act. While the Authority may be subject to challenge if it goes beyond the powers outlined in the legislation, the substantive decisions it makes are not open to challenge. In R *(on the application of Assisted Reproduction and Gynaecology Centre) v Human Fertilisation and Embryology Authority*, Wall J stated:

> [ART] is an area of rapidly developing scientific knowledge and debate, in which the Authority, as the licensing body established by Parliament, makes decisions and gives advice. It is not the function of the court to enter scientific debate, nor is it the function of the court to adjudicate on the merits of the Board's decisions or any advice it gives. Like any public authority, the Board is open to challenge by way of judicial review, but only if it exceeds or abuses the powers and responsibilities given to it by parliament ... [147]

One of HFEA's other major responsibilities is to oversee the licensing system detailed in the UK legislation. A range of ART activities require a licence and are outlined by the legislation.[148] Many aspects of ART practice can only be undertaken once a centre has been granted a licence, such as the use and storage of gametes and/or embryos. Carrying out such activities without

---

Authority, *Code of Practice* (8th edn, HFEA 2009).

143 Human Fertilisation and Embryology Act 2008 (UK), s 8(1)(ca).

144 Human Fertilisation and Embryology Authority (n 142) regulatory principles.

145 Human Fertilisation and Embryology Act 1990 (UK), s 25. See also, J Kenyon Mason and Graeme T Laurie, *Mason & McCall Smith's Law and Medical Ethics* (8th edn, OUP 2011) 254.

146 Human Fertilisation and Embryology Act 1990 (UK), s 25(6).

147 [2002] EWCA Civ 20 [15].

148 Human Fertilisation and Embryology Act 1990 (UK), s 11, sch 2.

a licence amounts to a criminal offence.[149] Once a licence is granted, there are a number of conditions automatically attached to it.[150] In addition to the standard conditions, the HFEA is also able to attach specific conditions to a licence and make recommendations aimed at improving practice within the centre seeking the licence.[151] The legislation divides licensed activities into four main categories.[152]

European law has also had some impact on this field. A Directive[153] issued to all European Union Member States requires ART providers to comply with specific requirements concerning human tissue and cells. The European Union Tissues and Cells Directive (EUTCD)[154] requires that any donation, procurement, testing, processing or storage of human gametes for the purposes of assisted reproduction must be licensed by the HFEA or be subject to an agreement with a licensed service.[155] Furthermore, as a condition of all licences, all donated sperm or eggs must be screened for disease and quarantined for six months, requiring the gametes to be frozen. The only exception to this requirement applies to a woman being inseminated by her partner's sperm.[156] Even in the latter instance, if sperm from a partner is to be stored, it must also be screened.[157] The EUTCD was incorporated into the 1990 legislative framework by the Human Fertilisation and Embryology Act 1990 (Amendment) Regulations 2006 (UK).

---

149 Human Fertilisation and Embryology Act 1990 (UK), sch 3.

150 Human Fertilisation and Embryology Act 1990 (UK), sch 2.

151 See Emily Jackson, *Medical Law: Text, Cases and Materials* (3rd edn, OUP 2013) 776–7.

152 See Human Fertilisation and Embryology Act 1990 (UK), s 11.

153 Under European Union law, a Directive is a form of secondary legislation and requires each European Union Member State to implement the measure specified within the Directive. It is the responsibility of each Member State to adopt the measure into domestic law and the Directive must be implemented within a specified time. In cases where a Member State fails to implement a Directive within that specified time, and an individual (or company) suffers damage as a result, it may be possible to bring a legal action against the government for failing to implement the Directive (or failing to implement it fully): *Francovich v Republic of Italy* [1995] ICR 722 ECJ Cases C-6 and 9/90.

154 Council Directive 2004/23/EC of 31 March 2004 on setting standards of quality and safety for the donation, procurement, testing, processing, preservation, storage and distribution of human tissues and cells [2004] OJ L102/48.

155 Human Fertilisation and Embryology Act 1990 (UK), s 4(1A). See also, Human Fertilisation and Embryology Authority, 'FAQs on EU Standards' (HFEA 2012) <www. hfea.gov.uk/fertility-clinic-questions-eu-standards.html> accessed 26 July 2014.

156 ibid.

157 ibid.

*Review of the Human Fertilisation and Embryology Act 1990*

Social attitudes concerning ART techniques have progressed significantly since the technology was first developed,[158] and this has occurred in tandem with rapid scientific advancements in the field. Inevitably, regulation in this field has the potential to become outdated alongside such developments,[159] and although the UK framework had attempted to address this issue by delegating discretion to the HFEA to update regulatory policy, there were aspects of the original legislative scheme that required urgent review.[160]

There were a number of factors that contributed to the need to update the UK legislative framework. In addition to some of the major scientific advances, the original legislative scheme was subject to a number of legal challenges.[161] Moreover, the legal recognition of same-sex relationships also had implications for questions of legal parentage in terms of children born into such families as a result of ART services. These factors (along with a number of others) have resulted in some of the most significant changes to the UK legislative framework since its inception in 1990.[162]

The legislative review process undertaken in the UK is one of the most systematic reforms of ART regulation in the Commonwealth. The process commenced in January 2004, when the Parliamentary Under Secretary for Public Health made an announcement stating that the UK Government had decided to review the 1990 legislation by way of public consultation, which was to be conducted by the Department of Health.[163] That same year, the House of

---

158 Department of Health (UK), *Review of the Human Fertilisation and Embryology Act: A Public Consultation* (2005) 6.

159 As Emily Jackson notes, '[t]he pace of scientific progress in the field of assisted conception means that primary legislation has an inevitable in-built obsolescence': Emily Jackson, *Regulating Reproduction: Law, Technology and Autonomy* (Hart Publishing 2001) 184.

160 See Fenton and Dabell (n 137); Marie Fox, 'The Human Fertilisation and Embryology Act 2008: Tinkering at the Margins' (2009) 17 Feminist Legal Studies 333.

161 There had been a number of significant cases that have challenged some of the provisions in the 1990 legislation: *R v Secretary of State for Health, ex parte Bruno Quintavalle (on behalf of Pro-Life Alliance)* [2001] EWHC Admin 918; *Rose v Secretary of State for Health and the HFEA* [2002] EWHC 1593; *R (Quintavalle) v Secretary of State for Health* [2003] UKHL 692; *Evans v Amicus Healthcare* [2003] EWHC 2161; *Leeds Teaching Hospitals NHS trust v A* [2003] EWHC 259 (QBD); *R (on the application of Assisted Reproduction and Gynaecology Centre) v Human Fertilisation and Embryology Authority* [2002] EWCA Civ 20; *R v Human Fertilisation and Embryology Authority ex parte Blood* [1999] Fam. 151.

162 See Christine Knight and Malcolm K Smith, 'Editorial: The Human Fertilisation and Embryology Act 2008' (2013) 32 New Genetics and Society 107.

163 Department of Health (UK) (n 158).

Commons Science and Technology Committee also reviewed the law relating to ART. The Committee's report was published in March 2005[164] and the Government produced an official response to the report in August that same year.[165] In December 2006, following the consultation process, the Department of Health published its report.[166] A number of significant recommendations were made, including a proposal to merge the HFEA with the Human Tissue Authority (HTA) to form the Regulatory Authority for Tissue and Embryos (RATE).[167] The plans to merge the two bodies also fell within the scope of the UK's general review of 'arm's length bodies'.[168] The Department of Health then produced a draft Bill in May 2007, which implemented the proposed reforms within the existing legislation.[169] Following this, a motion was made in both Houses of Parliament to appoint a Joint Committee to scrutinise the proposals for legislation and the draft Bill was considered by the Joint Committee on the Human Tissue and Embryos (Draft) Bill.[170] The Government again issued a formal response to the Joint Committee's report.[171] In relation to the major proposal to establish RATE, the Joint Committee recommended that there was 'overwhelming and convincing' evidence for the Government to abandon the proposal.[172] This was similarly reflected in the Government's response to the Joint Committee's recommendations.[173]

---

164 House of Commons Science and Technology Committee (n 131).

165 United Kingdom, *Government Response to the Report from the House of Commons Science and Technology Committee: Human Reproductive Technologies and the Law* (Cm 6641, 2005).

166 Department of Health (UK), *Review of the Human Fertilisation and Embryology Act: Proposals for Revised Legislation (Including Establishment of the Regulatory Authority for Tissue and Embryos)* (2006).

167 ibid. 26–30.

168 In 2004, the UK Department of Health undertook a review of its 'arm's length bodies' (arm's length bodies are described as 'national organisations sponsored by the Department of Health undertaking executive functions'), as part of a wider programme 'to improve efficiency and cut bureaucracy': Department of Health (UK) (n 158) 37. The conclusions of the review were published by the Department of Health and included proposals to reduce the number of arm's length bodies from 38 to 20: Department of Health (UK), *Reconfiguring the Department of Health's Arm's Length Bodies* (2004).

169 Department of Health (UK), *Human Tissue and Embryos (Draft) Bill* (2007).

170 Joint Committee on the Human Tissue and Embryos (Draft) Bill, *Report of the Joint Committee of the House of Lords and House of Commons on the Human Tissue and Embryos (Draft) Bill, 2007: Vol I: Report* (Session 2006–2007, HL Paper 169-I, HC Paper 630-II).

171 United Kingdom, *Government Response to the Report from the Joint Committee on the Human Tissue and Embryos (Draft) Bill* (Cm 7209 2007).

172 Joint Committee on the Human Tissue and Embryos (Draft) Bill (n 170) 31.

173 United Kingdom (n 171) 6.

After this extensive process the proposals reached Parliament in the form of the Human Fertilisation and Embryology Bill 2007. Debate on the Bill commenced in the House of Lords in November 2007 and reached the House of Commons in May 2008. Some of the Bill's provisions were subject to considerable debate, resulting in a number of further changes. The House of Lords strongly agreed with the decision not to merge the HFEA with the HTA to form RATE.[174] Many members of the House also expressed approval in relation to the way in which the legislative framework was reviewed. For example, Baroness Williams of Crosby remarked that the Bill provided 'a remarkable counter-example of how to involve people in the deepest discussion on a matter of such complexity and importance'.[175] Furthermore, Baroness Tonge stated that:

[t]he Government must also be congratulated on the wide consultation on the Bill and on the fine work of the committee that scrutinised the draft Bill ... I wish all legislation could be dealt with in this way ... [176]

## Key Aspects of the UK Legislative Provisions

As with the position in Australia, the UK legislative framework addresses a number of specific issues concerning the provision of ART services. Importantly, the legislation and the HFEA's Code of Practice outline specific

---

174 Baroness Jay of Paddington stated: 'I simply say that I am delighted to see the disappearance of RATE. It is my very strong view that the right architecture for providing a clear statutory framework based on the principles of devolved regulation is now the backbone of the Bill': United Kingdom, House of Lords, *Parliamentary Debates* 19 November 2007, 677 (Baroness Jay of Paddington). Furthermore, Lord Jenkin of Roding also made similar observations: 'From the very moment that the merger [of the HFEA with the HTA] was announced, I thought that it was a rotten idea – I am on record as saying it. The idea survived for some three and a half years, but the Select Committee, and the evidence that it heard from almost every witness who referred to it, has put paid to it. I hope that the Minister will give a firm assurance that no attempt to resurrect RATE will be made. One reason for rejecting the proposal which certainly impressed me was that to treat human tissues and embryos as though they were equal entities, which the original title of the draft Bill and RATE would have provided for, would seem to devalue the importance of the embryo'. United Kingdom, House of Lords, *Parliamentary Debates* 19 November 2007, 683 (Lord Jenkin of Roding).

175 United Kingdom, House of Lords, *Parliamentary Debates* 19 November 2007, 685 (Baroness Williams of Crosby).

176 United Kingdom, House of Lords, *Parliamentary Debates* 19 November 2007, 670 (Baroness Tonge).

requirements, such as: the need for participants to provide informed consent[177] (which must be made in writing);[178] that detailed information must be provided to participants;[179] and that participants must have been given an *opportunity* to receive counselling.[180] As outlined below, the UK legislation also requires ART

---

177 Human Fertilisation and Embryology Act 1990 (UK), sch 3, para 1; Human Fertilisation and Embryology Authority (n142) guidance notes 5.1–5.29. There is an exception in relation to minors, with regards to consent for the storage of gametes: see Human Fertilisation and Embryology Act 1990 (UK), sch 3, para 9.

178 Human Fertilisation and Embryology Act 1990 (UK), sch 3, para 1; Human Fertilisation and Embryology Authority (n 142) guidance note 5.13. Consent must also remain 'effective', meaning that it must not have been withdrawn (Human Fertilisation and Embryology Act 1990 (UK), sch 3, para 1(3)), and where the woman receives treatment with her partner either party is able to vary or revoke consent up until the embryo is implanted (Human Fertilisation and Embryology Act 1990 (UK), sch 3, para 4; see also *Evans v United Kingdom* (European Court of Human Rights, Grand Chamber, Application No 6339/05, 10 April 2007)). The consent of the participants must also state the maximum length of storage of any gametes or embryos (particularly if this is to be less than the statutory storage period) and state what is to be done with the gametes or embryos should the patient die or become incapable of withdrawing or revoking consent (Human Fertilisation and Embryology Act 1990 (UK), sch 3, para 2(2)).

179 Before providing treatment to any woman, the woman (and her partner if applicable) should be given the following information: (a) the centre's policy on selecting patients; (b) the centre's statutory duty to take account of the welfare of any resulting or affected child; (c) the expected waiting time for treatment; (d) fertility treatments available; (e) the likely outcomes of the proposed treatment (data provided should include the centre's most recent live birth rate and clinical pregnancy rate per treatment cycle, verified by the HFEA, and the national live birth rate and clinical pregnancy rate per treatment cycle); (f) the nature and potential risks of the treatment, including the risk of children conceived having developmental and birth defects; (g) the possible side effects and risks to the woman being treated and any resulting child, including ovarian hyperstimulation syndrome (OHSS); (h) in the case of fresh egg donation, the screening requirement of the donor and the risk of infection for the recipient; (i) the availability of facilities for freezing embryos, and the implications of storing embryos and then using embryos; (j) the importance of informing the treatment centre about the eventual outcome of the treatment (including if no live birth results); (k) the centre's complaints procedure; and (l) the nature and potential risks (immediate and long term) of IVF/ICSI with in vitro matured eggs, including reference to the clinic's experience: Human Fertilisation and Embryology Authority (n 142) guidance note 4.2. Information must also be given about the cost of treatment and any other specific aspect of treatment that may prove relevant in the circumstances of the patient(s): Human Fertilisation and Embryology Authority (n 142) guidance notes 4.3, 4.4.

180 Human Fertilisation and Embryology Act 1990 (UK), ss 13(6), 13(6A), 13A (as amended). See also sch 3, para 3, which also stipulates a number of further situations concerning counselling.

providers to prioritise the welfare of children who may be born following the
provision of ART services.

## Access to assisted reproductive technology services

The UK legislation does not impose eligibility criteria to exclude certain
individuals from accessing ART services. Therefore, access to services is not
restricted in the same way as some of the Australian jurisdictions outlined
above. However, there is a requirement that those providing treatment services
consider the welfare of children who may be born following the provision of
such services, which is reflected in the legislation as follows:

> A woman shall not be provided with treatment services unless account has been
> taken of the welfare of any child who may be born as a result of the treatment
> (including the need of that child for supportive parenting) and of any other
> child who may be affected by the birth.[181]

The pre-amended version of the 'welfare clause' required ART providers to
consider the child's 'need for a father' (instead of the need for 'supportive
parenting'). The requirement to consider the child's need for a father was based
on the view that it was 'better for children to be born into a two-parent family,
with both father and mother'.[182] There was considerable debate surrounding
the issue of whether treatments should be limited to married couples when the
1990 legislation was first enacted,[183] and the requirement to consider the child's
'need for a father' was implemented as a compromise for those who argued that
access should be limited to married couples.[184] The original welfare principle
under the UK legislation has been heavily criticised, particularly in terms of
it being applied inconsistently by different ART providers.[185] There was also
concern that the requirement discriminated against some women seeking to
access treatment services on the basis of their marital status or sexuality as the
requirement to consider the child's need for a father would, in principle, restrict
the accessibility of treatments to heterosexual couples. However, it has been

---

181  Human Fertilisation and Embryology Act 1990 (UK), s 13(5) (as amended).

182  Warnock (n 78) [2.11].

183  An attempt to amend the eligibility criteria to restrict access to married couples
lost by one vote in the House of Lords: Margaret Brazier, 'Reproductive Rights:
Feminism or Patriarchy' in John Harris and Søren Holm (eds), *The Future of Human
Reproduction: Ethics, Choice and Regulation* (OUP 1998).

184  Jackson (n 159) 197.

185  See Emily Jackson, 'Conception and the Irrelevance of the Welfare Principle'
(2002) 177 Modern Law Review 176; Emily Jackson, 'Rethinking the Pre-conception
Welfare Principle' in Kirsty Horsey and Hazel Biggs (eds), *Human Fertilisation and
Embryology: Reproducing Regulation* (Routledge Cavendish 2007) 47–68.

noted that in practice, the requirement did not operate to exclude single and lesbian women from accessing treatment.[186]

As a result of the major review of the law that was undertaken in the UK, the requirement to consider the child's 'need for a father' was replaced with the need for 'supportive parenting'.[187] This change was underpinned by evidence to suggest that it is not necessarily the gender of a child's parents that is fundamental, but the availability of two supportive parents. The Report of the Joint Committee states:

> We have found persuasive the evidence presented to us that a loving, supportive family network is more important for a child's development than the gender of the second parent ... [188]

Therefore, ART providers in the UK are required to ensure that the child will be born into a supportive environment. The Code of Practice issued by the HFEA has defined supportive parenting as:

> ... a commitment to the health, well being and development of the child. It is presumed that all prospective parents will be supportive parents, in the absence of any reasonable cause for concern that any child who may be born, or any other child, may be at risk of significant harm or neglect.[189]

In order to comply with this statutory duty (which is a condition of any licence granted to an ART centre), an assessment of the risk of harm to the child to be born must be undertaken[190] before providing treatment services.[191] Consequently,

---

186 The Joint Committee on the Human Tissue and Embryos (Draft) Bill heard evidence stating that the provision 'does not prevent someone having access to fertility treatment as a single woman, whether she is heterosexual or gay': see (n 170) 61. Furthermore, as noted by Lord Mackay of Clashfern, the requirement 'does not debar people from getting IVF when no father is in the offing but it requires the child's need for a father to be considered as a factor in the welfare of the child': United Kingdom, House of Lords, *Parliamentary Debates* 10 December 2007, 38 (Lord Mackay of Clashfern).

187 Human Fertilisation and Embryology Act 2008 (UK), s 14(2). For a discussion of the reform process surrounding the welfare clause and the parenthood provisions under the legislation, see Julie McCandless, 'Cinderella and Her Cruel Sisters: Parenthood, Welfare and Gender in the Human Fertilisation and Embryology Act 2008' (2013) 32 New Genetics and Society 135.

188 Joint Committee on the Human Tissue and Embryos (Draft) Bill (n 170) 65.

189 Human Fertilisation and Embryology Authority (n 142) guidance note 8.11.

190 Human Fertilisation and Embryology Authority (n 142) guidance note 8.3.

191 Treatment services means 'medical, surgical or obstetric services provided to the public or a section of the public for the purpose of assisting women to carry

as outlined in subsequent chapters, the UK regulatory approach seems to prioritise the notion of harm as a guiding factor of relevance in determining whether ART services should be refused to prospective participants. In this sense, a risk assessment is made in relation to each patient undergoing treatment (including the patient's partner, where applicable), and is to be carried out in a non-discriminatory way.[192] When carrying out the assessment, the centre is required to take account of the circumstances of the patient (and the patient's partner) that are likely to cause significant harm or neglect to the child to be born or to an existing child of the family.[193] Factors that should be taken into account include previous criminal convictions, family protection measures in relation to existing children and incidents of domestic violence.[194] Furthermore, any circumstances that impact on the ability of those seeking treatment to care for children in the future (such as psychological disorders or alcohol/substance abuse, or any medical conditions having the same effect) must also be taken into account.[195] Where factors are apparent to the centre, they are required to seek the patient's consent before obtaining information from third parties such as the patient's general practitioner, or any agencies or authorities.[196]

### Regulation of pre-implantation genetic diagnosis

The UK legislation directly addresses PGD,[197] and the HFEA's Code of Practice adds further detail to the legislative provisions.[198] The legislation specifically permits licensed centres to carry out 'practices designed to secure that embryos

---

children'. Human Fertilisation and Embryology Act 1990 (UK), s 2(1) (as amended); Human Fertilisation and Embryology Authority (n 142) guidance note 8.1.

192  Human Fertilisation and Embryology Authority (n 142) guidance note 8.7.

193  Human Fertilisation and Embryology Authority (n 142) guidance note 8.3.

194  Human Fertilisation and Embryology Authority (n 142) guidance note 8.10.

195  Human Fertilisation and Embryology Authority (n 142) guidance note 8.10.

196  Human Fertilisation and Embryology Authority (n 142) guidance note 8.13. Prior to a review of the welfare principle undertaken by the HFEA, there was a requirement for ART centres to undertake a background check into the history of the patient(s), but the HFEA moved towards a presumption in *favour* of providing treatment unless there were circumstances to suggest that any child born will be at a risk of significant harm or neglect: Human Fertilisation and Embryology Authority, *Tomorrow's Children, Report of the Policy Review of Welfare of the Child Assessments in Licensed Assisted Conception Clinics* (2005).

197  Schedule 2 of the legislation addresses the activities that may be licensed under the legislative framework. Paragraph 1 of the schedule addresses the use of embryo testing techniques, stating that 'A licence … may authorise any of the following in the course of providing treatment services – (b) procuring, keeping, testing, processing or distributing embryos … (d) other practices designed to secure that embryos are in a suitable condition to be placed in a woman'. Paragraph 1ZA also outlines a number of permitted uses of PGD. See Human Fertilisation and Embryology Act 1990 (UK), sch 2.

198  Human Fertilisation and Embryology Authority (n 142) guidance notes 9–10.

are in a suitable condition to be placed in a woman',[199] and this encompasses
the use of embryo screening practices.[200] Any centre in possession of a licence
will be subject to a number of standard conditions and although some of those
conditions relate to the use of PGD, an ART centre must only undertake embryo
screening for purposes authorised by the HFEA, as stipulated in the licence.[201]

The Code of Practice outlines detailed guidance concerning PGD, which
covers the use of embryo screening for diagnosing genetic conditions, tissue
type and establishing sex.[202] The legislation prohibits the practice of sex
selection unless there is a risk that the participants will give birth to a child
with a sex-linked genetic disorder.[203] For the provision of all PGD services, the
centre must ensure that suitable staff are employed,[204] which includes ensuring
that the team involved with undertaking PGD techniques includes a clinical
geneticist and a genetic counsellor (this would also be necessary for compliance
with the usual counselling and information-giving requirements outlined under
the statutory framework).[205]

In relation to the diagnosis of genetic conditions, the HFEA Code of
Practice states that PGD should be used to detect a heritable condition only
if there 'is a significant risk of a serious genetic condition being present in
the embryo'.[206] In deciding whether the condition is sufficiently serious to
warrant PGD, the centre should consider the circumstances of those seeking
treatment rather than the particular condition that the embryo will be tested
for.[207] Similarly, the Code of Practice outlines a number of further factors to

---

199 Human Fertilisation and Embryology Act 1990 (UK), sch 2, para 1(1)(d).

200 See Human Fertilisation and Embryology Authority (n 142). See also *R (on the
application of Quintavalle) v Human Fertilisation and Embryology Authority* [2005] 2 All ER 555.

201 See conditions outlined in Human Fertilisation and Embryology Authority (n
142) licence condition T89.

202 Human Fertilisation and Embryology Authority (n 142) guidance note 10.

203 Human Fertilisation and Embryology Act 1990 (UK), sch 2, para 1ZB.

204 Human Fertilisation and Embryology Authority (n 142) guidance notes 10.1–10.3.

205 Human Fertilisation and Embryology Authority (n 142) guidance note 10.2.

206 Human Fertilisation and Embryology Authority (n 142) guidance note 10.6.

207 Human Fertilisation and Embryology Authority (n 142) guidance note 10.5.
The Code of Practice outlines a number of factors that should be considered when
contemplating the use and appropriateness of PGD, as outlined in guidance note 10.7.
The use of PGD to prevent hereditary disease is an extremely controversial subject,
especially in deciding which disorders may be *serious* enough for the purposes of using
PGD. See Jonathan Glover, *Choosing Children: Genes, Disability, and Design* (OUP 2006);
David King, 'Preimplantation Genetic Diagnosis and the "New" Eugenics' (1999) 25
Journal of Medical Ethics 176; David Resnik, 'The Moral Significance of the Therapy-
Enhancement Distinction in Human Genetics' (2000) 9 Cambridge Quarterly of
Healthcare Ethics 365; Rosamund Scott, 'Choosing between Possible Lives: Legal

be considered in relation to pre-implantation tissue-typing.[208] Although these specific requirements are outlined in Chapter 3, it is worth noting that when PGD is used to establish tissue type in conjunction with the diagnosis of a genetic disease, the specific considerations relevant to pre-implantation tissue-typing are to be made *in addition* to the requirements listed in relation to the detection of genetic conditions.[209]

The HFEA has played an important role in developing PGD policy (particularly in relation to pre-implantation tissue-typing). Prior to the recent legislative reforms, the 1990 legislation did not specifically deal with embryo selection technologies in detail. However, as the technology has advanced, the HFEA has responded to such developments by issuing regulatory policy in relation to specific uses of the technology. In this regard, the policy and decision-making powers of the HFEA have been subject to legal challenge by way of judicial review. In a case concerning the use of embryo selection technologies for the purpose of establishing tissue type, it was argued that the HFEA was acting outside the scope of its powers.[210] The House of Lords held that the HFEA was acting within its powers and it was confirmed that the use of PGD in this context falls under the scope of the legislation, as it is a practice 'designed to secure that embryos are in a suitable condition to be placed in a woman'.[211] While the decision to permit the practice of pre-implantation tissue-typing was noted to be a controversial one, Lord Brown held that the case was 'all about the scope of a power, not about its exercise'.[212] He also stated that while 'suitability is for the woman, the limits of permissible embryo selection are for the authority'.[213] It was also noted that should the HFEA overstep its powers by allowing ART centres to use embryo selection technologies for purposes that fall outside the scope of the legislation, Parliament is able to pass regulations to restrict such use.[214] Furthermore, Lord Hoffman held that the

---

and Ethical Issues in Preimplantation Genetic Diagnosis' 26 Oxford Journal of Legal Studies 153; Loane Skene and Janna Thomson (eds), *The Sorting Society: The Ethics of Genetic Screening and Therapy* (CUP 2008).

208 Human Fertilisation and Embryology Authority (n 142) guidance notes 10.21–10.28.

209 The Code of Practice outlines a number of factors that should be considered when contemplating the use and appropriateness of PGD: Human Fertilisation and Embryology Authority (n 142) guidance note 10.21.

210 R *(on the application of Quintavalle) v Human Fertilisation and Embryology Authority* (n 200).

211 ibid.; See Human Fertilisation and Embryology Act 1990 (UK), sch 2, para 1(1)(d).

212 R *(on the application of Quintavalle) v Human Fertilisation and Embryology Authority* (n 200) 566.

213 ibid. 570.

214 ibid. 562. See Human Fertilisation and Embryology Act 1990 (UK), s 3(3)(c).

decision of the HFEA seems ' … exactly in accordance with the duty of the authority to keep the state of the art under review'.[215]

## Reflecting on the Regulatory Landscape

The regulatory framework in the UK is an example of a flexible and relatively liberal approach to ART regulation. Although the UK legislation addresses many aspects of ART, it does not attempt to address all aspects of ART practice. Instead, it delegates responsibility to the statutory body so that the HFEA can address specific issues as they arise and issue regulatory policy where necessary.

The significant process of review conducted by the UK Government provides an example of a comprehensive, thorough and thoughtful response to the issues raised within the sphere of ART. Nevertheless, there are aspects of the reformed legislative framework that require further consideration. As detailed in Chapter 8, the approach to pre-implantation tissue-typing is one of those issues in need of further attention. Although the HFEA has played an important role in developing regulatory policy on this specific topic, the reformed legislation now addresses this issue directly and is arguably more restrictive than the previous approach developed by the HFEA.

Importantly however, the legislative framework in the UK does not restrict access to ART services in the same way that services are restricted in some Australian jurisdictions. The key factor relevant to determining whether ART services should be provided or refused is the welfare assessment. The removal of the requirement to consider the child's 'need for a father' supports a move towards a wider notion of access, which does not discriminate against individuals (or couples) on the basis of marital status or sexuality. Furthermore, it is important to note that access to PGD is not restricted on the basis of statutory eligibility criteria, as with some of the Australian jurisdictions.

Arguably, the UK framework seeks to promote greater freedom in the context of reproductive decision-making compared to the approaches in some Australian jurisdictions. As discussed in Chapter 6, the UK's approach arguably prioritises the notion of harm as a basis for justifying intervention with reproductive decision-making.

## Conclusion

This chapter has provided the necessary foundations for understanding the regulatory frameworks applicable to the delivery of ART services in Australia

---

215 R *(on the application of Quintavalle) v Human Fertilisation and Embryology Authority* (n 200) 565.

and the UK. The different approaches are explored further in Chapter 3, in the specific context of the accessibility and regulation of pre-implantation tissue-typing. As will become clear, the difference between regulatory approaches more generally has a significant impact on the availability and use of embryo selection technologies. Moreover, this background also provides a foundation for unpacking the underlying normative principles that are guiding regulation in this field and therefore, most importantly, providing the basis for evaluating current approaches to pre-implantation tissue-typing. Finally, an understanding of the regulatory frameworks currently in place in the selected jurisdictions – including the principles underpinning these approaches – is fundamental in considering how regulation on the topic of pre-implantation tissue-typing can, and should, respond in circumstances where a family wishes to create a saviour child.

# Chapter 3

# Regulating Access to and the Delivery of Pre-implantation Tissue-typing Services

## Introduction

This chapter focuses on the more specific issue of accessibility to and regulation of embryo selection technologies in circumstances where assisted reproductive technology (ART) services are sought for the purpose of conceiving a saviour child. Importantly, the demand for in vitro fertilisation (IVF) in this particular context is not based on a medical problem that has rendered the woman or her partner infertile, nor is it based solely on the risk of passing on a genetic condition to a child who is conceived following the provision of ART services (although the technology may also be used for this purpose in some instances). The factor driving the couple to seek access to ART services in this context is their wish to help their sick child, who requires a transplantation of tissue from a compatible donor, to prevent the sick child's health from deteriorating. On this basis, the reason for seeking access to ART services is based on the circumstances of a person who is not a recipient of those services.

Before reviewing the regulatory position concerning this specific issue, it should be noted that the technique used to determine an embryo's tissue type does not, strictly speaking, 'diagnose' the embryo's genetics. Rather, the purpose is to establish the human leukocyte antigen (HLA) type of the embryo. The term 'pre-implantation genetic diagnosis' (PGD), however, can be used as an umbrella term to encompass embryo selection technologies for purposes other than identification of specific *genetic* characteristics.[1] Essentially, the physical process involved in the embryo biopsy procedure is the same irrespective of

---

1 PGD is also used as a general term to describe other techniques such as aneuploidy screening, which involves screening the embryo for chromosomal abnormalities so that those embryos which do not show abnormalities can be implanted in order to try and achieve a higher pregnancy rate. Similarly, this process does not involve the 'diagnosis' of a particular condition, but falls under the heading of PGD. See Pasquale Patrizio and others, 'High Rate of Biological Loss in Assisted Reproduction: It is in the Seed, Not in the Soil' (2007) 14 Reproductive Biomedicine Online 92.

whether the purpose is to detect a genetic condition or to establish the tissue type of an embryo (or for some other reason, such as determining the sex of an embryo). This chapter therefore considers how access to ART services is restricted in circumstances where they are sought for this specific purpose, and considers the regulatory requirements that must be complied with in such circumstances. The discussion in this chapter sets the scene for the analysis and evaluation that follow in the subsequent chapters, which also highlight the underlying normative principles that guide the regulatory approach in this context.

## Access to Assisted Reproductive Technology Services for Pre-implantation Tissue-typing

The ART regulatory landscape outlined in Chapter 2 provides the necessary background for understanding how the regulatory landscape impacts on the accessibility of pre-implantation tissue-typing services. As discussed below, the eligibility requirements outlined in some jurisdictions impact significantly on the issue of access when ART services are utilised for the sole purpose of conceiving a saviour child. However, even where statutory requirements do not preclude access for this specific purpose, there is a general requirement outlined in all applicable jurisdictions, to consider the welfare of any child who may be conceived following the provision of ART services. In the context of a decision to conceive a saviour child, the requirement to consider the welfare of the prospective child may be relied upon as a basis for refusing ART services. In this respect, restrictions on access may therefore result even if prospective ART participants are not precluded by statute.

### Accessibility in Australia

As established in Chapter 2, legislation in South Australia, Victoria and Western Australia requires ART centres to limit services to those who are unable to conceive due to medical reasons (or in Victoria, where a pregnancy cannot be established without utilising an ART service), or to those at risk of passing on a genetic condition when conceiving naturally.[2] A medical need for ART services

---

2 In South Australia, the Assisted Reproductive Treatment Act 1988 (SA), s 9(1)(c) requires that ART services are only provided where the woman (or her male partner) appear to be infertile, or if the couple are at risk of transmitting a serious genetic defect, disease or illness to a child conceived naturally. In Victoria, the Assisted Reproductive Treatment Act 2008 (Vic), s 10(2) states that a woman or couple will be eligible for treatment if '(a) a doctor is satisfied, on reasonable grounds', that: '(i) in

is established where a woman is unable to conceive naturally either because she has a medical condition that prevents her from establishing a pregnancy or carrying a pregnancy to term, or because her partner has impaired fertility. Alternatively, this may be established if a couple is at risk of passing on a particular genetic condition when conceiving naturally so that IVF and embryo selection technologies can assist them in their desire to conceive a child who will be born free from a particular genetic condition or disease. Fundamentally, the fact that ART services are limited to individuals or couples who have a medical need for them has a significant impact on access in other contexts. However, it should be noted that in Victoria a review panel is able to grant access to services in some circumstances where the woman or couple do not meet the statutory criteria. The position in Victoria is unique and is considered later in this chapter. In the remaining Australian jurisdictions where access to ART services is not limited by statutory eligibility criteria, clinics may choose to limit ART services to those who have a medical need for them.[3] Where this is so, it may indirectly impact upon the accessibility of such services where they are intended primarily for the creation of a saviour child, which would therefore require prospective participants to seek access to services at a different clinic (which could require them to travel interstate).

There have been a number of cases where families have sought to create tissue-matched children who may offer the prospect of curing a sick child who is suffering from a *genetic* condition; the couple seeking access to ART services intend to use embryo selection technologies to select an embryo that is not only free from the genetic condition their sick child is suffering from, but to *also* ensure that the prospective child matches the sick child's tissue type. In this context, pre-implantation tissue-typing is considered to be ancillary to the main reason that the couple wish to utilise IVF and PGD, which is to prevent the transmission of a genetic condition. In such circumstances, these families will not be excluded from accessing services in the relevant jurisdictions, as they fall within the statutory eligibility criteria (or the clinic's policy).

---

the woman's circumstances, the woman is unlikely to become pregnant other than by a treatment procedure'; or '(ii) the woman is unlikely to be able to carry a pregnancy or give birth to a child without a treatment procedure'; or '(iii) the woman is at risk of transmitting a genetic abnormality or genetic disease to a child born as a result of a pregnancy conceived other than by a treatment procedure, including a genetic abnormality or genetic disease for which the woman's partner is the carrier'; and '(b) a presumption against treatment does not apply to the woman'. In Western Australia, the Human Reproductive Technology Act 1991 (WA), s 23(a) permits licensed ART clinics to provide services where they 'would be likely to benefit' a woman or a couple who are unable to conceive 'due to medical reasons', or 'whose child would be likely to be affected by a genetic abnormality or disease'.

3 *JM v QFG* [2000] 1 Qd R 373; *Morgan v GK* [2001] QADT 10.

Alternatively, consider a family that similarly wishes to conceive a saviour sibling to treat a sick child. In this instance, the sick child suffers from a condition that is not genetic, but developed after birth. Similarly, the child's condition can be treated by way of transplantation from a tissue-matched donor. The driving factor encouraging the couple to seek access to IVF services is not based upon a desire to prevent transmission of a genetic condition, but is instead based upon the wish to select an embryo for implantation of the same tissue type as the couple's sick child. In this context, the couple would not be eligible for treatment in a jurisdiction (or an individual clinic) where narrow eligibility criteria are imposed. Thus, the need for treatment in this latter example is not based on the medical need of the participants or the child that may be born as a result of the treatment, but is instead focused on the medical need of a sick child.

This distinction raises an important issue in relation to the accessibility of IVF for pre-implantation tissue-typing. In those jurisdictions where no eligibility criteria are imposed, the technology is more widely accessible.[4] The normative analysis that follows in this book considers whether there is any justification for imposing restrictions on the accessibility of pre-implantation tissue-typing based on these differing cases. As discussed below, a distinction between these two examples was initially drawn by the United Kingdom (UK) regulator, the Human Fertilisation and Embryology Authority (HFEA), which meant that access to services was only granted in circumstances where a couple wished to utilise embryo selection technologies for the purpose of avoiding transmission of a genetic condition. This distinction received significant criticism.[5]

In Chapter 2, I provided a more general perspective of the regulatory position concerning access to ART services. The purpose of doing this was to clearly demonstrate how the general restrictions on access indirectly impact on pre-implantation tissue-typing. The normative evaluation that follows in the subsequent chapters will not consider whether these more general restrictions are justified, in the sense that the state is justified in limiting access to ART by indirectly preventing certain classes of people from accessing services (such as single and lesbian women who do not have a 'medical need' for treatment).[6]

---

4 Michelle Taylor-Sands, 'Selecting "Saviour Siblings": Reconsidering the Regulation in Australia of Pre-implantation Genetic Diagnosis in Conjunction with Tissue-typing' (2007) 14 Journal of Law and Medicine 551.

5 See Stephen Bellamy, 'Lives to Save lives – The Ethics of Tissue Typing' (2005) 8 Human Fertility 5; Sally Sheldon and Stephen Wilkinson, 'Hashmi and Whitaker: An Unjustifiable and Misguided Distinction?' (2004) 12 Medical Law Review 137.

6 The restriction is indirect and does not impact on *all* single and lesbian women: those women who are unable to establish a pregnancy because they are not engaging in heterosexual sexual intercourse (some have referred to this as 'social infertility') will

Furthermore, as will become apparent in Chapters 5 and 6, my analysis is focused on whether the *state* can justifiably impose restrictions on ART services in circumstances where they are intended for the creation of a saviour child. Therefore, restrictions imposed by individual ART clinics may fall outside the scope of this analysis. However, if it is established that the normative analysis supports a wider notion of access where IVF is utilised for the purpose of creating a saviour child, one possible option open to regulators is to ensure that ART policy (such as legislation or guidelines) permits access to IVF for this specific purpose. If this is so, the legislation in the relevant jurisdictions could specifically address the issue of access to services for this particular purpose, and it would not be open for individual clinics to impose their own restrictions where services are sought for the creation of a saviour child.[7]

One of the distinguishing factors in the Australian context is that the restrictions in place have not been consciously imposed by the state's decision to purposely limit the availability of IVF for pre-implantation tissue-typing. Legislators did not envisage this particular use of PGD when the statutory eligibility criteria were first implemented. Instead, services have been restricted to those who have a medical need for them and this *indirectly* restricts the availability of the technology in this specific context. Arguably, where regulation indirectly impacts on the accessibility of IVF for pre-implantation tissue-typing, regulators should be aware of this. And as the regulatory bodies or state health departments in the relevant jurisdictions have a responsibility to monitor developments in the sphere of ART, this would include an obligation to take note of how the eligibility criteria impact on the accessibility of services in this context.

Furthermore, where state bodies have reviewed the law and reported on such issues, the state will be aware of the impact that restrictive policies have on the accessibility of services. This was the case in Victoria following the review of the law by the Victorian Law Reform Commission (VLRC).[8] The final report of the VLRC proposed that wider eligibility criteria should be implemented in order to prevent the discrimination that arises as a result of

---

be prevented from accessing services in some jurisdictions. Where a woman can show that she is unable to conceive due to medical reasons, she will be able to gain access to services, regardless of her marital status or sexual orientation. See Chapter 2.

7 It is acknowledged that there is a distinction to be made between requiring the state to *refrain from restricting* reproductive liberty for certain purposes (such as pre-implantation tissue-typing) and requiring the state to *actively protect* the reproductive liberty of individuals for such purposes.

8 See Victorian Law Reform Commission, *Assisted Reproductive Technology and Adoption: Final Report* (2007).

the imposition of narrow eligibility criteria.[9] As discussed in Chapter 2, the law in Victoria has been updated and the change in the statutory eligibility criteria is reflective of the VLRC's suggestions. This legislative change is likely to widen access in circumstances where ART services are utilised for the purpose of conceiving a saviour child. If the statutory eligibility criteria cannot be satisfied in such circumstances (perhaps because a couple are at no risk of transmitting a genetic condition to a child when conceiving naturally and could establish a pregnancy naturally), an application can be made to the Patient Review Panel to seek authority for an ART clinic to provide IVF services. A family seeking access to IVF and pre-implantation tissue-typing could therefore make an application to the Patient Review Panel.[10] The Panel is required to make an assessment in accordance with the guiding principles under the legislation[11] and must be satisfied that the treatment is for a therapeutic goal.[12] The Panel must also be satisfied that the treatment is consistent with the welfare of any child that may be born.[13] In this regard, the welfare principle forms part of the assessment for determining whether access to ART services should be granted. The application of the welfare principle is considered below.

It is therefore clear that in some Australian jurisdictions ART services are restricted by legislation, which has a significant impact on the accessibility of services for families who are seeking to create a saviour child. If the normative analysis that follows in the subsequent chapters supports a more liberal approach to reproductive decision-making in this context, this provides a basis to argue that statutory eligibility criteria require amendment. To some extent this has been achieved in Victoria. However, the fact that prospective participants seeking access to IVF for pre-implantation tissue-typing are required to apply to the Patient Review Panel in some circumstances is unsatisfactory; this requirement applies only to those families who are not at risk of transmitting a genetic condition to future offspring (couples who are at risk of transmitting a genetic condition would fall within the eligibility criteria). Given that the intention of families in both circumstances is to conceive a tissue-matched donor child, the different requirements that apply to families based on the contextual circumstances do not appear to provide sufficient justification for applying different standards to each.

---

9  ibid. 67.

10  Assisted Reproductive Treatment Act 2008 (Vic), ss 10(1)(b), 15(1)(b).

11  See Chapter 2, p. 20.

12  Assisted Reproductive Treatment Act 2008 (Vic), s 15(3).

13  Assisted Reproductive Treatment Act 2008 (Vic), s 15(3).

## Accessibility in the United Kingdom

It was established that in the UK, the HFEA is responsible for monitoring the use of embryo selection technologies. As discussed below, following reform of the UK legislation, there are now limits placed upon the use of embryo screening technologies in circumstances where they are intended for the creation of a saviour child (there are also limitations placed upon the use of the technology in other circumstances).[14] These limitations are analysed in Chapter 8. Interestingly, before the legislation was reformed in this way, the HFEA played a significant role in developing regulatory policy on this specific issue.

In 2001, the HFEA was presented with an application from an ART centre seeking to undertake pre-implantation tissue-typing for the benefit of the Hashmi family. The Hashmis were at risk of conceiving a child with beta-thalassaemia (the same condition with which their child, Zain was suffering). The couple wished to access IVF and utilise embryo selection technologies to ensure that any embryo implanted as part of a treatment process was free from the genetic condition affecting Zain, and to also ensure that the embryo's tissue type matched Zain's. The HFEA granted permission to the centre for this purpose.[15] That decision was subsequently challenged by way of judicial review. When the matter was heard by the House of Lords, it was held that the scope of the HFEA's regulatory powers extended to determining the boundaries of permissible embryo selection, and that pre-implantation tissue-typing is a technique that can be used to ensure that an embryo is 'suitable'[16] for implantation. (The term 'suitable for implantation' is one used within the legislative framework.)[17]

In subsequent decision-making, the HFEA stated that the accessibility of the technology would be limited to cases where the participants are at risk of transmitting a genetic condition when conceiving naturally.[18] The implication of this restrictive policy was that those seeking to utilise IVF for the sole purpose

---

14  See Gerard Porter and Malcolm K Smith, 'Preventing the Selection of "Deaf Embryos" Under the Human Fertilisation and Embryology Act 2008: Problematizing Disability?' (2013) 32 New Genetics and Society 171.

15  Human Fertilisation and Embryology Authority, 'HFEA to Allow Tissue Typing in Conjunction with Preimplantation Genetic Diagnosis', press release, 13 December 2001 <http://www.hfea.gov.uk/961.html> accessed 10 August 2014.

16  Human Fertilisation and Embryology Act 1990 (UK), sch 2, para 1(1)(d).

17  R *(on the application of Quintavalle) v Human Fertilisation and Embryology Authority* [2005] 2 All ER 555 (in particular, see Lord Hoffman, at 560).

18  Human Fertilisation and Embryology Authority, 'HFEA Confirms that HLA Tissue Typing May Only Take Place when Preimplantation Genetic Diagnosis is Required to Avoid a Serious Genetic Disorder', press release, 1 August 2002 <http://www.hfea.gov.uk/935.html> accessed 10 August 2014.

of establishing the tissue type of an embryo (and not to establish a genetic condition) would not be granted access to do so.[19] In this respect, the regulatory body's approach represented a very restrictive view of when ART services should be available for the purpose of utilising embryo selection technologies; a precautionary approach was adopted with the HFEA concluding that the technology should only be available as a 'last resort'.

In 2002, the HFEA confirmed its initial approach when presented with a further application made on behalf of the Whitaker family. The HFEA refused to grant a licence for pre-implantation tissue-typing in this instance because the couple were at no greater risk of conceiving a child with a genetic condition. The Whitakers sought access to IVF and to utilise embryo selection technologies so that a saviour sibling could be created in an attempt to cure their child who was suffering with Diamond Blackfan anaemia (a condition that onsets after birth and is not genetically detectable).[20] In this context, the Whitaker family were not prevented from accessing the technology on the basis of general eligibility criteria imposed by legislation (as is the case in some Australian jurisdictions), but on the basis of a conscious decision made by the HFEA, which imposed restrictions on IVF for this purpose. Importantly, the HFEA subsequently amended its policy to widen the accessibility of IVF for the use of embryo selection technologies in circumstances where the technology is used for the sole purpose of establishing tissue type (subject to the other conditions outlined within the applicable policy, which is considered below).[21]

The distinction that was originally made between the Hashmi and Whitaker families went against the advice of HFEA's own ethics committee, which recommended that the technology should be available even in cases where the sole purpose of embryo screening is to establish tissue type.[22] The HFEA was subject to a significant level of criticism for the way in which it developed the tissue-typing policies and for the reasoning that was provided to restrict the accessibility of technology in some cases but not in others.[23] The HFEA stated that the distinctions made were drawn on the basis of ethical reasoning and underpinned by consideration for the welfare of any children born as a result.[24]

---

19 ibid.

20 ibid.

21 Human Fertilisation and Embryology Authority, 'HFEA Agrees to Extend Policy on Tissue Typing', press release, 21 July 2004, <http://www.hfea.gov.uk/763. html> accessed 10 August 2014.

22 Ethics Committee of the Human Fertilisation and Embryology Authority, *Ethical Issues in the Creation and Selection of Preimplantation Embryos to Produce Tissue Donors* (2001).

23 See Bellamy (n 5); Sheldon and Wilkinson (n 5); House of Commons Science and Technology Committee, *Human Reproductive Technologies and the Law* (2005) 109–13.

24 House of Commons Science and Technology Committee, *Human Reproductive Technologies and the Law* (2005) 109–13.

The arguments and reasoning put forward for the distinction are considered in Chapters 6 and 7. However, the significance of the welfare principle in this context will first be considered.

## Accessibility of ART Services and the Relevance of the Welfare Principle

In Australia, in the jurisdictions that rely on the National Health and Medical Research Council's (NHMRC) guidelines, ART centres are required to place the welfare of the child to be born as paramount.[25] The various statutory approaches similarly make reference to this principle. In Victoria, the requirement is contained in the legislation's guiding principles, requiring the welfare of any child born (or to be born) to be classed as paramount.[26] Similarly, paramount importance is to be placed on the principle under the South Australian legislation.[27] In Western Australia, clinics are required to ensure that the welfare of the child to be born is 'properly taken into consideration'.[28] Under the New South Wales legislation, one of the objects of the Act is to protect the interests of a person born as a result of an ART procedure.[29] Finally, in the UK, the welfare provision must be considered by clinics offering ART procedures and the welfare principle acts as the main factor for deciding whether access to treatment should be granted at all.[30]

It is evident that there is a consistent requirement across all relevant jurisdictions to consider the welfare of any child who will be born as a result of providing ART services. 'Paramount' importance must be given to the welfare principle in some jurisdictions. A literal interpretation of that term would require the principle to be placed above *all* other considerations (including the interests and welfare of the applicants). Applying the principle in this way may prove problematic, particularly if the welfare of a child who is not yet born is to be placed over the interests of those individuals seeking access to services. Additionally, there is also a requirement outlined in the UK context by the HFEA's Code of Practice, to consider the welfare of any other child who may be affected by the birth of the child who may be born.[31] Michelle Taylor-

---

25 National Health and Medical Research Council, *Ethical Guidelines on the Use of Assisted Reproductive Technology in Clinical Practice and Research* (2007) [2.5], [5.1].

26 Assisted Reproductive Treatment Act 2008 (Vic), s 5.

27 Assisted Reproductive Treatment Act 1988 (SA), s 4A.

28 Human Reproductive Technology Act 1991 (WA), s 4(1)(d)(iv).

29 Assisted Reproductive Technology Act 2007 (NSW), s 3.

30 Human Fertilisation and Embryology Act 1990 (UK), s 13(5).

31 Human Fertilisation and Embryology Authority, *Code of Practice* (8th edn, 2009) guidance note 8.2.

Sands observes that it is difficult to comprehend how the decision to conceive a saviour child can be in the interests of that particular individual, leading her to argue that the welfare principle should be applied in a more holistic way, in recognition of the child's welfare being inextricably intertwined with the interests of the family unit as a whole.[32] Remarkably, there is little guidance on how the principle is to be applied in the context of ART. The next section seeks to ascertain the purpose of the principle in order to assess its relevance in the specific context of conceiving a saviour child.

### General application of the welfare principle

In the context of the UK framework, the HFEA has stated that the welfare principle is to be applied as a means of assessing whether any child born following the provision of ART services will be at risk of significant harm or neglect.[33] To some extent then, this assessment requires a consideration of the individual circumstances of those seeking access to services, which may include judgments about the 'suitability' of the prospective participants as parents. Factors of relevance to the welfare assessment include certain criminal convictions (such as violence or abuse, or alcohol or substance abuse).[34] The centre is required to conduct an interview with the patient(s) to obtain a medical and social history.[35] If the information provided suggests that there is a risk of significant harm or neglect to any child who may be born, the centre is required to gain the consent of the participant(s) prior to approaching an individual, agency or body for further information that will be relevant to the assessment.[36] Refusal to consent to this process does not automatically equate to a refusal of treatment.[37] This approach is quite different to previous policy issued by the HFEA on this issue, as ART centres were previously required to conduct background checks in relation to prospective patients. This requirement was removed following a consultation undertaken by the HFEA, with the Authority recommending that there should be a presumption in favour of providing treatment.[38]

In Australia, there is no equivalent policy guidance provided by regulators to direct ART centres on how the welfare principle should be applied. Michelle

---

32 Michelle Taylor-Sands, *Saviour Siblings: A Relational Approach to the Welfare of the Child in Selective Reproduction* (Routledge 2013).

33 Human Fertilisation and Embryology Authority (n 31) guidance note 8.3.

34 ibid. guidance note 8.10.

35 ibid. guidance note 8.9.

36 ibid. guidance note 8.13.

37 ibid.

38 Human Fertilisation and Embryology Authority, *Tomorrow's Children: Report of the Policy Review of the Welfare of the Child Assessments in Licensed Assisted Conception Clinics* (2005) 10–11.

Taylor-Sands highlights the difference in terminology between the UK's welfare principle and the Australian approaches, which adopt more general language encompassing assessments about the 'welfare' and 'interests' of prospective children.[39] She further notes that it is disappointing that the VLRC did not address how this principle should be applied in its Final Report[40] – a significant shortcoming of the largest review of law and policy on the topic of ART in Australia. This lack of guidance ultimately leads to a position where ART service providers apply the principle inconsistently, based on very different reasoning.[41]

In Victoria, it is a requirement that all participants provide consent for the centre to conduct a child protection order check.[42] If the check reveals that an order was made to remove a child from the custody of the prospective participants, a presumption against treatment may be imposed. Similarly, if a criminal record check reveals that the participant(s) have been convicted of certain sexual and/or violent offences, a presumption against treatment will be imposed.[43]

It is interesting to note that the former statutory framework in place in South Australia also required participants to sign a statutory declaration stating that they had no previous serious convictions involving violence or child abuse, or that there was no history of alcohol or substance abuse.[44] This requirement is no longer found in the reformed statutory framework in South Australia. In the UK, the HFEA has moved towards a presumption *in favour* of treatment, which is rebutted where there is evidence to suggest that a child born following the provision of ART services will be at risk of significant harm or neglect. As a result, prospective participants are no longer subjected to routine background checks. In Victoria, however, there has been a shift in the opposite direction under the reformed legislative scheme: the new provisions impose compulsory background checks upon those seeking services and in some circumstances a presumption *against* accessing treatment will be imposed. In such circumstances, the participants would have to make an application to the Patient Review Panel

---

39  Taylor-Sands (n 32) 46.

40  ibid. Victorian Law Reform Commission (n 8).

41  Rachel Thorpe and others, 'In the Best Interests of the Child? Regulating Assisted Reproductive Technologies and the Well-being of Offspring in Three Australian States' 26 International Journal of Law, Policy and the Family 259.

42  Assisted Reproductive Treatment Act 2008 (Vic), s 11(1)(d).

43  Assisted Reproductive Treatment Act 2008 (Vic), s 14(1)(b). See *ABY & ABZ v Patient Review Panel (Health & Privacy)* [2011] VCAT 1382; *ABY & ABZ v Secretary to the Department of Health (Human Rights)* [2013] VCAT 625.

44  See South Australian Council on Reproductive Technology, *Regulations under the Reproductive Technology Act 1988 – Reproductive Technology (Code of Ethical Clinical Practice) 1995*, reg 11(1).

to gain access to services.[45] In this respect, the Victorian approach is, in some circumstances, more precautionary and is therefore suggestive of a more restrictive position concerning the question of access to services. In contrast to this position, the UK approach reflects a move towards a more liberal perspective by virtue of the fact that prospective participants are presumed to be free to access ART services. As will be argued in Chapter 8, this presumption could be extended to the use of IVF in circumstances where parents wish to create a saviour child.

In the remaining Australian jurisdictions there are no similar requirements imposed by the relevant regulatory policies. Given that the welfare principle is of such fundamental importance to the accessibility of ART services in Australia, it is surprising that there is no detailed or comprehensive advice to clinics to outline how the principle should be applied in practice.[46] Some commentators have argued that due to the disparate range of approaches to determining how the welfare principle should be applied under the different Australian regulatory frameworks – where some states require compulsory criminal background checks and others leave the assessment in the hands of clinician – that this provides a basis for the child's welfare to be undermined.[47]

Arguably, when applied in the general context of ART services, the welfare principle equates to a suitability assessment for prospective parents. There may be a range of factors considered relevant to the risk assessment, but ultimately, the purpose is to assess the risk of significant harm or neglect for children born following the provision of services.[48] Some commentators have criticised the application of the welfare principle, noting that the decision to reproduce is inherently private and should not be subject to the scrutiny and intrusion of the state or the medical staff providing treatment services.[49] Ultimately, however, as the principle is aimed at safeguarding the prospective child's interests and

45 Assisted Reproductive Treatment Act 2008 (Vic), s 15.

46 See Karinne Ludlow, 'What About me? How Far Do We Go in the Interests of the Child in Assisted Reproductive Technology?' (2006) 6 Queensland University of Technology Law and Justice Journal 214.

47 Thorpe and others (n 41).

48 Michelle Taylor-Sands has argued that the welfare assessment in this context should adopt a relational approach and consider the circumstances and welfare of the family as a whole (n 32).

49 For a discussion of the welfare principle and the issue of parental suitability and how the principle applies in the UK context, see Emily Jackson, 'Conception and the Irrelevance of the Welfare Principle' (2002) 65 Modern Law Review 176; Emily Jackson, 'Rethinking the Pre-Conception Welfare Principle' in Kirsty Horsey and Hazel Biggs (eds), Human Fertilisation and Embryology: Reproducing Regulation (Routledge-Cavendish 2007); Jacqueline A Laing and David S Oderberg, 'Artificial Reproduction, the 'Welfare Principle', and the Common Good' (2005) 13 Medical Law Review 328.

to prevent children being born into circumstances where they are likely to be at risk of significant harm or neglect, the application of the principle in the general context of ART services amounts to a harm assessment. I will return to the relevance of this in the subsequent chapters.

### Applying the welfare principle to decisions to conceive a saviour child

Based on the above reasoning, it is reasonable to conclude that the welfare principle is most commonly applied as a harm assessment. The implication of this is that ART services may be refused in cases where there is evidence to suggest that a child will be subjected to significant harm or neglect as a result of the circumstances at hand. Consequently, if the main assessment is based upon assessing the risk of harm to a prospective child, in the saviour child context this assessment should take account of the specific circumstances of the family to determine whether the saviour child is at risk of significant harm or neglect. As I discuss in Chapter 6, harm-based arguments have certainly dominated the debate in this field, as it is argued that there are a range of potential 'harms' that a child who is conceived as a saviour, may succumb to.

Some of the potential 'harms' that might eventuate in this context, *may* be considered relevant when applying the pre-conception welfare principle in circumstances where the family are contemplating the conception of a saviour child. Notably, however, the factors of relevance in this regard are not clearly addressed by regulatory guidance. Even the UK guidance (discussed below), which is the most comprehensive of all the regulatory approaches, fails to address exactly how the saviour child's welfare should be determined. However, a common theme running through all of the regulatory frameworks in place across Australia and in the UK, is that there is a need to consider the prospective child's welfare. This extends to a consideration of how, if at all, the child's welfare may be affected by the embryo biopsy process. For example, according to the NHMRC guidelines, there is a requirement to establish that the use of PGD techniques will not adversely affect the welfare of any child born following the provision of IVF and PGD.[50] Yet, despite the prioritisation of the welfare principle, there is no guidance provided to determine how a saviour child's welfare *may* be compromised. Michelle Taylor-Sands highlights the difference in terminology between the UK's welfare principle and the Australian approaches, which adopt more general language encompassing assessments about the 'welfare' and 'interests' of prospective children.[51] She further notes that it is disappointing that the VLRC did not address how this principle should be applied – a significant shortcoming in the largest review of law and policy

---

50 National Health and Medical Research Council (n 25) [12.3].
51 Taylor-Sands (n 32) 46.

on the topic of ART in Australia – merely resulting in the conclusion that the child's best interests should remain the paramount consideration.

Without guidance to determine how the welfare principle should be applied in circumstances where a family wish to conceive a saviour child, there is a risk of an inconsistent approach. Research exists to suggest that this is the case concerning the pre-conception welfare principle more generally,[52] thus making it reasonable to conclude that the principle will be applied inconsistently when applied to families who are seeking to conceive saviour children. Some clinicians or ethics committees responsible for making welfare assessments may attribute greater weight to some of the perceived risks in these circumstances, compared to those prioritised by other clinicians or ethics committees responsible for determining whether services should be provided. Consequently, some families may be denied access to ART services because of factors that were considered relevant by 'gatekeepers' in one instance, when such factors may not be considered sufficient to justify imposing a barrier on access to services by others. This inconsistency may consequently result in unjustifiable interferences with reproductive decision-making in some cases.

The analysis that follows in the subsequent chapters considers the relevance of the welfare principle as a basis for intervening with reproductive decision-making in such circumstances. Based on the reasoning outlined above, I argue that the welfare principle is primarily aimed at assessing the risk of harm to the potential child in this context. In this sense, my argument is that the welfare principle does, or at least should, be underpinned by liberal reasoning; there should be a presumption in favour of allowing families to access ART services for this purpose unless there is a real risk of harm to the child who will be born. However, as outlined below, there are other normative factors that seem to be guiding the regulatory position on this issue, which can be identified upon closer examination of the different regulatory policies.

### Regulating Embryo Selection Technologies for the Selection of Saviour Children

Regulation concerning the issue of conceiving saviour children by way of ART services exists in all Australian jurisdictions, as well as in the UK. As discussed below, the Code of Practice in the UK is more considered and contains more detailed guidance on this topic, compared to the approach in Australia. In Chapter 2, it was established that the NHMRC guidelines are applicable in all Australian states and territories and are only overridden in the jurisdictions where PGD regulation addresses embryo selection technologies directly. Western Australia is the only jurisdiction to regulate PGD over and above the requirements

---

52 Thorpe and others (n 41).

outlined under the NHMRC guidelines. However, the regulatory requirements concerning PGD in Western Australia do not address pre-implantation tissue-typing, which means that the use of the technology for this purpose can be considered in accordance with the NHMRC guidelines, but is subject to the restrictions imposed on PGD more generally under the legislative framework.

As also detailed in Chapter 2, prior to the legislative reforms in Victoria, the former statutory body – the Infertility Treatment Authority (ITA) – closely monitored PGD. Victoria was the only Australian jurisdiction to address the specific issue of pre-implantation tissue-typing in addition to the requirements set out in the NHMRC guidelines. As a point of comparison, the former policy in Victoria is also outlined below, following examination of the relevant provisions of the NHMRC guidelines. Finally, the specific provisions relating to pre-implantation tissue-typing in the UK are also considered before reflecting upon the normative principles that underpin these different policies.

### Pre-implantation tissue-typing under the NHMRC guidelines in Australia

Under the NHMRC guidelines, ART providers are required to carefully evaluate any use of PGD and where the technology is utilised for the purpose of establishing an embryo's tissue type, this is only permissible in accordance with the following requirements:

- The intended recipient of tissue is a sibling, and in such instance, the clinic must seek advice from a clinical ethics committee (or where relevant, a state or territory regulatory agency).
- The relevant committee or agency must ascertain that:
  - pre-implantation tissue-typing does not adversely affect the welfare and interests of the child who may be born;
  - the medical condition of the sibling must be life-threatening;
  - there are no other means available for treating the condition;
  - the wish of the parents is to have another child as an addition to their family and not merely as a source of tissue.[53]

In addition to these factors, the requirements relating to the provision of information and counselling for PGD must also be complied with,[54] although these provisions do not address the specific issues associated with creating a tissue-matched donor. As discussed in Chapter 2, PGD is not generally monitored under the national guidelines and there are no reporting requirements

---

53  National Health and Medical Research Council (n 25) [12.3].
54  ibid.

for ART centres providing PGD services.[55] The use of embryo selection technologies for establishing tissue type is the only use of the technology under the guidelines that requires ART centres to gain formal approval. And apart from the few factors outlined above, there is no further guidance provided to assist with determining how a child born in this context may have his or her welfare and/or interests adversely affected. For this reason, there is no clear basis upon which an ethics committee (or other relevant body) is justified in preventing a clinic from providing IVF and PGD services for this specific purpose. This is a significant shortcoming in the guidelines, as there is a need to consider how individual families' differing circumstances may, or may not, impact on the prospective saviour child's welfare.

### Pre-implantation tissue-typing under the former regulatory policy in Victoria

Under the updated legislative framework, the Victorian Assisted Reproductive Treatment Authority (VARTA) is responsible for overseeing ART services in Victoria. Under the former statutory framework, the ITA oversaw the regulation of PGD techniques. A three-tier system of regulation existed requiring clinics to gain permission prior to undertaking PGD for certain purposes, including the detection and selection of embryos on the basis of tissue type.[56] It was initially expected that the VARTA would assume a similar responsibility for overseeing the regulation of PGD, as the new statutory body had updated the ITA's guidance concerning PGD and pre-implantation tissue-typing.[57] However, the statutory body has confirmed that it will not play a role in the future regulation of PGD techniques.[58] Regulation of embryo selection technologies is a matter to be

---

55 For a discussion of the ethical issues surrounding the general use of embryo selection technologies, see Rosamund Scott, 'Choosing Between Possible Lives: Legal and Ethical Issues in Preimplantation Genetic Diagnosis' (2006) 26 Oxford Journal of Legal Studies 153.

56 The three-tier system permitted the use of PGD under three categories: (i) cases for which no permission or notification is required to undertake PGD – this only applied to established uses as outlined in the PGD policy; (ii) cases that are not established did not require permission to be obtained, but the use of PGD was reportable to the ITA; and (iii) in cases where the use of the technology is novel, approval had to be obtained from the ITA (and clinics were also required to notify the Authority of such uses): Infertility Treatment Authority, *Genetic Testing and the Requirements of the Infertility Treatment Act 1995: Policy in Relation to the Use of Pre-implantation Genetic Diagnosis (PGD)* (Victoria Parliament 2008) 5–6.

57 Victorian Assisted Reproductive Treatment Authority, *Conditions for Use of Tissue Typing in Conjunction with Preimplantation Genetic Diagnosis (PGD)* (2010).

58 This information was provided by Tracey Petrillo, Senior Policy and Education Officer, Victorian Assisted Reproductive Treatment Authority: email communication

determined by individual clinics. This significant change seems to accord with the general spirit of the reformed statutory framework, which has attempted to adopt a 'light touch' compared to the previous approach. Consequently, it is no longer a requirement to gain approval from the Victorian statutory body, due to the fact that the policies developed by the former ITA and updated by the VARTA concerning PGD and pre-implantation tissue-typing are no longer in force.[59] In some respects, this change is a move in the right direction, given that the former tissue-typing policy explicitly excluded access to the technology in cases where the statutory eligibility criteria were not met. However, complete removal of the policy also raises a number of concerns.

As highlighted above, the NHMRC guidelines lack specificity as to how a saviour child's welfare may be adversely affected. For this reason, there is no clear threshold that can be relied upon by an ethics committee (or other relevant body) when determining whether access to ART services for the creation of a saviour child should be refused. The previous state-level guidance in Victoria elaborated on at least some of the factors that may be deemed relevant to this assessment. Importantly, the guidelines required ART clinics to establish the following factors:

- Approval to provide the technology must be obtained from an ethics committee at the institution where the procedure will be undertaken, and the final decision in relation to the application rests with the committee.
- Each application for pre-implantation tissue-typing will be reviewed on a case-by-case basis.
- The *genetic* condition of the sick child who will be treated must be severe or life-threatening.
- In relation to the clinical management of the affected child, all reasonable possibilities of treatment and sources of tissue for the affected child should have been explored.
- Comprehensive counselling (from a genetic counsellor and an approved counsellor) must be provided to address the implications of PGD for the selection of embryos on the basis of tissue type and that specific consideration should be given to the first guiding principle of the legislation (that the interests of the person to be born are of paramount concern).
- The procedure will only be available where the primary intended tissue recipient is a sibling.

---

from Tracey Petrillo to author (February 2011).

59 Confirmed by Tracey Petrillo, Senior Policy and Education Officer, Victorian Assisted Reproductive Treatment Authority: email communication from Tracey Petrillo to author (February 2011).

- If a relative has a similar genetic condition, a decision about further donation of cord blood or bone marrow resides with the parents of the child.
- The child born as a result of the procedure should only provide cord blood or bone marrow, and that the harvesting of 'hard' or non-regenerative organs is not acceptable.[60]

In addition to these factors, the ethics committee of the institution where the procedure would be carried out was also required to consider a number of further issues, including:

- the motivation and level of understanding of the parents in seeking to have an additional child;
- the issues that may arise where the birth of a child does not resolve the genetic condition for the existing sibling;
- the status of the child within the family and the relationships, which grow, with the growth of all children within the family.[61]

Given that the state-level guidance had been in force for some time before it was revoked, it is possible that in the future, Victorian ART clinics' ethics committees may make reference to some of these factors.

### Pre-implantation tissue-typing in the United Kingdom

Pre-implantation tissue-typing is directly addressed on the face of the UK legislation as a result of the recent statutory reforms. The legislation states that the HFEA can issue a licence to authorise embryo testing:

> In a case where a person ('the sibling') who is the child of the persons whose gametes are used to bring about the creation of the embryo (or of either of those persons) suffers from a serious medical condition which could be treated by umbilical cord blood stem cells, bone marrow or other tissue of any resulting child, establishing whether the tissue of any resulting child would be compatible with that of the sibling.[62]

In this context the reference to 'other tissue' of the resulting child does not include a reference to any whole organ of the child.[63] There are a number of requirements outlined in the legislation that must be satisfied to enable a couple

---

60 Victorian Assisted Reproductive Treatment Authority (n 57) 2–3.

61 ibid.

62 Human Fertilisation and Embryology Act 1990 (UK), sch 2, para 1ZA (1)(d).

63 Human Fertilisation and Embryology Act 1990 (UK), sch 2, para 1ZA (4).

to utilise pre-implantation tissue-typing in the UK. The ART centre's licence must authorise this specific use of the technology,[64] and the Code of Practice issued by the HFEA details a number of further requirements which clinics must adhere to.[65]

The Code of Practice emphasises the need for clinics to take into account a number of issues beyond the immediate implications of the treatment process. When considering whether to provide PGD services for the creation of a saviour sibling, the clinic must consider the circumstances of each case rather than the fact that the technology is sought to create a child as a potential cure for a particular condition.[66]

During the reform process of the UK legislative framework, it was proposed that the technology be limited to cases where the sick child is suffering from a life-threatening condition.[67] However, the Joint Committee on the Human Tissue and Embryos (Draft) Bill suggested that the term 'serious' should be adopted in place of 'life-threatening'.[68] The difference between the two terms may appear to be marginal, but during debate in the House of Lords some argued that the term 'serious' is too vague.[69] It could also be equally argued that the term 'life-threatening' is too restrictive. Thus, as noted by Baroness Finlay, the 'difficulty with [using the term] "life-threatening" is that you cannot wait until the child who is ill is actually dying: you need to think about the saviour sibling concept earlier'.[70]

---

64 See Chapter 2, pp. 47–50 for details of PGD licensing in the UK.

65 Human Fertilisation and Embryology Authority (n 31) guidance note 10.

66 ibid. guidance note 10.22.

67 United Kingdom, House of Lords, *Parliamentary Debates* 21 January 2008, 11–12 (Lord Lloyd of Berwick).

68 The Committee comment: '[w]e recognise that this is a delicate area. However, given the Government's apparent acceptance of the principle of selecting for "saviour siblings" we do not understand why the practice is limited to "life-threatening" conditions capable of treatment using umbilical cord blood stem cells. We recommend that the draft Bill be amended to substitute "serious" for "life-threatening"'.; Joint Committee on the Human Tissue and Embryos (Draft) Bill, *Report of the Joint Committee of the House of Lords and House of Commons on the Human Tissue and Embryos (Draft) Bill, 2007: Vol I: Report* (Session 2006–2007, HL Paper 169-I, HC Paper 630-II) [199].

69 For example, Baroness O'Cathain comments that the 'term "serious medical condition" is … simply too vague to be a sufficient safeguard in this highly controversial area. No doubt some would say that the regulator – the Human Fertilisation and Embryology Authority – will reject spurious applications for a licence, but that is putting yet another onus on the HFEA': United Kingdom, House of Lords, *Parliamentary Debates* 21 January 2008, 13–14 (Baroness O'Cathain).

70 United Kingdom, House of Lords, *Parliamentary Debates* 21 January 2008, 26 (Baroness Finlay of Llandaff).

As stipulated by the legislation, in order for pre-implantation tissue-typing services to be provided, the ill child who will benefit from the tissue donation must be suffering from a *serious* condition.[71] Neither the Code of Practice nor the legislation defines the term 'serious'. However, the Code of Practice does detail factors relevant to considering the 'seriousness' of the existing child's condition, including the:

- degree of suffering associated with the condition of the affected child;
- speed of degeneration in progressive disorders (where relevant);
- extent of any intellectual impairment;
- prognosis for the affected child in relation to all treatment options available;
- availability of alternative sources of tissue for the treatment of the affected child, now and in the future;
- availability of effective therapy for the affected child, now and in the future.[72]

The clinic is required to take account of the welfare of any child born following the provision of ART services. As discussed above, the requirement to consider the welfare of children born following the provision of ART services is a factor of key importance. In the context of pre-implantation tissue-typing, there are a number of matters outlined by the Code of Practice that are applicable to the welfare of any child who is born. These include the need to consider:

- any possible risks associated with embryo biopsy for the child who is born;
- the long-term emotional and psychological implications;
- whether the treatment of the affected child is likely to require intrusive surgery (and whether this is likely to be repeated);
- any complications or predispositions for the child who may be born associated with the tissue type to be selected.[73]

Additionally, the clinic is also required to consider the circumstances of the family as a whole, including:

- their previous reproductive experience;
- their views and the affected child's views of the condition;
- the likelihood of a successful outcome for the affected child, taking into account the reproductive circumstances of the participants

---

71 Human Fertilisation and Embryology Act 1990 (UK), sch 2, para 1ZA (1)(d).
72 Human Fertilisation and Embryology Authority (n 31) guidance note 10.23.
73 ibid. guidance note 10.24.

(that is, number of embryos likely to be available for testing in each treatment cycle, the number likely to be suitable for transfer, whether carrier embryos may be transferred and the number of cycles likely to be undertaken);

- the likely outcome of treatment for the affected child;
- the consequences of an unsuccessful outcome;
- the demands of IVF and pre-implantation testing on them while caring for an affected child;
- the extent of social support available.[74]

In addition to the factors outlined above, the Code of Practice also stipulates that clinics are required to provide participants with:

- information about the tissue-typing tests to be performed;
- an explanation of the latest evidence about any risk associated with the biopsy procedure for any child who is born;
- information concerning the overall likelihood of a successful outcome for the affected child, including:
  - the likelihood of an embryo with appropriate tissue type being available for transfer following IVF, biopsy and genetic testing;
  - the likelihood of a child being born as a result, taking into account the circumstances of the people seeking treatment and their previous reproductive experience;
  - the likelihood of tissue from that child providing a successful treatment;
  - the limitations of the treatment for the affected child;
- the likely impact of the proposed procedure on all family members involved;
- information about other sources of treatment, counselling and social support available.[75]

As is clear, the UK approach requires an extensive consideration of the use of the technology, including its implications for the particular family seeking access to the services. This approach requires ART clinics to work through the potential issues with the family. However, the policy goes further than this; the Code of Practice requires that clinics implement adequate arrangements for contacting and inviting the families involved to take part in long-term follow-up studies relating to the physical and psychological development of children born

---

74  ibid. guidance note 10.25.
75  ibid. guidance note 10.26.

as saviour siblings and to also ensure that there is continued support available to families following the procedure.[76]

In principle, it appears as though ART services are not heavily restricted in the UK, as legislation does not limit services to those who are at risk of transmitting a genetic condition when conceiving naturally. However, the regulatory approach adopted in the UK is more detailed than the Australian approach. The Code of Practice addresses the implications of the technology extensively by requiring the provision of significant information in relation to this specific use of PGD. It also requires the ART centre to explore the long-term and psychological implications of undergoing treatment for the creation of a saviour sibling with the family. In Chapter 8 I argue that a number of the requirements imposed under the UK framework are overly restrictive.

## General ART Regulatory Requirements Relevant to Pre-Implantation Tissue-Typing

As outlined in Chapter 2, ART centres are required to adhere to a number of general regulatory requirements under the relevant frameworks in Australia and the UK. There are aspects of those frameworks that have relevance in the more specific context of pre-implantation tissue-typing. Importantly, these requirements may apply to some factors that are not directly addressed by a specific tissue-typing policy. Some matters of particular significance in this respect are the provisions relating to consent and information-giving, and the obligations concerning the provision of counselling.

### Consent to treatment and the storage of reproductive material

The requirement to provide consent to ART procedures applies across all of the jurisdictions examined.[77] Consent provides the justification for the physical contact involved in the procedure and some aspects of the IVF process are particularly intrusive. Therefore, all couples seeking access to pre-implantation tissue-typing services will need to provide a valid, written consent. In addition to addressing all relevant aspects of the treatment, the consent should specifically address the technique that will be performed which will include (but is not limited to) details of the stages in the IVF procedure, the relevant aspects of the PGD process, and the details of the embryo biopsy procedure that the embryos created will be subjected to. It is also important for the family to consider the risk that the biopsy

---

76 ibid. guidance note 10.28.

77 Assisted Reproductive Technology Act 2007 (NSW), s 17; Assisted Reproductive Treatment Act 2008 (Vic), s 11; Human Reproductive Technology Act 1991 (WA), s 22(1); NHMRC (n 25) 9; Human Fertilisation and Embryology Act 1990 (UK), sch 2, para 1.

process *may* have some impact on the success of establishing a pregnancy during the IVF process and this should be discussed as part of the consent process.

The UK tissue-typing policy is the only policy to address the more specific issues relating to consent in this context. Although most of the other jurisdictions have not implemented specific tissue-typing policies, as discovered in Chapter 2, the NHMRC guidelines and the other remaining statutory approaches require that information is provided to those undergoing ART services and this includes information relating to PGD techniques. These general requirements state that clinics should provide detailed information in the context of pre-implantation tissue-typing even though the specific policies addressing this issue do not directly stipulate this.

In addition to addressing the specifics of the procedures to be performed, consent will also need to address the storage of any reproductive material (such as gametes and/or embryos) if the couple wish to store such material. This will be likely in cases where a number of tissue-matched embryos are identified as a result of the PGD process.

### Information-giving and counselling

As mentioned above, it is necessary for prospective ART participants to be provided with relevant information concerning the procedure(s) that they will undergo and the techniques that will be used on their gametes and embryos. It was mentioned that the UK tissue-typing policy is the only policy to address information-giving in this context. Notably, however, the pre-implantation tissue-typing policy previously in place in Victoria required that comprehensive counselling should be provided to participants in order to address the implications of undergoing IVF for this specific purpose. The policy does not refer to information-giving. However, to successfully provide counselling services in this context – remembering that counselling is mandatory for all participants undergoing ART services in Victoria – there is an implication that it is necessary to provide the relevant information in this context (otherwise, such considerations are not possible as part of the counselling process). In this respect, the requirement to provide information overlaps with the counselling process.

In the remaining Australian jurisdictions, the general provisions relating to information-giving and counselling under the NHMRC guidelines are relevant. The guidelines specifically state that for the participants to make informed decisions about treatment involving PGD, they must be given 'up-to-date, objective [and] accurate information' concerning the technology (these factors are required in addition to the general information-giving and counselling requirements contained in the guidelines).[78] However, the factors

---

78 National Health and Medical Research Council (n 25) [9.7].

outlined in the guidelines are primarily concerned with the implications of using the technology for detecting *genetic* conditions in the embryo, not with the implications of using IVF for the creation of a tissue-matched child.[79] Therefore, within the majority of Australian jurisdictions, there is no specific guidance that provides clinics with the relevant information that they should be providing to prospective ART participants who seek to conceive a tissue-matched child. In some respects, however, it may be possible to argue that there is a duty to provide information in accordance with the common law principles on information disclosure. In the decision of *Rogers v Whitaker*,[80] the High Court of Australia held that medical professionals have a duty to disclose material information (including risks inherent in treatment procedures) for which a reasonable person in the patient's position would attach significance to.[81] This requirement is a patient-focused approach[82] and therefore requires the clinician to disclose information that is relevant to the individual circumstances of the patient or family in question.[83] On this basis, it may be possible to argue that clinicians providing ART services have a duty to disclose risks (or material information) that may be relevant to a particular family undergoing IVF for the purpose of utilising pre-implantation tissue-typing. However, the likelihood of these issues being explored in depth by the relevant clinicians at the pre-conception stage is questionable, based on the fact that counselling in this context is not mandatory (except in Victoria) and the information-giving provisions for this specific issue are inadequate (with the exception of the approach in the UK, outlined above).

---

79 For example, some of the specific issues to be addressed in relation to PGD include information regarding the likelihood of false positive and false negative results in the process, the implications for children born with particular genetic conditions and some considerations for selecting against such conditions: National Health and Medical Research Council (n 25).

80 (1992) 175 CLR 479; (1992) 109 ALR 625.

81 Ibid.; see also *Rosenberg v Percival* (2001) 205 CLR 434. This duty is also outlined in legislation in some Australian jurisdictions: Civil Liability Act 2003 (Qld), s 21; Civil Liability Act 2002 (Tas), s 21; Wrongs Act 1958 (Vic), s 50.

82 Ian Kerridge, Michael Lowe and Cameron Stewart, *Ethics and Law for the Health Professions* (4th edn, The Federation Press 2013) 357.

83 A similar position has also been adopted by the UK Supreme Court in the recent decision of *Montgomery v Lanarkshire Health Board* [2015] UKSC 11. It should be noted, however, that in the context of the UK regulation, the information-giving requirements for pre-implantation tissue-typing under the Code of Practice are extensive and for this reason there may be no need to argue that the common law duty on information disclosure should apply.

## The Underlying Normative Principles

When reflecting on the policies outlined above, it is clear that the regulatory response has been guided by a range of different normative principles. In this regard, my focus so far has been on the relevance of the welfare principle in terms of its application as a harm assessment. This is certainly relevant when determining the issue of access to ART services, particularly in those jurisdictions where access is predominantly determined by the application of the welfare principle. However, some of the regulatory requirements outlined above impose a number of conditions that appear to be focused on reasoning other than an application of the welfare principle – at least as it is applied in the form of a harm assessment. Some of this reasoning is highlighted below by an examination of some of the particular requirements outlined in the policies.

One condition imposed on the use of pre-implantation tissue-typing services, is that they should only be provided when the existing sick child is suffering from a 'serious' or 'life-threatening' medical condition and that there are no other options available for treating the sick child's condition. Limiting the use of the technology to cases where the existing sick child is suffering with a serious condition seems to reflect the view that a child should not be created as a source of tissue unless there is a significant potential benefit in doing so. In this regard, the creation of a saviour child is justifiable in circumstances where there is a *significant benefit* for the sick child or the family as a whole. This may imply that there is no such utility in cases where the sick child is suffering with a less than 'serious' condition, or where there is no threat to the child's life. Such an approach may be intended to reflect the view that the technology should only be available in cases where it will bestow a significant benefit on the family, thus rendering one family more 'deserving' than another. In this regard, the requirement could be interpreted as an assessment of the utility in a particular family's decision to create a saviour sibling.[84]

In the chapters that follow, I question the extent to which reasoning based on the prospective utility of a family's decision should provide a basis for restricting access to the technology. This requirement leads me to ask: if a family's reason for wanting to access the technology is 'less deserving' (based on the fact that there is a requirement to establish that the affected child is suffering from a less than 'serious' condition), does this provide a sufficient basis for intervening with the family's decision to conceive a saviour child? There may be many factors that help us to explain why the circumstances behind one family's request render their wish to access pre-implantation tissue-typing

---

84 Note that some commentators have considered the issue of benefit to the family unit as a whole in line with a relational interpretation of the welfare principle: Taylor-Sands (n 32).

services more 'justified' or 'deserving' compared to the circumstances behind a different family's request. However, it is questionable whether the seriousness of the affected child's condition should be used as a basis for denying access to services. There is an important difference between arguing that one family has a more convincing case for accessing the technology compared to another, and saying that a family should be *prohibited* from accessing ART services for this purpose. In terms of the seriousness of the affected child's condition, it is not clear that this provides a justification for saying that the 'less deserving' family should not be able to access services. There may be instances where an affected child's condition is not serious, but the family is nevertheless committed to caring for the saviour child and ensuring that he or she is not subjected to harm once born.

As outlined above, pre-implantation tissue-typing services are also limited in cases where the family intend to harvest non-regenerative tissue from the saviour child. Although this provision appears to prohibit the possibility of a saviour sibling acting as an organ donor, it does not explicitly prohibit organ donation per se. Instead, access to ART services for the creation of a saviour sibling is not permitted if it is clear (at the pre-conception stage) that the parents *intend* to harvest an organ from the saviour child once born. The issue concerns the parents' intent at the time they seek access to ART services; questions concerning tissue donation will be determined in accordance with the relevant human tissue legislation in the applicable jurisdiction at the time of the prospective donation. This provision is obviously intended to protect a saviour child from being exposed to harmful donation procedures. Additionally, however, this restriction may be underpinned by deontological reasoning, which views the decision to conceive a saviour sibling as *inherently* wrong, because the parents' primary intention is to create a child as a tissue donor.[85] In such circumstances, the family's decision may appear to contradict the Kantian principle that we should not treat others solely as a means to an end. However, some commentators have challenged this Kantian principle in the saviour sibling context.[86] Nevertheless, in the chapters that follow I question the extent to which the deontological objections are relevant in this context. When imposing restrictions on the provision of pre-implantation tissue-typing services, what

---

85  See Robert Boyle and Julian Savulescu, 'Ethics of Using Preimplantation Genetic Diagnosis to Select a Stem Cell Donor for an Existing Person' (2001) 32 British Medical Journal 1240; Susan Wolf, Jeffrey Kahn and John Wagner 'Using Preimplantation Genetic Diagnosis to Create a Stem Cell Donor: Issues, Guidelines & Limits' (2003) 31 Journal of Law, Medicine & Ethics 327.

86  Sally Sheldon and Stephen Wilkinson, 'Hashmi and Whitaker: An Unjustifiable and Misguided Distinction?' (2004) 12 Medical Law Review 137.

role should deontological reasoning play in determining the extent to which the technology should be restricted (if at all)? Why should this underlying principle trump assessments based on harm, when it is clear that the general regulatory approach prioritises the welfare of the child to be born as the guiding factor of relevance when determining access to treatment?

Similarly, there is also a need to establish that ART services in this context are not provided merely because the family wishes to conceive a child as a source of tissue for a sick child. For example, in the context of the NHMRC guidelines this is expressed by the requirement to establish that the parents intend to have another child as an addition to their family and not merely as a source of tissue. This aspect of the regulatory approach also appears to be underpinned by deontological reasoning. The concern is the child may not be valued as an individual who is worthy of respect in his or her own right; instead, the child's value may be represented in terms of the ability to cure a living person. Arguments such as these may similarly help us to establish whether the circumstances and motivation behind a family's decision appear to be more ethically justifiable in some cases compared to others. However, this also raises the question as to whether the family's motivation (assuming that it is possible to genuinely assess this), should provide a convincing basis to prevent them from accessing pre-implantation tissue-typing services. In such circumstances, although the desire to create a tissue-matched child as a source of tissue may be one of the driving factors behind the couple's decision to utilise ART services, if the family is nevertheless committed to loving and caring for that child once he or she is born, should the fact that they did not originally plan on having another child provide a basis for denying them access to ART services?

Finally, the availability of tissue-typing services is also limited based on the relationship between the intended tissue donor and the intended recipient of blood or tissue products. For example, the UK legislation – since the legislative reforms in 2008 – now limits the use of the technology to cases where the intended recipient of tissue is a sibling of the saviour child. Prior to this legislative change, the HFEA had determined that the technology should not be used in circumstances where the intended recipient is a parent.[87] The HFEA Ethics Committee had observed that in cases where the intended recipient is a parent, the purpose 'appears *prima facie* to be morally less acceptable than selecting an embryo to provide tissue to treat a sibling, as it seems to replace concern for another with concern for oneself'.[88] However, there is no evidence to suggest that children created for the benefit of other family members are

---

87 Human Fertilisation and Embryology Authority Ethics Committee, *Ethical Issues in the Creation and Selection of Preimplantation Embryos to Produce Tissue Donors* (2001) <http://www.hfea.gov.uk/docs/ELC_5_july03.pdf> accessed 10 August 2014.

88 ibid. [2.21].

at risk of being subjected to a greater level of harm than in cases where the recipient is a sibling. This raises the question of whether state intervention with reproductive decision-making is justified in circumstances where conduct appears to be 'morally objectionable', even though such conduct may not result in harm to others (or at least, where such conduct will not result in *greater* harm to others than in different circumstances where the same conduct is considered to be less 'morally objectionable').

The questions I have outlined above are important to bear in mind when considering my analysis of the regulatory position that follows in the remaining part of this book. Ultimately, I seek to demonstrate that while some of these principles provide a helpful starting point in the ethical debate that surrounds the creation of saviour children, they are not necessarily relevant in terms of providing the basis for a restrictive regulatory position that determines when access to the technology should be prohibited. Restricting reproductive decision-making in this way requires a much stronger justification.

## Conclusion

This chapter considered how the different regulatory approaches in Australia and the UK control the delivery of pre-implantation tissue-typing services. The impact of the regulatory frameworks is that there are some inconsistencies between jurisdictions in terms of access to ART services for the purpose of creating a saviour child. Fundamentally, it was determined that in some Australian jurisdictions, the question of access depends upon whether the couple are at risk of transmitting a genetic condition. In a similar way, access was originally restricted in the UK by the HFEA when issuing regulatory policy on the specific topic of pre-implantation tissue-typing, but this restrictive approach was later changed. One factor that distinguishes the Australian approach from the earlier position adopted in the UK, is that access to ART services for this purpose in the relevant Australian jurisdictions is *indirectly* restricted by general statutory eligibility criteria. Such requirements were implemented before regulators were aware of the potential use of embryo selection technologies for the creation of saviour children.

This chapter also considered the relevance of the welfare principle, which also plays a significant role in determining the question of access to ART services in the relevant jurisdictions. It was established that at a general level, the principle seeks to restrict access to services where there are particular factors to indicate that the child will be at risk of significant harm or neglect. In this sense, the principle is applied as a means of assessing the suitability of the participants as parents, by assessing the risk of harm to a prospective child born following the provision of ART services. In the following chapters, the scope of the harm assessment will be considered and the various harms relevant to the conception of a saviour child will be evaluated.

Finally, this chapter also provided an outline of the specific regulatory provisions relevant to the delivery of IVF and pre-implantation tissue-typing services. The different approaches in Australia and the UK were considered to determine how the regulatory guidance impacts on the accessibility of the technology. Moreover, the general regulatory requirements relevant to the delivery of ART services were considered in terms of how they may apply in cases where the technology is used to create a saviour child. It was established that some of the regulatory provisions imposed under the wider frameworks also impact on some of the specific matters relevant to the delivery of pre-implantation tissue-typing services (such as information-giving and counselling). Lastly, in order to set the scene for the evaluation that follows in the subsequent chapters, I have outlined some of the underlying normative principles that seem to be guiding the regulatory approach on this issue. Questions were raised in relation to which principles *should* guide regulation in this field and how best to balance the principles of relevance. It is the normative issues to which I now turn.

# Chapter 4
# Liberty and Reproductive Decision-Making

## Introduction

To what extent should an individual be free to determine his or her own decisions, and when is it acceptable for the state to impose restrictions upon individual choice? The answers to these questions are complex and require an exploration of concepts such as 'liberty' and 'autonomy'. The aim of this chapter is to determine the extent to which an individual *should* be free to make his or her own choices, by considering when state intervention in individual decision-making is acceptable, and to consider how this approach may apply to reproductive decision-making.

As a starting point, it can be noted that legislatures in Western democratic societies are guided by the notion of liberalism,[1] which requires the state to refrain from interfering with individual liberty unless there is sufficient justification for such intervention.[2] It has been observed that this approach is firmly embedded within Western culture 'even if it is an ideal rarely realised in practice'.[3] This can be said to represent the view that individuals are best placed to make decisions in relation to matters that impact directly upon them. As noted by Deech and Smajdor, 'there is a presumption in law that people should be free to exercise their rights' concerning issues that most closely affect themselves and their families.[4]

The view that individuals should be at liberty to make their own decisions has been applied extensively in the context of reproductive decision-making.[5] The literature relevant to the notion of reproductive liberty is considered in this chapter, to determine how the concept may be relevant to the more

---

1 Sheila McLean, *Modern Dilemmas: Choosing Children* (Capercaillie Books 2006) 9.

2 Nils Holtug, 'The Harm Principle' (2002) 5 Ethical Theory and Moral Practice 357, 357.

3 Colin Gavaghan, *Defending the Genetic Supermarket: The Law and Ethics of Selecting the Next Generation* (Routledge-Cavendish 2007) 35.

4 Ruth Deech and Anna Smajdor, *From IVF to Immortality: Controversy in the Era of Reproductive Technology* (OUP 2007) 68.

5 See Erin Nelson, *Law, Policy and Reproductive Autonomy* (Hart Publishing 2013).

specific issue of regulating the creation of saviour siblings. However, before
turning to consider the notion of reproductive liberty I first outline the notion
of liberalism in a more general sense. As discussed below, there are important
foundational principles that must be determined, which help to establish
when state intervention (such as regulation that imposes limits on decision-
making) is justified. A regulatory approach underpinned by liberal reasoning is
primarily permissive and will refrain from intervening with individual liberty
unless there is sufficient justification for doing so. In this regard, the fact that
a large majority of individuals may oppose certain types of conduct or view
it as contrary to their own beliefs or values is not considered as sufficient
to justify state intrusion. As noted by Jeanne Snelling, individuals 'should
be free to make their own choices in the light of their own values, whether
or not these choices and values are acceptable to the majority', unless there
is an adequate justification for the state to intervene.[6] Importantly then,
the justificatory basis for intervention must also be established and this is
explored in Chapter 5.

I should also again mention the fact that the liberal perspective is not the
only standard that can be adopted for evaluating whether certain reproductive
decisions using assisted reproductive technology (ART) services should be
permitted. Importantly, however, these wider justifications do not provide
a strong basis for interfering with decision-making, even though they may
heavily influence the bioethical debate. The liberal approach is deeply
embedded in Western democratic societies and this provides a strong basis for
adopting it as an evaluative tool, in terms of analysing the current regulatory
approaches. As will be discussed, this principle has gained considerable force
in the context of reproduction and is regarded as the dominant principle
for analysing reproductive decision-making.[7] Other normative approaches
have also been used to argue against, or in favour of, greater freedom in the
context of reproductive decision-making, and these too will be considered
so that they can be distinguished from the liberal approach. First, however, I
outline John Stuart Mill's liberal approach, as Mill is regarded as one of the
most influential philosophers in terms of developing a modern liberal theory.
Mill's work forms the foundation of the liberal approach that I adopt and this
therefore provides the basis of the framework for the analysis that follows in
the subsequent chapters.

---

6 Jeanne Snelling, 'Embryonic HLA Tissue Typing and Made-to-Match Siblings:
The New Zealand Position' (2008) 9 Medical Law International 13, 27.

7 See Rosalind McDougall, 'Acting Parentally: An Argument against Sex Selection'
(2005) 31 Journal of Medical Ethics 601.

## John Stuart Mill's Liberal Approach

John Stuart Mill was an influential English philosopher best known for his writings on utilitarianism and liberalism. In his essay 'On Liberty', Mill paid particular attention to the sphere of social philosophy concerned with 'the nature and limits of the power which can be legitimately exercised by society over the individual'.[8] The realm of Mill's work on the subject of liberty was concerned not only with legal or political freedom, but also with 'social, intellectual, psychological and religious freedom'.[9] 'On Liberty' was published in the mid-nineteenth century during a time where many social freedoms were restricted in Victorian England.[10] The oppressions with which Mill was concerned were not necessarily *legal* limitations on freedom. He mentions that '[p]rotection ... against the tyranny of the magistrate is not enough: there needs protection also against the tyranny of the prevailing opinion and feeling; against the tendency of society to impose, by other means than civil penalties, its own ideas and practices as rules of conduct on those who dissent from them'.[11]

In 'On Liberty', Mill was advocating for liberalism beyond the realms of pure legal control. As one commentator notes, '[w]hat [Mill] saw as his problem was to stop the "likings and dislikings of society" from being the determining factor in the rules of conduct which society enforced by opinion or by law'.[12] For Mill, imposing the views of the majority on all of society prevents the pursuit of 'individuality'.[13] Mill expected that the law would reflect the opinion of the majority and it was for this reason that the tyranny of the majority was feared.[14] Thus, Ryan notes that the 'course of the argument in [On] Liberty ... is much more concerned with the intrusion of social pressures on the individual in matters which are not strictly matters of right and wrong than with the legal enforcement of morals'.[15] Importantly, as Ryan observes, where there is no 'right' or 'wrong' viewpoint or answer on a particular issue, a response underpinned by liberal theory is likely to conclude that the morals of others

---

8 John Gray (ed), *John Stuart Mill, On Liberty and Other Essays* (OUP 1991) 05.

9 Alan Ryan, 'John Stuart Mill's Art of Living' in J Gray and G W Smith (eds) *J. S. Mill On Liberty in Focus* (Routledge 1991) 162, 163.

10 For a fascinating account of Mill's philosophy, see I Berlin, 'John Stuart Mill and the Ends of Life' in John Gray and G W Smith (eds), *J. S. Mill On Liberty in Focus* (Routledge 1991) 131–61.

11 Gray (n 8) 9.

12 Alan Ryan, *The Philosophy of John Stuart Mill* (2nd edn, Palgrave Macmillan 1987) 235.

13 Gray (n 8) 9.

14 ibid.

15 Ryan (n 12) 235.

should not be imposed upon the individual. Importantly, liberalism does not seek to endorse or disapprove of particular conduct per se, as may be the case with, for example, an analysis underpinned by deontological reasoning. As noted by Charlesworth, by failing to intervene with the conduct of an individual, the law is not expressing an opinion on the morality of the particular matter at issue, but is simply declaring that such conduct 'is out of bounds for state intervention and the criminal law'.[16]

For Mill, an individual's choice (or the pursuit of 'individuality') that does not accord with the opinion of the majority should only be restricted with good reason:

> No one indeed, acknowledges to himself that his standard of judgment is his own liking; but an opinion on a point of conduct not supported by reasons, can only count as one person's preference; and if the reasons, when given, are a mere appeal to a similar preference felt by other people, it is still only many people's liking instead of one.[17]

Mill builds on this approach and proposes that the Harm Principle should act as a threshold for justifying state intervention. Under this approach, intervention with individual liberty is justified when decision-making will cause harm to others. It is the Harm Principle that is therefore regarded as the key threshold in terms of justifying state intervention with liberty and this principle is defined in Chapter 5.

Importantly, according to Mill, the pursuit of individuality should be protected even if harm will result to the decision-maker, as 'compulsion, either in the direct form in the pains and penalties for non-compliance, is no longer admissible as a means to [an individual's] own good, and justifiable only for the security of others'.[18] Consequently, Mill was primarily concerned with ensuring that the state did not coerce the conduct of individuals unjustifiably and that 'he is not concerned to limit warning, advice, education, and exhortation'.[19] Ryan notes that 'Mill goes to great lengths to explain that it is only *coercion* that he wishes to eliminate, and that the motive for doing so is in part to allow the use of more appropriate ways of showing our concern for other persons' well-being'.[20]

---

16 Max Charlesworth, *Bioethics in a Liberal Society* (CUP 1993) 17–18.

17 Gray (n 8) 10.

18 ibid. 15.

19 Ryan comments that 'he is not concerned to limit warning, advice education, and exhortation': (n 12) 236.

20 ibid.

## Liberty and Utilitarianism

Liberalism is only one of a number of subjects that Mill wrote about. Subsequent interpretation has attempted to reconcile 'On Liberty' with Mill's other works, particularly his utilitarian perspective. In 'Utilitarianism', Mill comments that 'actions are right in proportion as they tend to promote happiness, wrong as they tend to promote the reverse of happiness'.[21] The approach in 'Utilitarianism' is ultimately concerned with evaluating, at a critical level, the rightness of actions according to the outcome those actions produce.[22] In simple terms, a utilitarian is concerned with the maximisation of happiness. For example, in the context of the use of embryo selection technologies, a utilitarian analysis would be concerned with evaluating the acceptability of reproductive choices by weighing the 'good' outcomes against the negative consequences.[23] At this stage, it can be acknowledged that there are overlaps between these two approaches. Thus, in pursuing individual choice it could be argued that a person will maximise his or her happiness if they are at *liberty* to exercise such free choice.

The subsequent interpretation of 'On Liberty' together with 'Utilitarianism' has been influenced by the fact that Mill considers his arguments concerning the notion of liberty to appeal only to utilitarian considerations.[24] Gray has paid particular attention to the interpretation of 'On Liberty' and its relationship with Mill's other works. He notes that one of the main criticisms of the liberal approach is that a truly committed utilitarian would only be concerned with analysing the rightness or wrongness of conduct to the extent that it produces the most desirable outcome and would not therefore require another theory (such as that proposed in 'On Liberty') to analyse conduct.[25] Gray goes on to comment that at times, the adoption of the principle in 'On Liberty' may not only require departure from the principle of utility, but would require utilitarianism to be completely disregarded.[26] This is because it is not always possible to follow

---

21 ibid.

22 Mill's approach to the theory of utilitarianism was built upon that of Jeremy Bentham for evaluation, distinguishing between 'higher' and 'lower' pleasures: see Nigel Warburton, *Philosophy: The Classics* (3rd edn, Routledge 2006) 153–9.

23 It is accepted that this is a very simplistic proposal of utilitarianism and there are difficulties in defining when outcomes are 'good' or 'bad' and how they should be weighed.

24 Mill comments: 'It is proper to state that I forgo any advantage which could be derived to my argument from the idea of abstract right, as a thing independent of utility': Gray (n 8) 15. See John Gray, *Mill on Liberty: A Defence* (2nd edn, Routledge 1996) 1; see also Holtug (n 2) 380, who comments that a reading of 'On Liberty' focused on freedom is uncharitable, as Mill 'explicitly confirms his commitment to utilitarianism'.

25 Gray, ibid. 4.

26 ibid.

a strictly utilitarian approach, especially at a practical level where decisions need to be made in absence of a higher, critical thought process:

> Mill recognises that we cannot always be calculating consequences; we need in our everyday life precepts or rules more specific in their content than the Principle of Utility itself.[27]

Gray seems to be suggesting that the principles of utility and liberty are distinct and that the 'accepted' interpretation of Mill's philosophy has focused too heavily on trying to reconcile the two principles with the conclusion that they are incompatible. Gray has focused on the similarities between the two approaches and notes that the 'liberty principle must be other than an application of the Principle of Utility, for that matter, if it is to have any special tenderness for liberty'.[28]

Essentially, what can be taken from this analysis is that Mill's liberal approach is a principle of non-intervention that promotes autonomous decision-making and 'individuality'.[29] Utilitarianism, however, is concerned with analysing the rightness or wrongness of conduct based on the 'good' consequences that flow from that conduct. Therefore, Mill's notion of liberalism is not directly concerned with evaluating the actual outcome of conduct or the outcome that results from the pursuit of individuality, but is instead focused on enabling an individual to pursue his or her chosen course of conduct without state intervention or restriction.[30] Gray concludes that Mill's liberal theory imposes moral constraint on the pursuit of happiness rather than promoting happiness as a concept in itself, and is accordingly a theory of *justice* rather than of the good.[31] In summary, therefore, a liberal approach facilitates the pursuit of individuality or individual decision-making, but places limits upon such choices where serious harm to others may result. This is fundamentally different to assessing the extent to which an individual's decision is ethically acceptable based on the good or bad consequences that flow therefrom, in terms of the extent to which it maximises happiness.

---

27 ibid.

28 ibid.

29 See also Steven McLean, '"The Fertilising Conflict of Individualities": HG Wells's *A Modern Utopia*, John Stuart Mill's *On Liberty* and the Victorian Tradition of Liberalism' (2007) *Papers on Language and Literature* (Southern Illinois University 2007) 166–89; Chin Liew Ten, *Mill on Liberty* (Clarendon Press 1980) 68–85; John Gray, 'Mill's Conception of Happiness and the Theory of Individuality' in J Gray and GW Smith (eds) (n 9) 190–211.

30 It could be argued that Mill's other works were to be read in tandem with 'On Liberty' in order to evaluate the actual conduct of individuals and their autonomous decisions.

31 Gray (n 29) 8.

Another important aspect of Mill's approach is the notion of individuality. Gray notes that Mill's liberal doctrine is 'almost unintelligible when taken out of the context of the conception of happiness and the theory of individuality'.[32] However, the concept of individuality has links with both utilitarianism and liberalism. In relation to utilitarianism, the pursuit of individuality is essentially based on utility; if the pursuit of individuality results in good outcomes for the individual concerned, then the notion of individuality is therefore linked to the 'good' that results (for example, utility is relevant to evaluating the pursuit of individuality). It would seem that 'On Liberty' is not so much concerned with the way in which individuality should be pursued. Instead, freedom (or liberty) *enables* the pursuit of individuality, irrespective of the outcome that results. As summarised by Nys, the essential character in 'On Liberty' is about the *pursuit* of individuality:

> People should be allowed to engage in 'experiments of living'; they should be able to live their lives according to their own values, i.e. their own conceptions of the good. Put differently, the question of utility, that is, which way of life brings the most happiness, cannot be solved a priori, nor is it settled by mere discussion. Instead, the value of a certain way of life should be 'proved practically'. If people are deprived of the liberty of experimentation then, although they might act in correspondence with a valuable path in life, they would still fail to experience its rightness. Even if they are carefully kept out of harm's way, even if they are paternalistically protected from practical error, they will never come to experience a 'living truth'.[33]

Having established that there is a distinction between the concepts of 'utilitarianism' and 'liberalism', I should emphasise that my theoretical framework is based on the notion of reproductive *liberty*, which is underpinned by the liberal perspective rather than an analysis based on utility. However, before considering the notion of reproductive liberty, it may prove useful to differentiate the notion of liberalism further, by considering how other normative values can be distinguished from the liberal approach.

## Distinguishing Mill's Liberal Approach

Although some philosophers may not necessarily agree about the interpretation and application of Mill's liberal approach,[34] others have found Mill's philosophy

---

32 Gray (n 24) 14.

33 Thomas Nys, 'The Tacit of Competence in J. S. Mill's *On Liberty*' (2006) 25 South African Journal of Philosophy 305, 313–4.

34 See, for example, Chin Liew Ten (n 29) 1–9, 42–51; Alan Ryan (n 9) 162–8.

to provide a useful starting point from which to analyse the acceptability of certain reproductive techniques. Notwithstanding the strong support for the liberal perspective, further theories and principles, such as utilitarianism, autonomy and reproductive rights, have also been used as a basis to support reproductive decision-making without restriction by the state. While these other principles may also potentially provide a basis for analysing reproductive decision-making (either ethically or from a regulatory perspective), they are essentially different in character.

## Liberty and Autonomy

Autonomy relates to the notion of 'self-rule' or the ability for individuals to make their own decisions.[35] Beauchamp and Walters comment that personal autonomy 'refers to personal self-governance: personal rule of the self by adequate understanding while remaining free from controlling interferences by others and from personal limitations that prevent choice'.[36] In this regard, it has been noted that contemporary accounts of autonomy adopt a more individualistic view in relation to the concept, than may have been considered by philosophers such as Immanuel Kant.[37]

Autonomy interacts with a varying range of principles and is wider than the concept of liberty. As observed by Jackson, autonomy 'encompasses a cluster of interests such as liberty, privacy and freedom of choice'.[38] In line with this view, Gavaghan similarly notes that while a number of commentators have accepted the concepts of autonomy and liberty as being closely related, they are not synonymous.[39] Gavaghan further notes – citing Beauchamp and Childress[40] – that autonomy comprises of two different components, including: 'independence from controlling influences' and the 'capacity for intentional action'.[41] Accordingly, an individual's choice is regarded as autonomous when it fulfils these two principles. Nelson also notes that there are certain 'authenticity conditions' relevant to the exercise of autonomy: such conditions 'describe the

35 Emily Jackson, *Medical Law: Text, Cases and Materials* (OUP 2006) 14.

36 Tom L Beauchamp and LeRoy Walters, *Contemporary Issues in Bioethics* (6th edn, Wadsworth 2003) 22.

37 Nelson (n 5) 12–13.

38 Jackson (n 35) 14.

39 Colin Gavaghan, 'Deregulating the Genetic Supermarket: Preimplantation Screening, Future People, and the Harm Principle' (2000) 9 Cambridge Quarterly of Healthcare Ethics 242, 244; Gavaghan (n 3) 13.

40 Tom L Beauchamp and James F Childress, *Principles of Biomedical Ethics* (5th edn, OUP 2001).

41 Gavaghan 'Deregulating the Genetic Supermarket: Preimplantation Screening, Future People, and the Harm Principle' (n 39) 244.

ability to reflect on and endorse or identify with one's "first-order" desires, so that one is able to act on values that in some concrete sense are one's own'.[42] The *capacity* and *ability* to make decisions are pre-requisites for the exercise of autonomous decision-making. Fundamentally, however, an individual can only exercise his or her autonomous choice when *at liberty* to do so. Liberty is central to the notion of autonomy and although the concepts of liberty and autonomy overlap, they are nevertheless distinct.

In their work, Beauchamp and Walters formulated a number of ethical 'principles' to guide practical decision-making in the arena of bioethics, with autonomy featuring as one of the four key principles. Gavaghan has observed that autonomy is given significant status in modern bioethics and it is identified as an intrinsically valuable concept.[43] Autonomy certainly has value as a means of promoting the interests of the individual by enabling decision-making and thereby maximising individual interest.[44] This view is centred on a utilitarian analysis of the benefits of permitting individual choice. In his work on the legal and ethical aspects of embryo selection techniques, Gavaghan has noted that the principle of autonomy adds support to the notion of reproductive liberty, as a central element of respect for autonomy is that the individual is at liberty to choose and this in turn enables the individual's interests to be furthered.[45] Other commentators have also noted the value of autonomy in the context of reproductive decision-making.[46]

Significantly, the concept of autonomy might help explain *why* liberty is considered to be of value and therefore worthy of respect. It could be said that in the context of ART, the strength in allowing a liberal approach is that it *permits* autonomous reproductive choice. However, the exercise of reproductive decision-making requires the individual to have the *capacity* to make the decision at hand. In cases where the individual does not possess the requisite capacity, he or she will not be capable of employing autonomous choices.

Although there is no denying that the principle of autonomy is intrinsically valuable, its value is certainly diminished in cases where the individual is not at liberty to make a particular decision. Thus, Gavaghan observes that there is a value in respecting liberty for its own sake, as permitting individuals to make their own decisions may result in beneficial outcomes.[47] However, when liberty is restricted, the potential benefits that may arise from permitting individual choice

---

42  Nelson (n 5) 13.

43  See Beauchamp and Childress (n 40).

44  Gavaghan (n 3) 16–17.

45  See Gavaghan (n 3) 16–39.

46  See Nelson (n 5); Nicolette Priaulx, 'Rethinking Progenitive Conflict: Why Reproductive Autonomy Matters' (2008) 16 Medical Law Review 169.

47  Gavaghan (n 3) 18.

may be prevented and this may provide a basis for arguing that interference with liberty constitutes a form of 'harm' in itself.[48] Such reasoning certainly adds weight to the proposition that liberty is worthy of value. Thus, the *value* in respecting liberty – such that it leads to beneficial outcomes in the exercise of autonomous decision-making – tells us *why* liberty should be respected, but this does not necessarily help to determine the legitimate basis for state intervention in individual decision-making.

Before moving away from the principle of autonomy, some reference should also be made to the second condition cited as necessary for autonomous decision-making: the *capacity* for intentional action. This requirement has also been mentioned in relation to Mill's liberal approach, particularly in line with the notion of individuality. Nys notes that the requirement for a minimum level of competence – which is necessary for the *exercise* of liberty – is often taken for granted by scholars applying Mill's theory.[49] At the very heart of the liberal approach is the principle of non-intervention, which permits the individual to pursue his or her own choices without sanction from the state. However, the pursuit of individuality requires the individual to possess the requisite capacity that is necessary for the exercise of individual choice. Although the notion of capacity is a fundamental aspect of autonomous decision-making, it is *not* an essential pre-requisite for the liberal approach; an individual who lacks capacity is nevertheless *at liberty* to engage in a particular form of conduct. It may be that the individual's inability to make an autonomous decision (based on a lack of decision-making capacity) prevents the pursuit of individuality in such circumstances, but this does not change the fact that he or she may be at liberty to pursue a particular course of conduct.

Significantly, therefore, the notion of autonomy is concerned with the individual's ability to make informed decisions. Liberty, by contrast, facilitates the pursuit of individuality (and thereby allows the individual to make autonomous decisions), but it is predominantly concerned with establishing the legitimacy of state intervention in relation to certain types of conduct. Notably, in the specific context of ART services, there is an expectation that the decision to undergo fertility treatments is made by *competent* adults and this requirement is enshrined in the consent requirements across all relevant jurisdictions.[50]

In summary, examining concepts such as 'utility' and 'autonomy' demonstrates the value of respecting individual liberty, but these principles do not help to establish the legitimacy of state intervention concerning specific issues. Nevertheless, it is important to acknowledge that the principle of

---

48  ibid.

49  Nys (n 33) 318. Nys also goes on to note that this is made clear by Mill who only permits the liberty of choice to those 'in the maturity of their faculties'.

50  See Chapter 2, pp. 24, 25 and 44.

autonomy has gained significant recognition in modern ethical reasoning and has made the argument *for* liberty stronger, but it is nevertheless distinct from the concept of liberty and how the different principles are applied for the purpose of evaluating the legitimacy of state intervention in the context of accessing ART services for the creation of a saviour child.

## Liberty and Rights

A further distinction that needs to be made is the difference between being at liberty to do something and possessing a right to do the particular thing in question. Ringen notes that the concept of freedom stems from a *right* to choose.[51] This may be a valid assertion, but it is necessary to clarify exactly what the right to choose entails as it may be misleading to speak of the notion of rights in the context of liberty. Someone who has the liberty to act in a particular way does not necessarily have the *right* to fulfil that action (although there may be a right to *choose* to act in that way). For example, applying this to the decision to conceive by way of reproductive technologies, an individual or couple who seek to reproduce using such techniques may be at liberty to do so, but they may not have a *right* to gain assistance to fulfil their desire to conceive in this way. The question may depend on whether the individual has the means to fund such services or is eligible for public funding to provide access to reproductive technologies.[52] Given that conception with reproductive techniques requires significant assistance from trained professionals and the provision of highly technical services, it is unlikely that an individual can assert that they have a *right* to conceive using such services.[53] Warnock comments:

> I don't think there can be any question of rights in this area ... for some people it's never going to be possible to have their own biological baby ... if you find yourself to be infertile and need assistance to have a baby, it's difficult to know how far your right to get that assistance goes, and this is largely a matter of expense. It's an identical problem with ... a drug that ... [is] too expensive, you

---

51  Stein Ringen, 'Liberty, Freedom and Real Freedom' (2005) 42 Society 36, 36.

52  For a discussion relating to the availability of IVF on the UK's National Health System, see Laura Riley, 'Equality of Access to NHS-Funded IVF treatment in England and Wales' in Kirsty Horsey and Hazel Biggs (eds), *Human Fertilisation and Embryology: Reproducing Regulation* (Routledge-Cavendish 2007).

53  See Emily Jackson, 'Conception and the Irrelevance of the Welfare Principle' (2002) 177 Modern Law Review 176; Amel Alghrani and John Harris, 'Reproductive Liberty: Should the Foundation of Families be Regulated?' (2006) 18 Child and Family Law Quarterly 191.

can't expect to have it free, though you may have a right to pay – and I think an
exactly parallel argument can be used in the case of assisted birth.[54]

Despite the difficulties in framing the issue of access to ART services from a
rights perspective, this does not necessarily provide a basis for the state to claim
that it has a legitimate interest in restricting access to ART services, or that it
is justifiable to prohibit the use of embryo selection technologies as part of
that process. This argument is very different to the view that the state should
provide assistance to certain individuals to carry through their reproductive
choices. As Petersen notes, there are certain freedoms that can be extended to
reproductive decision-making, but such freedoms are not rights per se: they
amount to interests that constrain 'society from interfering with the exercise of
reproductive choice without justification'.[55] This position was summarised by
one submission to the review of ART undertaken by the House of Commons
Science and Technology Committee, observing that there is not 'an absolute
right to have children or to be provided with assistance to do so. At most
therefore, there seems to be a requirement that states do not place unreasonable
obstacles in the path of people who wish to have children'.[56] Essentially, the
distinction between having a right to be provided with assistance to conceive in
the form of ART techniques, compared to being at liberty to do so, rests on a
distinction that is drawn between positive and negative freedom.

The distinction between positive and negative freedom has traditionally
been made in philosophical writings relating to freedom and liberty.[57] As a
basic definition, the difference between the two spheres of freedom rests on
an element of control. In the context of negative liberty there is an *absence*
of control or constraint over the individual, as he or she has no obstacles
preventing the making of a choice. Positive freedom, however, involves
the individual possessing the ability and capacity for determining their own

---

54 The Open University, 'The Right to Have Babies' (2008) <http://open2.net/
ethicsbites/right-have-babies.html> accessed 31 August 2014; see also Mary Warnock,
*Making Babies: Is There a Right to Have Children?* (OUP 2002).

55 Kerry Petersen, 'Genetic Technologies and ART: Ethical Values, Legal
Regulation and Informal Regulation' in Ian Freckelton and Kerry Petersen (eds),
*Disputes and Dilemmas in Health Law* (The Federation Press 2006).

56 House of Commons Science and Technology Committee, *Human Reproductive
Technologies and the Law* (2005) 11. This comment was made in relation to the European
Convention for the Protection of Human Rights, which contains a number of provisions
that have relevance to the provision of ART services in the UK. The Convention was
directly incorporated into UK domestic law through the enactment of the Human
Rights Act 1998 (UK). Of particular relevance to the current discussion is art 8, which
contains the right to respect for private and family life.

57 Joel Feinberg, *Social Philosophy* (Prentice-Hall 1973) 12.

decisions.[58] Thus, an individual who does not have the means to pay for their own in vitro fertilisation (IVF) treatment may be 'free' to gain such treatment only so far as the state will assist them with their choice, and is therefore lacking complete control of their own fate in terms of determining the course of their reproductive decisions.

The application of Mill's liberal theory results in the conclusion that intervention in reproductive decision-making is only justified where the exercise of liberty in this context will result in harm to others (as defined in accordance with the Harm Principle, outlined in Chapter 5). And although this requires that state intervention should be kept to a minimum, in the sphere of emerging technologies – where profound ethical and social considerations are raised – some have argued that regulatory oversight and intervention by the state is likely to be inevitable. As Lloyd notes, in modern society, restraint and limitation of individual freedom is inevitable, but negative freedom requires that intervention is minimised in the interest of free choice.[59] Yet, there is a difference between minimalist intervention that preserves liberty as much as is possible, and a response based on precautionary measures, where certain practices or technologies are regulated, based on an unknown and undefined risk of harm, or based on moral grounds. In Chapter 6, the precautionary principle is considered further, to determine whether reliance on an undefined or speculative risk of harm may provide a sufficient basis for state intervention. However, for the reasons outlined above, it is clear that an approach underpinned by liberal reasoning is very different to an argument based on the notion of rights, which would require the state to assist individuals in their right to conceive using ART services. Having outlined the liberal approach in some detail, I now turn to consider its significance in the specific context of reproductive decision-making.

## Liberty and Reproductive Decision-Making

The concept of reproductive liberty is one that has been considered extensively in the body of literature on the topic of reproductive decision-making. Notably, however, it is a concept that can be applied to a range of different matters concerning reproduction. Erin Nelson, who argues in favour of the concept of reproductive autonomy (a concept that I consider below), has taken note of the contextual factors relevant to the origins of the dialogue concerning reproductive liberty and autonomy:

---

58  See Isaiah Berlin, *Two Concepts of Liberty* (Clarendon Press 1958).

59  Lord Lloyd of Hampstead and MDA Freeman, *Lloyd's Introduction to Jurisprudence* (5th edn, Stevens & Sons 1990) 146.

Many see the origins of reproductive autonomy as a concept arising out of the struggles over birth control and abortion that began in the mid-nineteenth century. Avoidance of coerced reproduction was the point – the battle for reproductive autonomy was a battle for women's right to control their own reproductive capacities by preventing or terminating unwanted pregnancies.[60]

Although the arguments concerning reproductive liberty may have indeed originated from debates relating to issues such as abortion and birth control, the view that reproductive decisions are matters that are best determined by the individual, without state intrusion, is central to the framework adopted for analysis in this book. Despite the historical origins of the notion of reproductive liberty, as will become clear from the discussion below, the liberal perspective is one that has gained considerable traction in the sphere of reproductive decision-making and has also been applied to the use of ART services. Mill's liberal perspective provides a strong basis for arguing in favour of a position of non-intervention in this context.

The report of the United Kingdom's (UK's) House of Commons Science and Technology Committee on the regulation of ARTs noted that 'the philosophical view that individuals should have the right to make private choices – such as reproductive decisions – free from the scrutiny of the state can be traced to John Stuart Mill'.[61] Similarly, Glover observes that this 'attractive principle can be borrowed from political philosophy and applied to ethics', when he considers the specific issue of using embryo selection technologies to prevent transmission of genetic disorders and disabilities.[62] Although this approach may indeed appear to be attractive for evaluating decision-making in this context, its application nevertheless raises difficulties. The Harm Principle is of central importance in terms of justifying when state intervention is appropriate, and as discussed in Chapter 6, it is a particularly difficult principle to apply to reproductive decision-making. Thus, Gavaghan notes:

> it is no easy thing to apply the Harm Principle to [the use of reproductive] technologies; as … the concept of 'harm' is not as straightforward as Mill … perhaps assumed, and it is especially problematic in relation to 'genesis questions', that is, decisions about who should be born.[63]

Despite the difficulties that may arise when applying a harm-based approach to questions surrounding reproduction, the liberal approach nevertheless provides

---

60 Nelson (n 5) 31–2 (footnotes omitted from the original text).
61 House of Commons Science and Technology Committee (n 56) 17.
62 Jonathan Glover, *Choosing Children: Genes, Disability and Design* (OUP 2006) 74.
63 Gavaghan (n 3) 37–8.

a suitable starting point for determining that there should be a presumption against state intrusion in terms of reproductive decision-making. John Robertson has paid particular attention to the question of whether there should be a presumption in favour of reproductive liberty.[64] His approach has been noted as one of the most influential views on the topic of reproductive liberty.[65] Although Robertson's approach does not directly rely on Mill's liberal theory, it does resemble something very similar to it, as it is strongly underpinned by the view that reproductive decision-making should only be restricted where the exercise of reproductive choice results in harm to others.

Robertson observes that there are different values at stake in the context of modern reproductive techniques, as such technologies have the potential to generate 'controversy, bewilderment, and fears of larger social effects'.[66] He further comments, 'initial wonder at their marvels is usually followed by a nagging sense of discomfort because of the way in which they change nature and could harm children, family, women and society'.[67] Robertson's central argument is that procreative liberty should be given presumptive priority and in cases of conflict, opponents of particular techniques should be required to demonstrate the potential harms.[68] Robertson implicitly supports an application of the Harm Principle when he notes that in some cases, there may be evident harm that rebuts the strong initial presumption in favour of the freedom to decide.[69] Robertson does, however, incorporate a utilitarian justification for his approach. This is clearly evidenced by his view concerning the use of embryo selection technologies for the selection of genetic traits, where he argues that there:

> [I]s a presumptive right to procreate because of the great importance to the individuals of having biological offspring – personal meaning in one's own life, connection with future generations, and the pleasures of child rearing. If a person thought that she would realize those benefits only from a child with particular characteristics, then she should be free to select offspring to have those preferred traits. The right to procreate would thus imply the right to take actions to assure that offspring have the characteristics that make procreation desirable or meaningful for that individual.[70]

---

64 John A Robertson, *Children of Choice: Freedom and the New Reproductive Technologies* (Princeton University Press 1994).

65 Nelson (n 5) 32.

66 Robertson (n 64) 15.

67 ibid.

68 ibid. 16.

69 ibid. 17.

70 ibid. 152–3.

Robertson appears to incorporate language based on the notion of rights and utility when framing his argument in favour of reproductive choice, suggesting that the concept of liberty (which can be justifiably curtailed in cases where serious harm will ensue) is not the only principle that he regards as relevant to this argument. Importantly, however, Robertson maintains that by adopting a presumptive liberal position concerning procreative choice, a fuller analysis of the core interests at stake will eventuate:

> By asking what procreative freedom demands, we can see how much presumptive choice individuals should have over the use of these techniques. By asking what is really at stake in the objections raised, we can see what value should be assigned to competing ethical and social concerns. This requires a careful analysis of both the asserted procreative interest and the asserted harms, so that procreative choice will be limited only when truly weighty concerns are present.[71]

Robertson notes that reproduction is fundamentally respected because of its centrality to personal identity, meaning and dignity.[72] He further argues that this importance elevates the notion of being at liberty to reproduce to a moral right that cannot be limited except for very good reason.[73] As outlined above, the language of rights (even moral rights) does not sit squarely within the liberal framework that I am advocating for. However, an important factor that can be taken from Robertson's position (and one that is explored further in Chapter 5) is that in circumstances where the presumptive position is challenged (based on the potential for establishing harm to others), state involvement should not necessarily adopt a *prohibitive* approach; it may be that other forms of regulatory intervention may successfully minimise the harm in question. Robertson's approach in this respect argues in favour of non-coercive methods and this is of particular significance to the harm approach outlined in Chapter 5 and the proposed regulatory approach put forward in Chapter 8.

Robertson also argues that certain reproductive decisions may require state intervention based on an assessment of whether or not they are 'responsible'.[74] This notion of reproductive responsibility is used primarily in the context of involuntary contraception and sterilisation, and prenatally caused harm.[75] As noted by Nelson, state intervention is permissible under this approach when

---

71 ibid. 18.
72 ibid. 30.
73 ibid.
74 ibid. 78–80.
75 Nelson (n 5) 33.

'on balance, individual reproductive decisions are irresponsible'.[76] Yet, the factors of relevance for assessing whether a particular reproductive decision is 'irresponsible' are not entirely clear. If we were to accept that this standard could potentially apply in the context of using ART services for the creation of a saviour child, there may be a number of factors that help to support the view that a family's decision is 'responsible'. Thus, the conception of a saviour child may prove successful in promoting the interests of the entire family and avoid the death of one of the family members. Perhaps on this basis, a family's decision could be regarded as 'responsible' (although, I accept that some may also argue to the contrary, to claim that a decision to conceive a saviour child is irresponsible). Nevertheless, the notion of 'responsible' decision-making does not, in my view, provide a sound basis for state intervention with reproductive decisions (particularly where the regulatory response *prohibits* the use of ART services for this purpose), although it may well provide grounds to argue that a particular reproductive decision is or is not ethically justifiable.

The restrictions currently in place in some Australian jurisdictions (and the restrictions previously in place in the UK), which preclude access to ART services for the creation of a saviour child, are guided by the welfare principle.[77] Thus, the primary factor of relevance under each of the relevant regulatory approaches is the extent to which the reproductive decision will impact on the welfare of a potential child who may be born following the provision of ART services (or how the decision may impact on existing children of the family). As discussed in Chapter 6, this requires a focus on assessing the potential harm to a child who may be born as a result of the reproductive decision in question. However, the extent to which a decision is 'responsible' is not necessarily relevant to whether a specific reproductive decision will cause harm to a prospective child (or to others).

It is therefore clear that a fundamental factor of relevance to Robertson's presumptive approach is the extent to which a reproductive decision will cause harm to others. If a presumptive liberal approach is accepted in the context of reproductive decision-making, the key issue when determining whether state intervention is justified is to determine whether intervention is necessary to prevent (or at least minimise) the risk of harm to others. The issue of what constitutes harm to others is addressed in Chapter 5. Importantly, however, Robertson is not the only commentator that adopts a presumptive position in favour of reproductive decision-making; other scholars have adopted similar reasoning. These approaches are considered below.

---

76 ibid.
77 See Chapter 3, pp. 61–6.

## Liberty, Reproductive Decision-making and the Views of other Commentators

Other commentators have similarly noted the significance of the liberal position in the context of reproductive decision-making, with the observation that state intervention in reproductive choice should only occur where there is strong justification for such intervention. Rosalind McDougall has noted that the prevailing approach in analysing reproductive decision-making is to prioritise the concept of parental procreative liberty.[78] She also notes the relevance of the Harm Principle in relation to the liberal perspective, stating that the 'procreative liberty framework is a harm-based approach to reproductive ethics that posits a criterion of right action' and that ' ... under this framework a reproductive choice is morally permissible if it is not (significantly) harmful'.[79] McDougall has analysed the permissibility of using embryo selection technologies from a virtue ethics perspective. Nevertheless, McDougall clearly acknowledges the significance of the liberal perspective.

In the context of reproductive decision-making, Emily Jackson has argued in favour of the principle of procreative *privacy* (this concept can arguably be distinguished from the principle of procreative *liberty*). Jackson's argument begins with the proposition that an individual's bodily integrity is inviolate and that interference with natural procreation would contravene this principle.[80] She justifies this by arguing that an individual has a right to pursue his or her own life choices, noting similarly to Robertson that there is individual importance in being able to reproduce.[81] Jackson's central argument is that it is not justifiable to subject infertile people to a 'parenting suitability' assessment (by applying the welfare principle) simply because they require ART services to conceive. In this regard, she argues that women (and where relevant, their partners) should have the right to make reproductive decisions in privacy and without scrutiny:

> My claim is that we should refrain from scrutinising the pre-conception decisions of adults who intend to bring about a child's creation just as we would if they had happened to be able to conceive naturally. Notice that this is not the same as saying that people have a *right* to be provided with infertility treatment. On the

---

78  McDougall (n 7) 601.

79  ibid.

80  Jackson (n 53) 177; see also, Emily Jackson, 'Rethinking the Pre-conception Welfare Principle' in Kirsty Horsey and Hazel Biggs (eds), *Human Fertilisation and Embryology: Reproducing Regulation* (Routledge-Cavendish 2007) 47–68.

81  ibid.; see also Priaulx (n 46).

contrary, my argument here is much more modest. It is simply that we should each have the liberty to shield certain personal decisions from public scrutiny.[82]

Jackson's approach is broader than the liberal perspective; her central thesis is that reproductive decisions are worthy of respect on the basis that they are private and should not be subject to the scrutiny of others. However, this view does not necessarily extend to an analysis of the potential harmful consequences of specific reproductive decisions (in fact, it seems to suggest the opposite in some respects, as she is arguing that the pre-conception welfare principle should *not* be applied to screen out prospective ART participants). As Jackson's approach requires the state to refrain from intervening with the private reproductive decisions of others, this position is, in some ways, very similar to the one I am advocating. However, importantly, Jackson has framed her argument from the perspective of the rights of prospective parent(s) to make private reproductive decisions. My argument, on the other hand, is framed from the perspective of the state's legitimate interest in restricting access to ART services; it is not necessarily focused on establishing the *right* to access ART services or the right to reproductive privacy. Notwithstanding this distinction, I acknowledge that the outcome under either theoretical approach may be the same. Therefore, to some extent it is likely that these two positions seek to forward the same purpose despite the difference in the theoretical bases underpinning them.

Erin Nelson's approach to the issue of reproductive decision-making is also worthy of consideration, particularly when formulating an argument that is framed from the perspective of the legitimate exercise of state power over the individual. Nelson's approach is centred on the notion of reproductive *autonomy*, although she does also use the term to encompass the concept of liberty.[83] Above, I distinguished the notion of autonomy from that of liberty. This distinction is particularly important for framing my argument, which is underpinned by the liberal perspective, rather than that of autonomy. Nelson observes that autonomy is linked to liberalism, but states that 'autonomy is critical as a means of protecting the individual from the State, or protecting a space for individual decision making and self-governance'.[84] What appears to be particularly important to Nelson is that the state not only refrains from intervening with reproductive decision-making, but also actively works towards a framework that facilitates and encourages *autonomous* decision-making. She comments:

From a traditional liberal point of view, as long as neither men nor women are coerced into reproducing, or sterilised without their consent, or prohibited

---

82 Jackson (n 53) 178.
83 Nelson (n 5).
84 ibid. 15–16.

from choosing technological means of reproducing, all is well. But, as a richer conception of autonomy helps to highlight, all is not well when we fail to acknowledge the uneven effects of reproductive decision making (and reproduction itself) on men and women, and particularly on women who are multiply disadvantaged.[85]

When developing her approach to reproductive autonomy, Nelson also outlines some of the criticisms of the liberal approach. She comments:

> ... procreative liberty is a negative liberty; in essence, it requires no more of the State (or others) than a hands-off, permissive approach. While this perspective is preferable to one permitting significant restrictions on reproductive choice, it is ultimately unsatisfactory, as it will undoubtedly result in the denial of meaningful reproductive choice for those who are economically and socially disadvantaged.[86]

This is certainly a valid criticism that requires consideration. However, this view also needs to be considered in line with the scope of Nelson's analysis of reproductive autonomy, which is focused on a much wider evaluation of reproductive decision-making. Thus, Nelson goes on to consider the role of liberalism in relation to issues such as abortion – an issue that has divisive views on how the law protects (or should protect) the autonomy of women, particularly in the United States. Nelson also observes that there are equality issues in the context of reproductive decision-making that are not adequately addressed by the 'hands-off' liberal approach, particularly around the fair allocation of resources. She further observes that an approach based on privacy rights, 'privileges the reproductive choices of those with wealth and power, and discounts both "'private' obstacles" to reproductive choice and government interference (short of coercion) that constrains reproductive decision making'.[87] Nelson's view in relation to liberal theory is that it misses 'too many things, especially things that are important to women's ability to exercise meaningful reproductive choice',[88] and she therefore argues that it is not safe to assume that an individual will make an autonomous decision simply because she is at liberty to choose.[89]

Ultimately, Nelson's quest is to formulate a richer and deeper understanding of what reproductive *autonomy* might entail and to this end, her work must be commended. Yet, as she acknowledges in the quote above, according to a pure

---

85  ibid. 47.
86  ibid. 34.
87  ibid. 35 (footnotes from original source omitted).
88  ibid. 47.
89  ibid. 48.

libertarian approach, as long as 'neither men nor women are ... prohibited from choosing technological means of reproducing, all is well'.[90] In this respect, all is not well. In Chapter 3 it was established that access to ART services for the purpose of conceiving a saviour child is prohibited in some Australian jurisdictions. The fact that the state has adopted a system of regulation that *prohibits* access to ART services in this context (either directly as a result of the imposition of statutory eligibility criteria, or indirectly by an application of the welfare principle) requires contemplation of whether such restrictions are justifiable. In this sense, the question of the legitimacy of state intervention in the sphere of reproductive decision-making is the necessary starting point. Thus, before we can design a regulatory framework that may assist in facilitating autonomous decision-making in this context (which, I agree, is desirable), it is first necessary to consider whether state-imposed barriers that prevent access to ART services in this context should be removed. For this purpose, it is the liberal perspective that provides the starting point. Factors that may help to assist families with making informed, autonomous decisions, can then be subsequently considered once it is determined (if at all) that the state has no legitimate role in restricting the accessibility of ART services for this purpose.

Colin Gavaghan has also adopted a liberal perspective when analysing the regulatory issues surrounding embryo selection technologies.[91] Gavaghan acknowledges that a presumption in favour of liberty can be justified by reference to a number of principles, including respect for autonomy (as an intrinsically valuable concept); the value of individual decision-making as a means of promoting positive outcomes (a utilitarian approach); or on the basis that reproductive decision-making is worthy of respect in its own right (presumption in favour of reproductive liberty).[92] All of these factors strengthen the case for procreative liberty. However, as discussed above, while these principles support an analysis underpinned by liberal reasoning, they do not provide a basis upon which to determine the legitimacy of state interference with reproductive decision-making.

## ART Regulatory Policy and the Liberal Presumption

There is a further justificatory basis that can be relied upon to support the adoption of the liberal approach for analysing the bounds of state intervention with reproductive decision-making. Significantly, the liberal perspective is deeply embedded within the current regulatory approach relevant to ART services. The relevance of the pre-conception welfare assessment was considered in Chapter

---

90 See text accompanying (n 85).
91 Gavaghan (n 3) 23.
92 ibid.

3 and it was established that in the UK context, there is a presumption in favour of providing ART services, subject to a harm assessment (applied in the form of the welfare principle). This approach is referred to in the policies developed by the Human Fertilisation and Embryology Authority (HFEA). For example, the review of the welfare principle undertaken by the HFEA in 2005 led to the statement that 'there is now a presumption to provide treatment, unless there is evidence that any child born to an individual or couple, or any existing child of their family, would face a risk of serious harm'.[93] This presumption is also firmly stated in the HFEA's report on sex selection:

> [T]he decision to have children ... is an area of private life in which people are generally best left to make their own choice and in which the state should intervene only to prevent the occurrence of serious harms, and only where this intervention is non-intrusive and likely to be effective.[94]

Given that the liberal perspective has been afforded priority under the ART regulatory framework, both from a theoretical and a policy perspective, it may prove difficult to dislodge this view when considering the extent to which the state can justifiably intervene with reproductive decision-making.


## Conclusion

In this chapter, I have outlined the liberal approach of John Stuart Mill in 'On Liberty'. Mill's theory prioritises the principle of liberty and regards state interference as unjustifiable, unless it can be established that serious harm will result to others in the absence of intervention. The liberal perspective is not concerned with taking a particular moral standpoint on specific matters per se. Instead, it adopts a 'hands-off' approach. This principle is firmly embedded in modern democracies; as noted at the beginning of the chapter, the concept of liberty is firmly embedded within Western democratic society even if it is an ideal rarely recognised in practice.[95]

Liberty was distinguished from concepts such as utilitarianism, autonomy and rights-based approaches. Liberal theory requires the state to refrain from intruding on the liberty of the individual. It does not require the state

---

93 Human Fertilisation and Embryology Authority, *Tomorrow's Children: Report of the Policy Review of Welfare of the Child Assessments in Licensed Assisted Conception Clinics* (HFEA 2005) 1.

94 Human Fertilisation and Embryology Authority, *Sex Selection: Options for Regulation* (HFEA 2003) 33.

95 Gavaghan (n 3) 35.

to provide positive assistance to enable individuals to fulfil their reproductive choices, although, as highlighted above, commentators such as Nelson view the state's role as requiring something more than a hands-off approach in order to facilitate truly autonomous reproductive decision-making. Most importantly, however, the primary purpose in outlining the liberal perspective was to consider its relevance to *reproductive* decision-making and for my analysis this is focused on reproductive decisions in the context of ART. It was established that the principle of liberty is deeply embedded within the realms of reproductive decision-making and this has been confirmed by a number of commentators. The notion of reproductive liberty has gained considerable traction in the literature, thus supporting a presumptive approach in favour of non-intervention. And a number of commentators have similarly concluded that there is a strong interest in reproductive decision-making, which leans towards the existence of such a presumption. Quite frequently, however, the underlying liberal perspective is intertwined with other normative viewpoints, such as autonomy and utilitarianism. Indeed, it cannot be contested that these additional normative perspectives provide us with an influential view on *why* the notion of reproductive liberty is worthy of respect. However, concepts such as autonomy and utilitarianism do not necessarily provide us with a basis for determining when state intervention is justified.

At the heart of Mill's liberal theory is the view that state intrusion with individual decision-making is unjustified unless it can be established that harm to others will result without such intervention. My argument is that the presumptive position favoured by the liberal approach should be similarly adopted concerning the issue of access to ART services for the conception of a saviour child. Significantly, this is subject to a determination of the extent to which particular reproductive decisions will (or may) harm children who are conceived in this way, or how such decisions may potentially harm others. It is to the concept of harm that I now turn, so that the principle can be adequately explored in the chapters that follow.

# Chapter 5
# The Harm Principle as a Means for Justifying State Intervention and Regulation

## Introduction

The significance of the liberal approach to reproductive decision-making was outlined in Chapter 4. It was established that a presumptive position in favour of reproductive liberty requires the state to take a 'hands-off' approach in terms of determining the issue of access to assisted reproductive technology (ART) services. This also requires a non-restrictive approach to the use of embryo selection technologies. Importantly, however, this presumptive position is rebuttable and, consequently, it is necessary to determine the relevant standard or 'threshold' that provides the justification for such rebuttal (thereby legitimising state intervention). For this purpose, the central aspect of Mill's liberal approach is the Harm Principle.

The focus of this chapter is to establish the scope of the Harm Principle. This principle determines the extent to which the state can legitimately intervene with the liberty of individuals. The fundamental aspect of the Harm Principle is that state interference with liberty is only justified in circumstances where the conduct of a person or group of people is likely to result in serious harm to others. It is therefore necessary to establish what is meant by 'harm to others'. For this purpose, I consider the principle as outlined by Mill and expand upon this with some basic definitions and consider how other commentators have subsequently defined the notion of harm. This is then followed by an examination of how the principle may apply to reproductive decisions.

## The Harm Principle

The Harm Principle has been used to defend a number of moral and ethical issues, ranging from the sale and distribution of pornography to the practice of euthanasia.[1] It is clear that the principle has been raised in many areas of

---

1 See Thomas Nys, 'The Tacit of Competence in J. S. Mill's *On Liberty*' (2006) 25 South African Journal of Philosophy 305; Steven D Smith, 'Is the Harm Principle Illiberal?' (2006) 51 The American Journal of Jurisprudence 1.

social policy and has been used to establish the type of conduct that should be subject to criminal sanction.[2] For example, in England, the question of whether homosexuality should be the subject of criminal prosecution was addressed in the Wolfenden Report in 1957,[3] which, in essence, applied Mill's Harm Principle to conclude that while some members of society may be offended by homosexual behaviour, they are not actually *harmed* by it.[4] As established in Chapter 4, the liberal approach is not concerned with evaluating the morality of specific conduct per se; instead, it is concerned with determining how the conduct of one or more individuals impacts on others. Ultimately, Mill was concerned with, as he put it, one very simple principle:

> [T]he sole end for which mankind are warranted, individually or collectively, in interfering with the liberty of action of any of their number, is self-protection. That the only purpose of which power can be rightfully exercised over any member of a civilized community, against his will, is to prevent harm to others.[5]

## Defining Harm

One of the most important tasks is to appropriately define the notion of harm. The difficulty is that the term is vague, ambiguous and capable of use in a wide range of contexts. It can be used to describe differing degrees of injury or damage to person or property. Importantly, it is necessary to determine the extent to which the Harm Principle encompasses these different types of 'harm'. Does it cover all types of harm in a broad sense, or is there a more narrow definition that must be formulated for the purposes of defining the threshold point at which state intervention is justified?

The *Australian Oxford Dictionary* defines the word 'harm' as 'damage' or 'injury'.[6] Similarly, the *Macquarie Dictionary* also defines the term to mean 'damage' or 'injury', but also adds the terms 'hurt', 'moral injury', 'evil' or 'wrong'.[7] These definitions alone do not provide a basis for applying the Harm Principle, although they do provide us with a starting point. As Feinberg notes,

---

2 Joel Feinberg, *Social Philosophy* (Prentice-Hall 1973) 21.

3 Committee on Homosexual Offences and Prostitution, *Report of the Committee on Homosexual Offences and Prostitution* (HMSO 1957).

4 Nils Holtug 'The Harm Principle' (2002) 5 Ethical Theory and Moral Practice 357, 357–89.

5 John Gray (ed), *John Stuart Mill, On Liberty and Other Essays* (OUP 1991) 14.

6 *The Australian Oxford Paperback Dictionary* (4th edn, OUP 2006) 378.

7 *Macquarie Concise Dictionary* (4th edn, Macquarie Library 2006).

the term 'harm' is a 'useful peg' and works as a 'convenient abbreviation' for complicated moral and value judgments that may be underlying its use.[8]

According to Riley, the term 'harm' represents a form of 'perceptible damage' suffered against one's wishes, requiring something more than mere dislike.[9] On Riley's analysis, harm arises in a number of forms including 'physical personal injury (not excepting death), forcible confinement, financial loss, damage to reputation, broken promises (contractual or otherwise) and so on'.[10] Most people would agree that physical personal injury is a form of harm, but other examples are more problematic. For example, a person can suffer harm and this can occur irrespective of whether another person's conduct has caused the particular harm in question. In this context, harm is synonymous to the term 'damage' as it conveys that an individual has suffered some form of damage rather than trying to describe how that damage was inflicted. An act of 'harming', on the other hand, relates to the *conduct* of an individual (or group of people) responsible for causing the alleged damage. As Feinberg notes, an 'act of harming is one which *causes* harm to other people' (emphasis added).[11] The Harm Principle is ultimately concerned with harm prevention (by way of intervening with individual liberty) and can therefore be seen as a basis for preventing the very *conduct* that causes harm.

The way in which the infliction of harm is described may also be relevant to defining the principle. For example, Feinberg draws a distinction between being *harmed* and suffering from a *harmful* condition; in the case of a *harmed* condition the person may suffer some kind of damage, but this will only amount to a *harmful* condition if it is likely to cause further harm:

> A blistered finger may be to some small degree a *harmed condition*, but unless the finger is on the hand of a concert pianist or a baseball pitcher, it may not be at all *harmful* (emphasis added).[12]

On this basis, a harmed condition may denote even a minimal level of damage, whereas a harmful condition implies a higher degree of harm or damage and may involve repeated harms. As Gavaghan explains, a 'harmful condition is

---

8 Joel Feinberg, *The Moral Limits of the Criminal Law: Harm to Others* (OUP 1984) 32.

9 Jonathan Riley, *Mill on Liberty* (Routledge 1998) 98. Riley does note that by implication, self-harm must be unintentional on this view.

10 ibid. Feinberg poses the interesting question of whether a person is 'harmed' when they are killed, or whether it is their surviving *interests* that are harmed (n 8) 79–91.

11 Feinberg (n 8) 31.

12 ibid.

one likely to give rise to further, future harms'.[13] One significant question that needs to be addressed is the extent to which the Harm Principle encompasses differing degrees of harm.

## Scoping the Harm Principle: On Liberty and Beyond

As Mill's theory forms the basis of the applicable framework, it is the natural starting point for attempting to clarify and scope the threshold under the Harm Principle. However, this appears to be an optimistic starting point as Mill's essay did not go into great depths to explain exactly what the term 'harm' should encompass.

### Problems in scope

Some have argued that Mill's determination of the Harm Principle is burdened from the start, as Mill differs in his analysis as to what exactly constitutes harm.[14] Mill asserts that harm involves the violation of 'certain interests which ought to be considered as rights'.[15] However, there is also a lack of detail as to what constitutes an 'interest'. As Nys notes, 'this merely reformulates the question: For what are these basic interests?'[16] The lack of precision in Mill's essay is also highlighted by Gray:

> Does he intend the reader to understand 'harm' to refer only to physical harm, or must a class of moral harms to character be included in any application of the liberty principle? Must the harm that the restriction on liberty prevents be done directly to identifiable individuals, or may it also relevantly be done to institutions, social practices and forms of life? Can serious offence to feelings count as harm so far as the restriction of liberty is concerned, or must the harm be done to interests, or to those interests the protection of which is to be accorded the status of a right?[17]

The essential basis of Mill's thesis is to determine the extent to which a particular form of conduct will cause harm to *others*. This has been interpreted to mean that the interests of an individual should be protected from invasion or damage.[18] Essentially, harm occurs when the *interests* of

---

13 Colin Gavaghan, *Defending the Genetic Supermarket: Law and Ethics of Selecting the Next Generation* (Routledge-Cavendish 2007) 52.

14 Nys (n 1) 321.

15 Gray (n 5).

16 Nys (n 1) 322.

17 John Gray, *Mill On Liberty: A Defence* (2nd edn, Routledge 1996) 49.

18 ibid. 50.

others are wrongfully infringed in some way.[19] The concept of infringing another person's interest is explored below. However, philosophers such as Feinberg have observed that nearly all human conduct impacts on others in some way or another,[20] and this therefore makes it difficult to argue that there is a sphere of personal action that impacts on no one other than the agent. And importantly, Mill was clear that self-regarding[21] conduct falls outside the scope of the Harm Principle:

> The only part of the conduct of any one, for which he is amenable to society, is that which concerns others. In the part which merely concerns himself, his independence is, of right, absolute. Over himself, over his own body and mind, the individual is sovereign.[22]

This comment has been heavily criticised as the sphere of private and public conduct overlap significantly. As noted by Berlin, 'anything a man does could, in principle, frustrate others; that no man is an island; that the social and the individual aspects of human beings often cannot, in practice, be disentangled'.[23] This view is particularly apparent in the context of moral issues that have differing and extreme viewpoints and therefore impact on a wide range of people in different ways.

The distinction between conduct that harms another person (or group of people) and conduct that is regarded as morally offensive is one that has generated significant debate. One clear example, referred to by the Hart/Devlin debate,[24] is the issue of homosexuality. When the UK Wolfenden Committee considered whether homosexual conduct should be de-criminalised, it was noted that while many people may be offended by homosexuality, people do not suffer harm as a result of the homosexual behaviour of autonomous adults. On this basis, it was concluded that homosexual conduct between consenting adults in private should not be the subject of criminal culpability.[25] Applying the same reasoning in the context of ART, it is clear that there are divergent views on the acceptability of certain reproductive practices.

---

19 ibid.

20 Feinberg (n 8).

21 For an analysis of self-regarding actions, see Chin Liew Ten, *Mill On Liberty* (Clarendon Press 1980) 10–40.

22 Gray (n 5) 14.

23 Isaiah Berlin, 'John Stuart Mill and the Ends of Life' in John Gray and G W Smith (eds) *J. S. Mill On Liberty in Focus* (Routledge 1991), 147.

24 See H L A Hart, *Law, Liberty and Morality* (Stanford University Press 1963).

25 ibid. 15.

The Harm Principle – as a basis for justifying state intervention – therefore requires something more than merely offensive conduct. It requires that the conduct of an individual or group of people causes harm to others. Any conduct that falls within the scope of the actor's own interests (and no other person's interests, unless he or she consents to such interference) will be classed as self-regarding therefore falling outside the scope of the Harm Principle.[26]

## Further consideration of the harm principle

Given that Mill's Harm Principle lacks the necessary detail for practical application, it is necessary to consider how other commentators have refined the principle. Feinberg has paid considerable attention to the notion of harming in his work, *The Moral Limits of the Criminal Law*.[27] He has considered Mill's central thesis (the Harm Principle) and has modified it based on the criticism levelled against it, while keeping true to 'Mill's liberal motivating spirit'.[28] Although the exact scope of the Harm Principle is still not universally agreed upon, Feinberg's work is widely respected and has been extremely influential in defining the scope of the Harm Principle.[29]

---

26 Mill also recognised that self-regarding actions have potential for self-harm. For example, this may occur in the form of self-injury, directly attributable to an individual's conduct. However, it may also occur as result of how another person reacts to the conduct of an individual. In the latter context, a person may shun or avoid an individual because they find the person's conduct insulting or offensive: see Riley (n 9) 92–4. Mill rejected these factors as grounds for coercing individual conduct, and advocated strongly against paternalism aimed at preventing self-harm (either as a direct or indirect result of a person's conduct). See Gerald Dworkin, 'Challenges to Self-Determination: Paternalism' in Joel Feinberg and Jules Coleman (eds), *Philosophy of Law* (6th edn, Wadsworth 2000) 271–81. Neither form of self-harm falls under the scope of the Harm Principle and paternalism is strongly rejected. However, those who lack the capacity for autonomous decision-making are unlikely to be free to exercise individual liberty without some level of paternalistic intervention, as the notion of paternalism was rejected only to the extent that it was imposed on those 'in the maturity of their faculties': see Nys (n 1) 318.

27 Feinberg (n 8). Volume 1 is entitled 'Harm to Others', Volume 2 'Offense to Others', Volume 3 'Harm to Self' and Volume 4 'Harmless Wrongdoing'.

28 Feinberg (n 8) 15.

29 Richard A Epstein, 'The Harm Principle – And How it Grew' (1995) 45 University of Toronto Law Journal 369, 370; Holtug (n 4); Gavaghan (n 13); Carson Strong, 'Harming by Conceiving: A Review of Misconceptions and a New Analysis' (2005) 30 Journal of Medicine and Philosophy 491; Douglas S Diekema, 'Parental Refusals of Medical Treatment: The Harm Principle as Threshold for State Intervention' (2004) 25 Theoretical Medicine 243.

Feinberg's approach is focused on the exercise of 'political power'[30] and the boundaries of the criminal law; it therefore applies more narrowly than what was anticipated by Mill. However, Feinberg's narrow focus does not jeopardise the Harm Principle as an evaluative tool. As detailed in Chapter 3, reproductive decision-making is limited by the *state* in some jurisdictions, either directly or indirectly. The intrusion on reproductive decision-making occurs by way of prohibition. On this basis, Feinberg's approach is equally applicable; Mill and Feinberg were concerned with determining the extent to which the state is justified in coercing individuals and limiting liberty by means of criminal sanction. In the context of embryo selection techniques, the form of coercion is not a threat of criminal sanction against those seeking to use the technologies (for example, the families seeking to create a saviour child). Instead, the relevant sanctions will be imposed against clinicians and scientists who perform such techniques without approval or in compliance with relevant legislation and/or guidelines.[31] In this respect, the interference with reproductive decision-making is *indirect*; ART centres and practitioners failing to comply with the relevant regulatory provisions may incur criminal liability and/or risk losing their accreditation status as an ART provider with the relevant professional body. Feinberg's approach is therefore capable of application to reproductive decisions in this specific context.

Irrespective of whether reproductive decision-making is restricted by way of direct or indirect coercion is not of great significance. As noted by Gavaghan, prospective parents seeking access to embryo selection techniques are 'victims' of indirect coercion.[32] It matters little that the force of the criminal law is not used against families *directly* as a means of coercion. The fact that criminal sanction is used as the basis for prohibiting certain reproductive decisions supports the view that the work of both Mill and Feinberg is relevant for analysis of the legitimacy of state intervention.

### Establishing the Harm Threshold

Feinberg outlines three categories of harm in the context of harming others:

1. harm in an extended or derivative sense;
2. harm as setbacks to interests;
3. harm as wrongdoing.

For the purpose of determining the relevant harm 'threshold', Feinberg argues that the Harm Principle is engaged when his second and third categories of

---

30  Feinberg (n 8) 3.
31  Gavaghan (n 13) 15.
32  ibid.

harm overlap: 'only setbacks of interests that are wrongs, and wrongs that are setbacks to interest, are to count as harms in the appropriate sense'.[33] Other commentators have similarly observed that Feinberg 'clearly defines "harm" as a *wrongful* set-back to interests'.[34] It is therefore the notion of wrongfully setting back an individual's interests that requires particular focus.[35]

## Harm as setbacks to interests

Feinberg proposes that harm arises through the thwarting, setting back or defeating of an *interest*.[36] As outlined above, the notion of interests was also important to Mill, although Feinberg defines the concept of an interest with much greater precision. Feinberg argues that the scope of the Harm Principle is not to protect an individual's 'wants' or 'desires', but is instead focused on protecting a person's most fundamental interests. For this purpose, Feinberg outlines two key interests. Feinberg first refers to what he terms, 'commercial-legal' interests,[37] noting that such interests encompass an individual's 'stake' in a particular matter.[38] He observes that a person has a 'stake in $X$ (whether $X$ be a company, a career, or some kind of 'issue' of events) when he stands to gain or lose depending on the nature of $X$'.[39] More relevantly to the context of reproductive decision-making, Feinberg adds to the notion of protectable interests with his second category, which encompasses an individual's 'welfare interests' (which he argues should be distinguished from a person's most ultimate

---

33  Feinberg (n 8) 36.

34  Hamish Stewart, 'Harms, Wrongs, and Set-Backs in Feinberg's *Moral Limits of the Criminal Law*' (2001) 5 Buffalo Criminal Law Review 47, 49.

35  Feinberg does also highlight the potential harm that may result from interfering with one's interest(s) in things such as objects or property. In this context, the harm suffered is by those who have interests in the objects or property. For example, he comments, that by 'breaking windows, the vandals have done direct harm to the interests of the building's owner; they have harmed the *windows* only in a derivative and extended sense'. It follows that in cases where objects or property are 'harmed' in a non-derivative sense (when no one has interests in them), more appropriate terminology for 'harm' would be 'damaged', 'broken', 'mangled', 'shattered', 'split' and so on. Significantly, such terms are capable of describing what can be done to 'a mere thing even if no person has an interest in it' but it would not follow that the *thing* was *harmed*. It is for this reason that damage to property or objects may constitute an interference with the interests of the individual who has an interest in the object or property remaining in its non-harmed state. If this is so, the interference with such an interest is relevant to Feinberg's second category of harming: Feinberg (n 8) 32–3.

36  ibid.

37  ibid. 33.

38  ibid.

39  ibid. 33–4.

goals or aspirations – categorised as 'ulterior interests').[40] Feinberg states that welfare interests consist of:

> Interests in the continuance for a foreseeable interval of one's life, and the interests in one's own physical health and vigor, the integrity and normal functioning of one's body, the absence of absorbing pain and suffering or grotesque disfigurement, minimal intellectual acuity, emotional stability, the absence of groundless anxieties and resentments, the capacity to engage normally in social intercourse and to enjoy and maintain friendships, at least minimal income and financial security, a tolerable social and physical environment, and a certain amount of freedom from interference and coercion.[41]

Relevantly then, Feinberg has therefore defined the scope of an interest within the meaning of the Harm Principle as:

- a 'commercial–legal' interest – that being a matter in which a person has a 'stake' and he or she stands to lose or gain;
- an individual's *welfare* interests (which does not necessarily encompass an individual's 'ulterior' interests) – Feinberg comments that '[w]elfare interests, to summarize, have the characteristics of bare minimality, stability, and durability'.[42]

Feinberg then moves on to consider the key issue of how an individual's interests can be set back. This is of fundamental importance to his framework:

> The test ... of whether such an invasion has in fact set back an interest is whether that interest is in a worse condition than it would otherwise have been in had the invasion not occurred at all.[43]

This approach requires a comparison of the individual's interests both before and after the alleged harmful event, to determine the extent to which his or her interests were set back. Importantly, this approach has been referred to as a 'baseline' approach, which is similarly shared by other commentators. For example, Nils Holtug notes that an event may harm an individual 'if and only if it renders her worse off than she would *otherwise* have been' (emphasis added).[44] He refers to this as a 'counterfactual baseline' assessment. This baseline approach

---

40  ibid. 37.
41  ibid.
42  ibid.
43  ibid.
44  Holtug (n 4) 368–9.

requires evaluating the impact on the individual's interests had the harm never occurred. As is discussed in Chapter 6, the application of the baseline approach in the context of reproduction is problematic.

### Harm and wrongdoing

Feinberg's notion of harming requires that a setback to an interest also constitutes a form of *wrongdoing*. Feinberg comments that a wrong occurs where a person's 'indefensible (unjustifiable and inexcusable) conduct violates the other's right, and in all but certain very special cases such conduct will also invade the other's interest and thus be harmful'.[45] Under this approach, a wrong is an unjustified invasion of an interest that is deemed to be of higher priority.[46] As Gavaghan notes, this means that the Harm Principle is invoked 'when the conduct in question interferes with an interest deemed in advance to be of high priority'.[47] Feinberg explains:

> The interests of different persons are constantly and unavoidably in conflict, so that any legal system determined to 'minimize harm' must incorporate judgments of the comparative importance of *interests* of different kinds so that it can pronounce 'unjustified' the invasion of one person's interest of high priority done to protect another person's interest of low priority. Legal wrongs then will be *invasions of interests* which violate established priority rankings (emphasis added).[48]

Imposing restrictions on liberty will nearly always require the balancing of competing interests, as an interference with liberty will involve restricting an individual's interest *in* liberty. Therefore, the interest in liberty must be balanced against the interests of those who will (or may) be harmed in the absence of such intervention. In this sense, it is necessary to consider the relevant competing interests at stake in order to prioritise them, in accordance with Feinberg's explanation above.

The concept of wrongdoing overlaps heavily with the notion of *interests*. Feinberg regards the Harm Principle as encompassing the setting back of some ulterior interests, where this occurs as a result of invading an individual's *welfare* interests. Importantly, however, thwarting an individual's welfare interests is also likely to amount to a form of *wrongdoing*, in circumstances where an individual

---

45 Feinberg (n 8) 34.
46 ibid. 35.
47 Gavaghan (n 13) 51.
48 Feinberg (n 8) 35.

has a *right* to have such interests protected.[49] Feinberg's consideration of wrongdoing displays this clearly, as he implicitly acknowledges that wrongdoing occurs when an individual's welfare *interests* are purposely set back:

> In a fair contest a loser may be unavoidably harmed, but when he is harmed by means of an attack on his welfare interests, he is not only harmed but doubly *wronged*: the indefensible infliction of harm on his welfare interest wronged him, and the defeat of his more ultimate interest … by foul means also wronged, as well as harmed, him (emphasis added).[50]

In essence, a wrong will occur whenever a person's interests are *unjustifiably* invaded. Notably, however, protectable interests are not necessarily limited to welfare interests and may involve any interest for which a person has a normative claim over (for example, a proprietary interest).[51]

Although Feinberg's work is regarded as 'the most influential in the ethics of harms and interests',[52] his notion of wrongdoing has been the subject of criticism. It has been suggested that he does not sufficiently distinguish between his second and third categories of harming. Stewart notes:

> Again and again, and usually implicitly rather than directly, Feinberg either abandons the wrongfulness component of his definition of harm, or assumes rather than justifies its operation. It would be more fruitful for Feinberg's project to identify clearly the separate roles that the concepts of wrong and set-back to interests might play … [53]

Furthermore, Feinberg's analysis of what he refers to as 'aggregative' and 'accumulative' harming, similarly rests on the concept of interests.[54] Harm in this context 'is defined not by an independent standard of wrongfulness, but in terms of setbacks to interests'.[55] However, while these further categories

---

49 Dennis J Baker, 'The Harm Principle vs Kantian Criteria for Ensuring Fair, Principled and Just Criminalisation' (2008) 33 Australian Journal of Legal Philosophy 66, 77–8.

50 Feinberg (n 8) 114.

51 Baker (n 49) 78.

52 Gavaghan (n 443) 52; John Harris, *Wonderwoman and Superman: The Ethics of Human Biotechnology* (OUP 1992) 88–92.

53 Stewart (n 34) 49.

54 Stewart states that 'Harms are "aggregative" where an activity as a whole is harmful, but many specific instances of it are not harmful and may even be beneficial' and that 'an activity causes "accumulative" harms where it is harmful if a lot of people engage in it, but not harmful if only a few do': ibid. 54–5.

55 ibid. 56.

involve a determination of the concept of interests, the essential aspect when determining whether an individual has been wronged, is to assess whether there was an unjustifiable interference with the individual's interest(s). In the analysis that follows, the notion of unjustifiably interfering with the interest(s) of others will be considered for the purpose of applying the relevant harm threshold.

John Harris has challenged Feinberg's notion of harming, by arguing that a harmed condition is one where an individual's 'interests *or* rights are frustrated' (emphasis added).[56] According to Harris, harm encompasses the frustrating of a person's rights *or* interests alone. Harris's fundamental disagreement with Feinberg is therefore that a person can suffer 'harm' solely by having his interests set back.[57] For example, if a person undergoes an elective surgical procedure, he or she will suffer a setback to his or her interests, even though the setback is only likely to be temporary (assuming the surgery is successful). On the basis of Harris's analysis, the individual suffers 'harm' in some sense due to that setback. In contrast, according to Feinberg's approach, the person is not harmed in the appropriate sense, as he or she is not wronged by undergoing the operation; the individual will (in most cases) provide consent for the procedure with the intention of achieving an overall benefit. In this context, it can be said that the setback to the patient's interests resulting from the procedure is outweighed by the benefit to be achieved by performing the procedure.[58] The setback in question is therefore *justified* on the basis of prioritising the interests at stake. Furthermore, in this specific example, the fact that the patient provides consent means that the performance of the operation does not violate the person's legal right and this would negate any possibility of wrongdoing. As Feinberg notes:

> Mill left no doubt about how his harm principle was to be interpreted on this question ... what a person consents to is not 'harm' in the requisite sense. It follows ... that no one can rightly intervene to prevent a responsible adult from voluntarily doing something that will harm only himself (for such a harm is not a 'wrong') ... [59]

Although Harris may be correct in some respects by arguing that an individual will be 'harmed' by having his or her interests set back to achieve a net benefit,[60] this approach is too wide to encompass the threshold of harming under the scope of the Harm Principle. As noted by Gavaghan, this formulation of the Harm Principle is problematic, because:

---

56  Harris (n 52) 92, cited in Gavaghan (n 13) 52.
57  Gavaghan (n 13) 51–4.
58  ibid. 53.
59  Feinberg (n 8) 116.
60  Gavaghan (n 13) 53.

it is possible to find in almost any act an interest somewhere, however trivial, that is thwarted or frustrated. Most troublingly, acts that clearly benefit an individual by promoting some of his most important interests in important ways will often involve the setting back of some other of his interests.[61]

It is for this reason that Feinberg requires an overlap between his second and third categories for the purpose of invoking the Harm Principle. And Feinberg contemplates such an objection, as he specifically excludes the possibility that wrongdoing alone constitutes harm in the appropriate sense when he considers the concept of 'harmless wrongdoing'.[62]

In terms of applying the Harm Principle as an evaluative tool, the overlap between Feinberg's second and third categories (as detailed above) will be adopted. The issue of wrongdoing will therefore be addressed by considering the priority of conflicting interests. In the context of reproductive decision-making, Gavaghan argues that because of the inherent importance of reproductive decisions the interest in reproductive liberty will normally be afforded high priority and interference with it 'will usually, on Feinberg's analysis, constitute both harms *and wrongs*' (emphasis added).[63] State-imposed eligibility criteria that preclude access to ART services for some individuals and couples therefore constitutes an interference with reproductive liberty, which in turn amounts to a form of harm. On this basis, the interest in reproductive liberty (which includes the ability to use techniques such as tissue-typing during the in vitro fertilisation (IVF) process) is deemed to be of high priority from the outset; this is an argument that was also put forward in Chapter 4 concerning the liberal framework. However, while the interest in reproductive liberty is deemed to be of value and worthy of protection, it will not always prevail over other interests. It may be outweighed in cases where the interests of *others* are wrongfully set back unless such liberty is restricted.

### Responding to Harm: Further Guiding Principles

Having established the 'trigger' at which state intervention becomes legitimised (at least in principle), it is important to highlight that the nature of the regulatory response depends upon a number of further factors. Fundamentally, engaging the harm threshold alone does not provide a basis for *prohibiting* specific conduct; it merely brings into play the state's legitimate interest in providing some form of regulatory response.

---

61 ibid.

62 See Joel Feinberg, *The Moral Limits of the Criminal Law: Harmless Wrongdoing* (OUP 1990).

63 Gavaghan (n 13) 52.

Before considering the principles that should guide the regulatory response, it is important to note that there are some interests regarded by Feinberg as universally protectable under the scope of the Harm Principle. Such interests include standard welfare interests 'in continued life, health, economic sufficiency, and political liberty'[64] noting that 'harm to *these* interests, at least, must be prevented'.[65] At the opposite end of the spectrum, Feinberg argues that there are some types of harm that should *not* be relied upon to justify regulatory intervention:

> ... bare minimal invasions of interest just above the threshold of harm are not the appropriate objects of legal coercion either, and a plausible version of the harm principle must be qualified to exclude them.[66]

Feinberg provides an example of rude and insulting remarks that 'not only "wound feelings" but indirectly harm the interest in personal efficiency by causing depression and anger sufficiently great to distract and debilitate',[67] stating that such an example should be excluded from the regulatory response. His reasoning is that while '[m]inor or trivial harms *are* harms ... legal interference with trivia is likely to cause more harm than it prevents ... '[68]

It has been established that some interests are universally protectable under the scope of the Harm Principle and that the thwarting of other interests may be so trivial, that there is no justifiable basis for regulatory intervention. It is necessary to consider how regulation should respond to the remaining scope of interests that *are* protected. Feinberg has formulated a number of 'mediating maxims' aimed at providing regulators with guidance as to when and how intervention with liberty is justified. He comments that the principles are:

> designed to suggest strategies for coping with uncertainties about how to apply the harm principle in tricky circumstances. They are meant to help the hypothetical legislator by providing his nearly vacuous guiding principle with a little more content, a little clearer direction.[69]

These principles may prove particularly useful in terms of proposing a suitable basis for regulation (if at all).

---

64 Feinberg (n 8) 188.
65 ibid.
66 ibid.
67 ibid. 189.
68 ibid. 216.
69 ibid. 188.

## Assessing the risk of harm

As the Harm Principle is ultimately concerned with reducing or eliminating the potential harm that may result from specific conduct, the first principle requires an assessment of whether the conduct in question is likely to result in the prospective harm in question.

In some instances, it may be evident that the outcome of a particular course of conduct will *always* result in harm (as defined under the threshold). If this is the case, the only way of minimising or eliminating that harm is to completely prohibit the conduct that causes it. Therefore, total prohibition will be justified if the harm can only be eliminated or minimised in such a way. However, in other cases, the certainty of predicting whether harm will eventuate may not be so clear-cut.

In some contexts, it may be that the harm in question will result in only a percentage of cases where liberty is exercised. For example, there may be a 20 per cent risk of a specific harm eventuating – that harm being 'Y' – when an individual undertakes 'X'. Therefore for every 10 instances of X, two of them are likely to result in Y. In relation to this particular example, the chance that the harm will eventuate could be based on probability and may not necessarily be dependent on the individual circumstances or characteristics of those who cause the harm in question.

In contrast to this, there may be some instances where the prospective harm in question is determined by reference to the individual factors of the person undertaking the potentially harmful activity. For example, a person with impaired vision *may* be more likely to have a road traffic accident if she fails to wear her glasses when driving, compared to a driver who has no visual impairment to her vision (there are of course a significant number of other variables that may impact on the likelihood of harm in this context, but assume hypothetically that the risk is caused by the impairment to vision). In the event that a motor vehicle accident occurs as a result of the fault of the driver with impaired vision, it will almost certainly amount to harm under the threshold (another driver may be injured, or his or her property is damaged as a result of the collision). In this context, it is the particular characteristics of the person who caused the harm that increased the risk of the harm occurring. Driving a motor vehicle is indeed a risky activity, but it does not follow that the state should prohibit driving altogether. The law does not need to restrict the liberty of all motor vehicle drivers to minimise the risk of the harm occurring (at least in relation to this particular example – where we assume that the accident was causally linked to the fact that the driver had impaired vision). Instead, less intrusive means can be adopted by the state, such as a requirement that those with impaired vision take appropriate measures to avoid the harm (for example, that they wear glasses or do not drive without them). As will be discussed in Chapter 8, in the context of ART services, it may be that the circumstances of a particular family – seeking to create a saviour child – may increase or decrease a particular risk of harm in their future child. However, it does not follow that a blanket prohibition on access to services should be applied.

Although an assessment of the likelihood that the harm will result is of critical importance in determining whether coercion or restriction of liberty is justified, this factor alone is not necessarily determinative of whether regulatory intervention is appropriate. As Feinberg notes:

> It will not do to simply say that only harm whose occurrence as a consequence of a given activity is *more probable* than not will justify preventative coercion. If the harm in question is very great, then a very small likelihood of its occurrence will do.[70]

It is therefore necessary to assess (where possible) the *risk* of the harm occurring; this is something that requires a balancing of the probability of the harm resulting, together with the seriousness or gravity of the harm in the event that it should occur.[71] Feinberg proposes:

> the greater the probability of harm, the less grave the harm need be to justify coercion; the greater the gravity of the envisioned harm, the less probable it need be.[72]

Some forms of harming are regarded as so severe, that the law should always seek to prevent them from occurring. For example, the intentional infliction of grievous bodily harm results in such severe injuries for the victim, that the state can justifiably interfere with the liberty of those who seek to inflict such harm. Importantly, state coercion of individual liberty is justified in such circumstances, even if the probability of the harm occurring is very low.[73] Consequently, applying this reasoning to reproductive decision-making, it can be said that the state may be justified in limiting the liberty of a family seeking to conceive a saviour child if, for example, the embryo biopsy procedure is likely to cause severe impairment or disability to a child who is born following the performance of such techniques. This *may* be justified on the basis of the severity of the risk, even where the probability of it occurring is relatively low (although, as discussed in Chapter 6, this harm-based argument is difficult to make out in circumstances where the individual who will be harmed, does not yet exist).

---

70  ibid. 190.
71  ibid. 191.
72  ibid.
73  ibid. 191.

In any given situation, there are a significant number of factors that may impact on assessing the risk of the harm, in terms of balancing the probability and severity. It would be extremely difficult to provide a universal formula that will prove successful in determining the regulatory response for *all* cases of harming. Therefore, the further guiding principles will always need to be considered in line with a specific set of circumstances.

In Chapter 6, I outline the range of potential harms relevant to the creation of a saviour child (or at least those commonly raised as 'harm-based' objections). The analysis will seek to establish whether:

- the potential harms can be regarded as invasions of fundamental welfare interests, which are therefore worthy of universal protection;
- the potential harms are so trivial that they are not worthy of protection under the Harm Principle (at least by way of the regulatory response which seeks to limit or restrict liberty);
- regulation should coerce or restrict liberty in response to a *risk* of harm (as established above) by considering the probability and severity of the specific risk of harm in question.

If it is determined that a *risk* of harm prima facie warrants regulatory intervention, it will also be necessary to consider the relevance of the other guiding principles outlined below. In some circumstances, less restrictive regulatory options may be available to minimise the risk of the relevant harm in question.[74] This approach has the potential to avoid unjustifiable and excessive restrictions on individual liberty, while implementing regulatory measures aimed at minimising specific risks of harm.

### Impact of regulation and preservation of liberty

Given that the interest *in* liberty is afforded presumptive priority, Feinberg also argued that the imposition of restrictions on the principle should be kept to a minimum (where possible). By considering the impact of regulatory intervention with liberty concerning specific conduct,[75] it is possible to establish whether a particular form of regulation (for example, prohibition or other, less restrictive regulatory options) can minimise the harm in a minimally restrictive way.

In some instances, prohibition of certain activities or conduct will impact differently on those who are seeking to exercise their liberty in a specific way. For example, a person who is using dangerous equipment in a careless manner

---

74 Feinberg considers a number of regulatory options (such as licensing systems) available to legislatures in order to minimise harm to others but preserve some element of individual liberty: ibid. 193–9.

75 ibid. 193–8.

will pose a greater risk of harm compared to those who use the equipment with
due care and caution. If the law prohibits everyone from using the equipment
in question, it may amount to an excessive restriction of individual liberty
for those who use the equipment safely. In this sense, the risk of harm to
others depends upon the circumstances of the particular person (or group of
people) in question; there may be specific factors that increase or reduce the
risk accordingly.

It may therefore be possible to implement regulatory measures to preserve
the liberty of the majority by restricting the liberty of those who pose a higher
risk of harm to others, or by imposing conditions upon all individuals who wish
to engage in the risky activity. For example, a licence-based system that permits
some members of society to engage in specific conduct, but requires that those
individuals comply with a set of conditions, will act to preserve liberty to a
greater extent than a regulatory approach that imposes a blanket prohibition on
the conduct in question. Such a regulatory approach does not aim to completely
eliminate the risk; the conditions are aimed at reducing the probability of the
harm eventuating or the severity of the harm if it were to eventuate.

Under a licensing scheme, liberty is preserved to a large extent, at least
for those who comply with the conditions stipulated by the regulator. An
obvious example of such a scheme is the requirement for motor vehicle drivers
to be licensed. Individuals are not at liberty to drive a car unless they have
demonstrated a level of competence and skill and have been awarded a licence
to drive.[76] Non-compliance with these conditions (either in the form of driving
without a licence, disregarding the rules of the road, driving in a dangerous
way and so on) may result in sanction or revocation of the licence and this
would impact on an individual's liberty to drive. Those who are more likely to
cause harm will therefore have *their* liberty infringed so that the liberty of other
individuals is preserved.

Alternatively, a particular regulatory measure can be imposed on all who
engage in a particular activity. The requirement for drivers and passengers
of motor vehicles to wear a seatbelt, takes account of the fact that there are
certain risks that can never be eliminated in relation to the conduct of others
(in this context, the risks are those created by persons responsible for driving
a vehicle, which are to a large extent, beyond the control of other road users).
Nevertheless, the requirement to wear a seatbelt is a measure that can potentially
reduce the severity of a motor vehicle accident while preserving the liberty (to a
large extent) of those who wish to engage in the conduct in question.

---

76 Of course, it should be noted that it is literally possible for any person to drive
a vehicle without a driving licence, and in such circumstances, there is an exercise of
liberty. However, if this happens, the law can be enforced in order to prevent the
conduct in question and the law therefore has the purpose of coercing individual liberty.

Importantly, therefore, by considering the impact of regulation on those who wish to exercise their liberty, it may be possible to adopt a regulatory position that is capable of minimising specific risks of harm, while effectively preserving liberty. Further restrictions on liberty may be imposed against certain individuals who pose an increased risk of harm to others (for example, those who have not demonstrated that they are capable of driving a motor vehicle safely and in accordance with standards that are set under a scheme of motor vehicle licensing). On this basis, it is therefore necessary to consider how regulation impacts on individual liberty, and to assess whether there are any options for regulation that may minimise a particular risk of harm without restricting the liberty of all individuals. Alternatively, in some circumstances, the only option open to the regulator may be to impose conditions on *all* individuals who engage in a particular course of conduct so that the probability or the severity of the harm is minimised in a particular context (for example, the requirement for all individuals to wear seatbelts when using a motor vehicle).

### Burden and proportionality of the regulatory response

The question of whether the state can justifiably limit liberty also depends on an assessment of the *burden* of implementing measures to protect against or minimise a particular risk. As already mentioned, the range of regulatory options open to the regulator in any given situation may be wide. However, the burden of implementing and maintaining measures to coerce individual liberty (as a basis for preventing harmful conduct) may be significantly high. In some cases it may be disproportionate to implement burdensome measures in response to a particular risk of harm, if the risk is relatively low.[77] The guiding principle of proportionality therefore requires policy makers to refrain from intervention unless the burden is proportionate to the *risk* of a particular harm. When considering a way forward for regulation in Chapter 8, this particular principle will be considered in the context of pre-implantation tissue-typing in order to determine the burden of the regulatory response (if any).

### The relevance of the guiding principles

The guiding principles outlined above will inform the analysis that follows in the subsequent chapters and will also be relevant in terms of proposing a way forward for the regulatory response to the issue of using IVF and pre-implantation tissue-typing for the creation of a saviour child.[78]

---

77  Feinberg (n 8) 189.
78  See Chapter 8.

## Summarising the Scope of the Harm Principle

To be of value as an evaluative tool, the Harm Principle needs to be capable of practical application. Having established that the notion of 'harm' is wide in scope and vaguely unhelpful without further clarity, definition and focus, I explored how the concept could be appropriately narrowed for the purpose of applying it to the issue of creating a saviour child. Most importantly, I outlined a number of principles that helped to focus the Harm Principle sufficiently, which can be summarised as follows:

1. Harm as a tool for normative evaluation is a broad concept *capable* of describing a wide range of injuries to the person, damage to property or interference with interests.
2. Mill's approach in *On Liberty* does not provide sufficient clarity in terms of determining the scope of the Harm Principle.
3. Mill's formulation of the Harm Principle has been interpreted to include harm as an invasion of another's *interests*.
4. Mill's work fails to provide a sufficient definition of which interests are to be protected under the scope of the Harm Principle.
5. Feinberg's work has received a significant level of respect in terms of defining the harm threshold as a wrongful setback to another person's interest(s).
6. A protected interest under the scope of the Harm Principle includes a legal–commercial interest (where an individual has a stake in something from which he or she may lose or gain) and what Feinberg refers to as 'welfare interests'. Ulterior interests fall under the scope of the Harm Principle only when they are thwarted as a result of a setback to a welfare interest.
7. A setback to an interest occurs where an interest is in a worse condition than it would have been had the harmful conduct not occurred (the counterfactual baseline assessment).
8. A wrong is an unjustified or inexcusable interference with an interest that is ranked of higher priority when weighed against a conflicting interest. A wrong that does not set back a person's interests falls outside the scope of the Harm Principle (Feinberg refers to this as 'harmless wrongdoing').
9. When a person's interests are set back in order to gain a net benefit (as considered by John Harris), he or she is not 'harmed' unless there is a harm *on balance*.
10. Self-regarding harms (harms to which consent is given) do not fall under the scope of the Harm Principle.

11. The Harm Principle therefore encompasses an overlap between setbacks to *interests* that are wrongs, and wrongs that are setbacks to interests.

12. To guide the regulatory response when the harm threshold is triggered, a number of principles should be considered:

    * Some interests are of universal application and should always be protected under the scope of the Harm Principle.
    * Minor or trivial harms just above the threshold are not protectable under the scope of the Harm Principle.
    * The higher the probability of the harm eventuating, the greater the justification for coercing liberty.
    * The greater the seriousness or gravity of the harmful conduct, the greater the justification for limitation of (or at least, intervention with) liberty.
    * The gravity and the probability of the harm should be considered together to identify the *risk* of harm.
    * As interference with liberty is itself considered a form of harm, regulators should adopt an approach that is the least restrictive of individual liberty when attempting to minimise the risk of harm in question.
    * The burden of implementing measures to guard against the harm should be proportionate to the risk.

The scope of the Harm Principle considered so far may need further exploration, specification and clarity as the analysis progresses. However, as a starting point, there are a number of principles that provide a more focused definition of the concept for application as a practical framework for guiding regulation on the issue of creating a saviour child.


## Conclusion

Formulating an appropriate harm definition is no simple task, given the ambiguity of the term. Mill failed to define the concept with precision, rendering his approach incapable of practical application. However, other commentators have added to Mill's approach, particularly Feinberg, who has provided a more specific definition of the notion of harm, as summarised above. Feinberg's theory of harming has received significant recognition and is influential. In the following chapter, the range of potential harms that have been raised in the debate will be considered, in order to ascertain whether any fall within the harm threshold. Most importantly, for this purpose, it is necessary to establish whether the use of IVF and pre-implantation tissue-typing for the creation of a saviour child, will (or may) result in the wrongful setback of the interests of others, as defined above. The key issue is to establish whether the threshold is (or will be) invoked in this specific context. In Chapter 8, the further guiding principles will be considered to formulate an appropriate regulatory response.

# Chapter 6
# Creating Saviour Children: What is the Harm?

## Introduction

Having outlined the framework in Chapter 5 that underpins the regulatory analysis, this chapter considers the range of potential harms that may result to a saviour child who is conceived as a tissue donor. These harm-based objections have been commonly cited in the body of literature that examines the issue of conceiving saviour children. The purpose of the analysis in this chapter is to determine whether the harm-based objections might provide a basis for justifying regulatory intervention. I should note that some commentators are critical of an approach that focuses predominantly on the notion of harm; thus, Kimberly Strong and others observe that a harm-focused analysis fails to acknowledge the significant benefits that might be attained for a family who conceive a saviour child by way of assisted reproductive technology (ART) services.[1] It is certainly important to acknowledge that there are significant benefits that might be achieved for families who conceive a saviour child by way of ART services. This utilitarian perspective might help to explain why the notion of benefit is equally important (if not more important) as the notion of harming in the sphere of *bioethical reasoning*. Thus, the benefit that might be achieved by the decision to conceive a saviour child may help to explain why a family's decision appears to be ethically sound when this is weighed against the risks of harm that are commonly cited in the debate. This is particularly so, as the harm-based objections are often viewed as speculative and uncertain. However, from a regulatory perspective, reliance on the utility of the family's decision appears to offer no compelling reason for discounting the harm-based objections if it is accepted that regulatory intervention is justified in cases where harm to others is likely to ensue. Essentially, as explored in Chapter 5, the liberal approach requires that the balance in favour of regulatory intervention is tilted in cases where the risk of harm can be established and it is this issue that I now explore in relation to the decision to conceive a saviour child. However, before analysing the specific harm-based objections it is useful to summarise how the

---

1 Kimberly A Strong and others, 'It's Time to Reframe the Savior Sibling Debate' (2011) 2 AJOB Primary Research 13, 22.

notion of harm is relevant to regulatory policy in the field of ART, as this
further demonstrates the significance of the harm-based objections.

## Liberty, Harm and Welfare

In Chapters 4 and 5 it was established that the liberal approach requires that
individual liberty is not restricted except in circumstances where harm will
result to others without state intervention. This concept has been applied in
the context of reproductive decision-making, where the use of ART services
is contemplated.[2] Significantly, as I discuss below, ART regulatory policy also
seems to prioritise a harm-focused approach in terms of applying the pre-
conception welfare principle. Although the welfare principle has been identified
as a relational concept by some,[3] and arguably represents a 'parental suitability'
test, as I discuss below, regulatory policy emphasises the need to apply this
important principle as a harm assessment.

### ART Regulatory Policy: A Harm Assessment?

Gavaghan notes that although welfare 'is not synonymous with "harm", it is …
difficult to conceive of any calculation of welfare that does not take account of
harm … '.[4] The concept of welfare is therefore somewhat wider in scope than
the Harm Principle. Nevertheless, the United Kingdom's (UK's) ART regulator,
the Human Fertilisation and Embryology Authority (HFEA), has consistently
emphasised that the principle should be applied as a pre-conception harm
assessment. To comply with the statutory duty imposed under s 13(5) of the
Human Fertilisation and Embryology Act 1990 (UK) (which is a condition
of any licence granted to an ART centre in the UK), the HFEA's Code of
Practice stipulates that a risk assessment must be undertaken to consider the
risk of harm to the child to be born (and any existing children) prior to the
provision of treatment services.[5] Access to services should only be denied

---

2 Jonathan Glover, *Choosing Children: Genes, Disability, and Design* (OUP 2006)
73–5; House of Commons Science and Technology Committee, *Human Reproductive
Technologies and the Law* (2005) 17. Both explicitly referred to Mill when considering the
issue of reproductive liberty: see Chapter 5.

3 Michelle Taylor-Sands, *Saviour Siblings: A Relational Approach to the Welfare of the
Child in Selective Reproduction* (Routledge 2013).

4 Colin Gavaghan, *Defending the Genetic Supermarket: Law and Ethics of Selecting the
Next Generation* (Routledge-Cavendish 2007) 42.

5 Human Fertilisation and Embryology Authority, *Code of Practice* (8th edn, HFEA
2009) guidance note 8.10.

where the circumstances suggest a likelihood of *significant* harm or neglect.[6] The risk assessment must be made in relation to each patient undergoing treatment (including the patient's partner where applicable) and the assessment is dependent upon the individual circumstances of each individual or family seeking access to treatment services.[7]

The review of the welfare principle undertaken by the HFEA in 2005 led to the statement that 'there is now a presumption to provide treatment, unless there is evidence that any child born to an individual or couple, or any existing child of their family, *would face a risk of serious harm*' (emphasis added).[8] This presumption is also firmly stated in the HFEA's report on sex selection:

> This is an area of private life in which people are generally best left to make their own choices and in which the state should intervene only to prevent the occurrence of serious harms, and only where this intervention is non-intrusive and likely to be effective.[9]

In Chapter 3, it was established that similar prominence is given to the welfare principle under the Australian regulatory regime. As discussed, jurisdictions such as Victoria are moving towards a more stringent process of screening prospective ART participants, which is underpinned by the aim to safeguard future ART children from harm.[10] It is therefore difficult to dislodge this dominant principle from the sphere of ART regulation, and in particular, from the pre-conception welfare principle. The discussion above therefore provides a strong basis for analysing the differing regulatory approaches from a harm-based perspective, although it is important to note that there are also other ethical and normative values at play in the web of ART regulation in place across Australia and the UK. The ethics or normative values underpinning the law in this regard are considered in Chapter 7.

## Harm and the Precautionary Principle

Regulation in relation to some aspects of ART services has progressed in an extremely cautious manner in Australia and the UK. The initial policy

---

6 ibid. guidance note 8.15.

7 ibid. guidance note 8.3.

8 Human Fertilisation and Embryology Authority, *Tomorrow's Children: Report of the Policy Review of the Welfare of the Child Assessments in Licensed Assisted Conception Clinics* (2005) 1.

9 Human Fertilisation and Embryology Authority, *Sex Selection: Options for Regulation* (2003) 33.

10 See *ABY & ABZ v Secretary to the Department of Health (Human Rights)* [2013] VCAT 625; *PQ v Patient Review Panel (Health & Privacy)* [2012] VCAT 291.

concerning pre-implantation tissue-typing issued by the HFEA restricted the
use of the technology to families at risk of transmitting a genetic condition
when conceiving naturally. The key reason for this was that the long-term
risk of harm to the child following the pre-implantation genetic diagnosis
(PGD) embryo biopsy process was not known.[11] When evaluating this initial
precautionary approach, the UK's House of Commons Science and Technology
Committee heard submissions from the then Chief Executive of the HFEA,[12]
who explained why tissue-typing was limited to cases where it was ancillary to
testing for a genetic condition:

> My own recollection of the initial [distinction] is that it was based on ethical
> and welfare of the child issues regarding the *benefit* to the embryo and the *risks*
> and *benefits* of the procedure itself, given that there might be no benefit to the
> embryo in one case and there would be in another case. It was not a legal issue
> (emphasis added).[13]

The House of Commons Science and Technology Committee expressed
concern with this precautionary approach.[14] It was noted that the decision of
the HFEA went against the advice of the body's own Ethics Committee[15] and
that while there may be possible risks inherent in the biopsy process, nearly all
medical practice carries risk.[16] It was further noted that the usual approach is
to fully advise patients of the risks involved in medical treatments so that an
informed decision can be made.[17]

One issue with the Committee's line of reasoning here is that the risks
involved in the biopsy procedure impact on the child to be born, who is unable
to knowingly accept those potential risks before his or her birth. Thus, although
there may be risks inherent in many medical procedures, ordinarily the notion
of accepting risk relates to those risks that concern the individual who is
providing informed consent to the particular procedure. Although prospective
ART participants may choose to accept risks inherent in the in vitro fertilisation

---

11 See Human Fertilisation and Embryology Authority, 'HFEA Confirms That
HLA Tissue Typing May Only Take Place when PGD is Required to Avoid a Serious
Genetic Disorder', press release, 1 August 2002 <http://www.hfea.gov.uk/935.html>
accessed 25 November 2014.

12 House of Commons Science and Technology Committee (n 2).

13 ibid. 111.

14 ibid. 122–3.

15 The HFEA disagreed with the Committee because 'of risks arising from embryo
biopsy and it was felt that the Ethics Committee had not taken proper account of the
absence of evidence of no risk': ibid. 122.

16 ibid. 123.

17 ibid.

(IVF) process, harm that may result to *others* falls outside this notion of self-regarding harms. In the context of PGD techniques, the parents are seeking to make a decision that might directly impact upon a child who may be born following those techniques. A more appropriate analogy is to therefore consider a parent who is consenting to a procedure on behalf of their incompetent child. In such a case, the parent is only lawfully permitted to make decisions that accord with the child's best interests.[18] The welfare principle is designed to protect and promote the interests of the child (or in the context of ART, the future child), where people are making decisions on behalf of the child or prospective child. In such circumstances, the Harm Principle is relevant because the parents' (or prospective parents') actions might impact on the welfare of *other people* (or potential people).

The above line of reasoning might be used as a basis of precaution to support restrictive PGD policies. The problem with regulatory precaution, however, is that it directly conflicts with the liberal approach to reproductive decision-making outlined in Chapter 4, as well as the presumption emphasised by the HFEA (as outlined above). In rejecting the precautionary principle, the House of Commons Science and Technology Committee observed that to justify restrictions on reproductive liberty, more than a mere risk of harm is required; actual evidence that harm will arise, or is likely to arise, must be present.[19]

The UK Government's response to the rejection of the precautionary principle by the House of Commons Science and Technology Committee was that there are instances where a precautionary response is warranted and that 'the potential harms that should be taken into account may not necessarily be susceptible to demonstration and evidence in advance'.[20] Others have expressed unease with a precautionary approach when regulating scientific and technological advance; former Justice of the High Court of Australia, Michael Kirby, explains as follows:

> Whilst [the precautionary] principle appears to be gaining increasing acceptance in the international community … it carries risks of its own. If taken too far, it

---

18 In *Department of Health and Community Services (NT) v JWB (Marion's case)* (1992) 175 CLR 218, the High Court of Australia held that parents are not legally entitled to consent to a non-therapeutic sterilisation on behalf of their intellectually disabled daughter, and approval was required by a court.

19 House of Commons Science and Technology Committee (n 2) 121. See also, Kerry Petersen, 'Genetic Technologies and ART: Ethical Values, Legal Regulation and Informal Regulation' in Ian Freckelton and Kerry Petersen (eds), *Disputes and Dilemmas in Health Law* (Federation Press 2006) 217, 222.

20 United Kingdom, *Government Response to the Report from the House of Commons Science and Technology Committee: Human Reproductive Technologies and the Law* (Cm 6641, 2005) 6.

could instil a negative attitude towards science and technology and encourage excessive regulation in the attempt to avoid *any* risks. Life is risky. Most technological innovations carry some risk. An undue emphasis on precaution, for fear of *any* risks, would not be good for science or technology or for the global economy or for innovation in thought as well as action.[21]

Ruth Deech and Anna Smajdor similarly express unease with a precautionary approach, referring to a European Commission Communication to European Union Member States, published in 2000, which urged that the precautionary principle should only be raised where a specific potential risk has been identified and evaluated.[22] With reference to this Communication, they comment:

> [The] risks have to be weighed against the freedom and rights of individuals, industries and organizations. The response in the case of risk should be proportionate, consistent, and open to revision. … Where a new technology is under consideration, according to the statement of the European Commission, it is only acceptable to act on the precautionary principle in relation to risks that have been identified as being connected with the new technology.[23]

Other commentators have dismissed the precautionary principle from the bioethical analysis in the saviour child context. Strong and others argue that without evidence to substantiate the harm-based objections, the validity of these concerns remains questionable.[24] The authors further comment that '[b]ioethics and clinical medicine are both ill-served by one-sided analyses and by adherence to moral claims that lack empirical foundation'.[25]

In support of a less restrictive regulatory approach in this field, it could be argued that PGD techniques are generally well established in the context of ART practice. The science has evolved rapidly since embryo selection technologies were first developed and these techniques are now performed on a routine basis. As discussed below, although there is no conclusive evidence to support the view that the embryo biopsy procedure is safe, there is no evidence

---

21 Michael Kirby, 'The Fundamental Problem of Regulating Technology' (Conference on the Ethical Governance of Information & Communications Technology and the Role of Professional Bodies, Australian National University, 1 May 2008) <http://www.hcourt.gov.au/assets/publications/speeches/former-justices/kirbyj/kirbyj_1may08.pdf> accessed 25 November 2014.

22 Ruth Deech and Anna Smajdor, *From IVF to Immortality: Controversy in the Era of Reproductive Technology* (OUP 2007) 151.

23 ibid.

24 Strong and others (n 1) 22.

25 ibid.

to the contrary to suggest that the process is harmful. Notably, however, the risks of harm that are often cited in the literature surrounding the creation of saviour children extend beyond the safety of PGD techniques. The prospective risks to the saviour child concern the physical and psychological risks of being conceived as a tissue donor. Although reference to such risks might appear to provide a basis for precaution, these particular risks of harm are speculative and unknown. As I discuss below, it is for this reason that a restrictive regulatory approach cannot be supported.

## Harm to the Saviour

Children are afforded particular protection by the state because of their vulnerable nature. This is demonstrated by the fact that legislation in Australia and the UK places the welfare or best interests of children as the paramount consideration when making decisions relating to them.[26] A saviour child who is conceived following pre-implantation tissue-typing might be exposed to a number of harms (or potential harms) arising from the fact that the child was purposely conceived as a tissue donor. Some of these potential 'harms' arise directly from the fact that the child is selected on the basis of his or her tissue type. These risks of harm include the potential impact on a child's physical development following the embryo biopsy procedure, or a risk of psychological harm that might arise from the child learning that he or she was selected on the basis of his or her potential to save the life of a sibling or relative.

Other potential harms that have been voiced in the debate are not so closely linked to the way that a saviour child is conceived, but nevertheless arise because of the intentions of the parents in conceiving the child. For example, the parents might intend to subject the saviour child to a tissue-harvesting procedure once he or she is born, for the benefit of an existing sick child or relative.

One of the most frequently cited objections to the argument that a *potential* child (who is yet to exist) can be harmed by the circumstances surrounding his or her conception, is that the only other alternative for that *particular* child is to not exist. This argument is referred to as the 'non-identity' problem, which was famously outlined by Derek Parfit.[27] I consider this particular line of reasoning below, in terms of its relevance to the saviour sibling context. The next part of this chapter, however, considers whether the potential harms outlined above are capable of

---

26 Family Law Act 1975 (Cth), s 60B(1); Children Act 1989 (UK), s 1(1). For example, under s 60B(1) of the Family Law Act 1975 (Cth), the object of the legislation relating to decisions involving children, is to ensure that the best interests of children are met by '(a) protecting children from physical or psychological harm ... '.

27 See Derek Parfit, *Reasons and Persons* (OUP 1984).

falling within the harm threshold set out in Chapter 5. Note that this is different
to stating that a potential saviour child will or might be harmed. Fundamentally,
it can be acknowledged that the prospective 'harms' relevant to the conception
of a saviour child are at least *capable* of falling within this harm threshold; they
concern potential interferences with the child's physical and psychological welfare
and therefore fall within what Feinberg termed, 'welfare interests'. The range of
harms is now considered in accordance with the harm-based framework.

### The Risk of Harm from the Embryo Biopsy Process

The technology used for determining an embryo's genetics (including the
determination of the embryo's human leukocyte antigen (HLA) type) has
advanced significantly in recent years. The process can be undertaken at
different stages of the embryo's development, but typically involves the removal
of one or more cells from the embryo for examination in the laboratory. When
PGD techniques were first developed, it was not clear whether the removal of
embryonic cells posed a risk of harm (or other implications) for children born
following this process.[28] This uncertainty largely explains why the technology
has been regulated in a restrictive way.

For the purpose of determining whether the potential impact of the embryo
biopsy process might fall within the scope of the Harm Principle (as outlined
Chapter 5), it is necessary to consider the notion of wrongfully setting back the
saviour child's interests. In Chapter 5 I considered how the notion of harming
ordinarily requires a determination of whether an individual's interests are
wrongfully set back to the extent that he or she will be in a worse condition
than they would have otherwise been had the alleged 'harmful conduct' not
occurred. As the harm assessment is applied by way of the pre-conception
welfare assessment, this requires a consideration of future potential harms and
contemplates how these might impact on the interests of a person who does
not yet exist. As I discuss below, this is problematic. However, leaving aside
the issue of whether a child can be harmed as a result of the circumstances
surrounding their conception, it can be noted that the *type* of harm in this
respect might fall within the scope of the Harm Principle.

The risk of harm that may result from the embryo biopsy procedure is that
the process poses a risk to the physical development of the child. The key issue
is essentially whether the embryo biopsy process is in fact unsafe or whether it

---

28 An editorial in *The Lancet* stated that 'embryo biopsy for PGD does not seem
to produce adverse physical effects in the short term, but it is too early to exclude the
possibility of later effects': Editorial, 'Preimplantation Donor Selection' (2001) 358 The
Lancet 1195, cited in Sally Sheldon and Stephen Wilkinson 'Should Selecting Saviour
Siblings be Banned?' (2004) 30 Journal of Medical Ethics 533, 535.

is likely to impact on the future welfare interests of the saviour child. Stephen Bellamy has considered the safety of PGD procedures in his analysis of the ethical issues raised by the creation of saviour children.[29] When considering the risk of harm posed by the biopsy process, he refers to a number of surveys relating to obstetric outcome following PGD, confirming that the procedure does not seem to have any adverse impact on the child's development.[30] Bellamy notes, however, that while there is no short-term evidence of adverse impact on the development of children born following PGD techniques, the long-term impacts on child development are still not clear.[31] Earlier findings on the safety of PGD techniques had concluded that the risk to the child from embryo biopsy procedures was 'no greater for PGD babies than those conceived naturally, indicating that neither IVF nor embryo biopsy poses a serious threat to embryos'.[32] More recently, a review of PGD conducted by a research centre in New Zealand also found that there seems to be no impact on children born following PGD processes, but noted the need for long-term studies.[33] The fact that there is no conclusive evidence to suggest that PGD practices are unsafe, has led some to argue that:

It seems disproportionate to permit these risks to be undertaken on a daily basis in the context of infertility, but to draw a regulatory line when it comes to conceiving a child who may also provide [a potential cure] for an existing seriously ill child, unless there are other arguments to justify prohibition.[34]

Importantly, however, it is not entirely certain whether PGD is completely safe. With developments in the scientific process relevant to PGD techniques and

---

29 Stephen Bellamy, 'Lives to Save Lives – the Ethics of Tissue Typing' (2005) 8 Human Fertility 5.

30 ibid.

31 ibid. 9.

32 European Society of Human Reproduction and Embryology Ethics Task Force, Françoise Shenfield and others, 'Taskforce 5: Preimplantation Genetic Diagnosis' (2003) 18 Human Reproduction 649; Yury Verlinsky and others, 'Over a Decade of Experience with Preimplantation Genetic Diagnosis: A Multicenter Report' (2004) 82 Fertility and Sterility 292, cited in Natalie R Ram 'Britain's New Preimplantation Tissue Typing Policy: An Ethical Defence' (2006) 32 Journal of Medical Ethics 278, 279.

33 Human Genome Research Project, *Choosing Genes For Future Children: Regulating Preimplantation Genetic Diagnosis* (2006 Dunedin) 164.

34 Jeanne Snelling, 'Embryonic HLA Tissue Typing and Made-to-Match Siblings: The New Zealand Position' (2008) 9 Medical Law International 13, 21. This view has also been expressed elsewhere. Deech and Smajdor note that there is no greater risk of harm to a child selected on the basis of tissue type compared to children born following the use of PGD generally: Deech and Smajdor (n 22) 68.

with emerging research on the safety of these procedures, it has been reported
that some of the processes used for obtaining embryonic cells appear to be
more harmful (at least in terms of embryonic development) than others.[35] For
example, 'blastomere biopsy' – which involves the removal of one or two cells
from the embryo once it has reached the eight-cell stage (referred to as the
'cleavage stage', which occurs three days after fertilisation) – has been reported
as less safe than trophectoderm biopsy, which is used to remove cells at the
'blastocyst stage' (five days after fertilisation).[36] The researchers involved in this
study observed that 'two of every five [embryos] that have day-three blastomere
biopsy will be harmed to a sufficient extent to yield them incapable of
implanting and progressing to term'.[37] Nevertheless, despite such conclusions,
this research supports the view that the impact of these PGD techniques
affects the likelihood of the embryo *implanting and progressing to term*; this does
not necessarily provide support for the claim that PGD techniques impact
negatively on the development of children who are actually born following
these techniques.

Notably, there is a need for further monitoring and research of the impact
of PGD techniques on children. Recent research suggests that the safety of
PGD techniques is not conclusive. A research study published in 2014, which
examined the impact of the PGD process on the embryos of mice, found
that blastomere biopsy caused male mice to experience peculiar behaviour
alterations and changes in body weight.[38] The authors of this study therefore
concluded that the process of blastomere biopsy has long-term effects on
post-natal development and behaviour in mice.[39] This led the research team to
state that PGD could be a risk factor for late-onset, neurodevelopmental and
metabolic disease predisposition.[40]

Although there is no conclusive evidence to support the view that children
born following PGD are 'harmed', recent research suggests that there is
nevertheless a need for long-term studies to assess the impact of this process.
Fundamentally, however, given the lack of conclusive evidence, PGD should
not be restricted without evidence to support the claim that it causes harm to
children born following such techniques. Given that pre-implantation tissue-

---

35  Katherine L Scott, Kathleen H Long and Richard T Scott, 'Selecting the Optimal
Time to Perform Biopsy for Preimplantation Genetic Testing' (2013) 100 Fertility and
Sterility 608.

36  ibid.

37  ibid. 613.

38  S Sampino and others, 'Effects of Blastomere Biopsy on Post-natal Growth and
Behavior in Mice' (2014) 29 Human Reproduction 1875.

39  ibid.

40  ibid.

typing involves the same physical risks as general PGD techniques, there is no justificatory basis for using the uncertain and unestablished risk inherent in embryo biopsy procedures as a reason to limit the accessibility of PGD services for the purpose of establishing tissue type.

The risk inherent in the biopsy procedure was one of the factors that influenced the restrictive approach initially adopted by the HFEA in the UK. The HFEA had concluded that the potential risk inherent in the biopsy procedure is acceptable in cases where the technique would prevent a child from inheriting a genetic disorder or disease. Accordingly, the benefit in preventing transmission of such disorders was seen as outweighing the marginal risk of harm that may eventuate to children born following PGD techniques. The corollary of this view is that the uncertain and marginal risk of physical harm from PGD techniques is not outweighed in cases where the techniques are used solely to establish tissue type. Although the HFEA later reversed its approach, thereby permitting PGD techniques to be used in cases where they are used only to determine tissue type, as discussed in Chapters 2 and 3, some Australian jurisdictions restrict the accessibility of PGD services to those who are at risk of transmitting a genetic condition.

One argument put forward for limiting tissue-typing services to cases where the primary purpose is to detect a genetic condition in the embryo (for example, where testing for tissue type occurs as an ancillary process to screening for a genetic condition), is that the potential harm in relation to the use of the biopsy procedure is outweighed by the benefit of having a child born free from the particular condition being screened out.[41] However, this argument should be considered carefully. This view is based on the assumption that the benefit accrued when using PGD for detecting genetic disease is the birth of a healthy child. This inevitably involves testing a number of embryos to establish which are free from the particular condition being tested for. If this is so, children born following the embryo biopsy have not necessarily accrued any particular benefit as they are in the same condition both before and after the biopsy procedure; their genetic make-up and characteristics have not been altered or 'benefited' in any way. This is an argument that has been made by Sally Sheldon and Stephen Wilkinson, who claim that no direct benefit is conferred upon an embryo subjected to biopsy in any way, except to the extent that it increases the probability of the embryo being implanted.[42] Furthermore, as I discuss below, the counterfactual baseline approach for assessing harm makes it difficult to assert that a child born in a healthy condition is 'benefited', as prior to birth, he or she has no interests that are capable of being furthered (or set back). Thus,

---

41  Ram (n 32) 278.

42  Sheldon and Wilkinson (n 28) 533–7. McLean also observes this same argument: Sheila McLean, *Modern Dilemmas: Choosing Children* (Capercaillie Books 2006) 82.

the harms (and benefits) of selection for this specific risk are the same whether testing for genetic disease, or solely to establish tissue type.[43]

For the purpose of establishing that the harm threshold is triggered, it will not suffice to show that the use of PGD techniques for the creation of a saviour child exposes a potential child to a *greater* risk of harm than when testing for genetic disease. More simply, the key factor for any circumstances where PGD techniques are contemplated is simply whether they are harmful. As Sheldon and Wilkinson comment:

> … a child welfare argument based on physical health considerations will either simply fail (because the evidence of harm is inadequate) or will prove too much, counting not only against the creation of saviour siblings, but against *all* uses of PGD. Either way, the argument doesn't successfully single out saviour sibling selection for especially restrictive treatment.[44]

There is no evidence to support the view that children born following the embryo biopsy process are harmed. Although there is clearly a need for long-term studies to monitor the impact of the embryo biopsy technique on the subsequent development of children born following this process, there is currently no evidence to support the view that children are likely to be negatively impacted by this process. For this reason, the risks relevant to the embryo biopsy process do not provide a compelling basis for limiting reproductive decision-making.

### A Psychological Risk of Harm if Selected as a 'Saviour'?

Some commentators have argued that there is a risk that children conceived as saviours might suffer psychological harm in learning that they were selected on the basis of their tissue type as a cure for a relative or family member.[45] As already discussed, in Australia and the UK, ART service providers are required to consider the welfare of the child to be born as a result of the services they provide. The welfare assessment is capable of encompassing the psychological implications of being selected as a saviour. Therefore, just like the potential risks associated with embryo biopsy techniques, the psychological welfare concerns

---

43 Ram (n 32) 279.

44 Sheldon and Wilkinson (n 28) 535 (emphasis in original).

45 Ram (n 32) 280; Stephen Wilkinson, *Choosing Tomorrow's Children: The Ethics of Selective Reproduction* (OUP 2010) 113. See also, Allane Madanamoothoo, 'Saviour Sibling and the Psychological, Ethical and Judicial Issues that It Creates: Should English and French Legislators Close the Pandora's Box?' (2011) 18 European Journal of Health Law 293.

are capable of falling within the notion of welfare interests under the scope of the Harm Principle.

Sheldon and Wilkinson outline two concerns in relation to the potential psychological impact on children born following pre-implantation tissue-typing:

[F]irst, that a future child may suffer psychological harm if she finds out that she were wanted not for herself, but as a means to save the life of a sibling; and second, that a child conceived for this reason is likely to enjoy a less close and loving relationship with its parents who are less likely to value and nurture the child given that they wanted it primarily to save the life of the sibling.[46]

The discussion relating to the risk of psychological harm in this context has not been confined to academic commentary. In the novel, *My Sister's Keeper*, Jodi Picoult creates the fictitious character of Anna, a 13-year-old girl, created as a tissue match in order to try and cure her sister, Kate, who is very ill with leukaemia. Although Picoult is exploring the boundaries of possibility in her fictitious novel, she does depict the very essence of the arguments at stake in this analysis. Picoult seeks to express how Anna may feel, knowing that she was conceived to save her sister:

I was born for a very specific purpose. I wasn't the result of a cheap bottle of wine or a full moon or the heat of the moment. I was born because a scientist managed to hook up my mother's eggs and father's sperm to create a specific combination of precious genetic material … It made me wonder, though, what would have happened if Kate had been healthy. Chances are, I'd still be floating up in Heaven or wherever, waiting to be attached to a body to spend some time on earth. Certainly I would not be part of this family. See unlike the rest of the free world, I didn't get here by accident. And if your parents have you for a reason, then that reason better exist. Because once it's gone, so are you.[47]

Although the character of Anna in *My Sister's Keeper* is fictitious, as Tsitas notes, 'the fiction writer is presenting only an exaggerated situation now happening in the realm of science rather than science fiction'.[48] The foundation of a child's conception has very real implications for the child's psychological development.

---

46 Sheldon and Wilkinson (n 28) 536. The authors acknowledge that both the Hashmi and Whitaker families denied that this was a possibility, stating that they wanted another child in any case.

47 Jodi Picoult, *My Sister's Keeper* (Allen & Unwin 2005) 7–8.

48 Evelyn Tsitas, 'The Role of the Creative Arts in Bioethical Debates' (2006) 6 Queensland University of Technology Law and Justice Journal 255, 260.

A child who discovers that he or she was selected based on their potential to cure another person, might be negatively impacted upon learning of this.

Sheldon and Wilkinson make an interesting comparison between children born as saviours and children born naturally, but are not of the desired tissue type and therefore unable to assist in the treatment of a sick sibling.[49] They comment that a child conceived naturally and born into a bereaved family is just as likely to suffer negative emotional and psychological consequences, particularly if the parents had hoped that the child would be of a compatible tissue type.[50] On this basis, it is argued that there may be potential advantages for the saviour child, who could 'benefit from [his or her sibling's] company and may well derive pleasure from knowing that [he or] she has saved' the life of the sibling.[51] Sheldon and Wilkinson observe that even if evidence supports the view that saviour children would be less happy than children who are not of a matching tissue type, this does not provide a valid justification for limiting reproductive liberty and preventing such children from being born.[52]

When addressing the psychological harms associated with selective reproduction, Michelle Taylor-Sands makes reference to the work of Erica Grundell,[53] noting that saviour children may feel as though the root of their existence is relevant only to fulfil the purposes of another individual.[54] Furthermore, Taylor-Sands highlights the incompatibility of selection with what Feinberg terms the child's 'right to an open future',[55] noting that this argument necessitates that the 'child's future interests or options should be kept open until that child has the capacity of self-determination'.[56]

It is difficult to assess the potential psychological harm that may result from being selected as a saviour, as it is not possible to determine this with any certainty. There is no published research that considers the psychological effects of conceiving a child as a saviour. Imposing restrictions on the accessibility of embryo selection technologies based on risks that are speculative is a precautionary regulatory response and represents a severe limitation to

---

49 Sally Sheldon and Stephen Wilkinson, 'Hashmi and Whitaker: An Unjustifiable and Misguided Distinction?' (2004) 12 Medical Law Review 137, 151–2.

50 ibid. See also Wilkinson (n 45).

51 Sheldon and Wilkinson (n 49) 151–2.

52 Sheldon and Wilkinson (n 28) 536. See also Wilkinson (n 45) 113.

53 Erica Grundell, 'Tissue Typing for Bone Marrow Transplantation: An Ethical Examination of Some Arguments Concerning Harm to the Child' (2003) 22 Monash Bioethics Review 45.

54 Taylor-Sands (n 3) 58.

55 Joel Feinberg, 'The Child's Right to an Open Future' in William Aiken and Hugh LaFollette (eds), *Whose Child? Children's Rights, Parental Authority, and State Power* (Rowman and Littlefield 1980) 124.

56 Taylor-Sands (n 3) 58.

procreative liberty. In accordance with the sentiment outlined at the beginning of this chapter, regulation in this field should not progress on a precautionary basis when there is no evidence of harm to the child.

Importantly, there are other, less restrictive regulatory means available to address the concern of psychological harm to saviour children – a matter that I consider further in Chapter 8. Additionally, follow-up studies could be undertaken to attempt to establish the long-term psychological implications of saviour selection.[57] By monitoring the impact of conceiving children as tissue donors, this would allow the speculative risk of harm in this context to be monitored, without imposing unjustified restrictions on the reproductive choices of some families.

A further problematic aspect of relying on the risk of psychological harm to justify a restrictive regulatory approach is that it is likely to prove difficult to establish that any adverse impact on the child's psychological welfare is linked directly to being selected as a saviour. Being born into a family with an existing health crisis might prove difficult for any child, irrespective of whether or not that child was selected on the basis of being a compatible tissue donor. The child's psychological development is likely to be influenced by other social factors within the family. As Bellamy notes, much will depend upon the way that the child is treated:

> [the speculative] difficulties are far from inevitable because much depends on how the situation is handled within the family. Certainly with love [and] care … there need be no major problem any more than there need be in the explanation of other less usual family circumstances such as adoption.[58]

This speculative risk of psychological harm does not provide a sufficient justificatory basis for imposing restrictions on reproductive liberty. By analogy, if harm-based objections were given the same priority in the context of natural reproduction, given that it is more likely than not that most children will experience some form of harm in their lives, this would require parents to refrain from reproducing whenever it is foreseeable that a *risk* of psychological harm may result to the prospective child (irrespective of how the child is conceived).

### Conceiving Child Donors: An Enduring Harm?

The view that a child who is purposely conceived as a donor might be harmed, has been identified by some commentators as the most important claim in the debate, as this potential harm relates to the saviour child per se and applies

---

57 Snelling (n 34) 23.
58 Bellamy (n 29) 7.

irrespective of whether a saviour child is conceived naturally or by way of ART services.[59] There are a number of different harms relevant to acting as a tissue donor that are outlined in the literature.

Once a saviour child is born, the umbilical cord blood can be harvested for the purpose of performing a transplant. In terms of physical harm, the use of blood stem cells from a child's umbilical cord poses no risks to the mother or the child born.[60] The placenta and umbilical cord would normally be discarded following birth and it is therefore difficult to argue that the harvesting of blood stem cells from the umbilical cord might impact on the child's welfare interests. As noted by Sheila McLean:

> It is generally anticipated that the cells used would be taken from the cord blood of the new baby. Normally the umbilical cord would simply be discarded, and its use has no physical impact on the child. There is, therefore, no bodily intrusion on the child, and no physical harm is caused.[61]

In the event that a transplantation procedure using the umbilical cord blood is unsuccessful, the family might contemplate the harvesting of blood products or bone marrow from the saviour child for the benefit of his or her sibling. Bone marrow transplants and stem cell transplants (referred to as 'hematopoietic stem cell transplants' (HSCTs)) are more invasive. Such procedures typically require the donor child to undergo a general anaesthetic for catheter insertion (to harvest stem cells) or for bone marrow collection from the hip.[62] The child undergoing the procedure will suffer some physical harm. He or she will be exposed to the risk of the anaesthetic, the pain involved in the procedure and will be in a worse physical condition than prior to the procedure (albeit only temporarily). Despite this, bone marrow harvesting has been described as relatively 'atraumatic' with the observation that the child would:

> ... suffer only temporary physical discomfort ... would not require a blood transfusion and there would be no long lasting physical effects from the procedure ... there may be some bruising and soreness for a day or two but

---

59 Strong and others (n 1) 21.

60 Mitchell S Cairo and John E Wagner, 'Placental and/or Umbilical Cord Blood: An Alternative Source of Hematopoietic Stem Cells for Transplantation' (1997) 90 Blood 4665, 4673.

61 McLean (n 42) 92.

62 Kendra D MacLeod and others, 'Pediatric Sibling Donors of Successful and Unsuccessful Hematopoietic Stem Cell Transplants (HSCT): A Qualitative Study of Their Psychosocial Experience' (2003) 28 Journal of Pediatric Psychology 223, 223. See also *Re Inaya (Special Medical Procedure)* [2007] FamCA 658.

many children … appear relatively unperturbed after initial post-operative recovery … If the procedure is performed in the morning, the child is often able to be discharged home by evening, or if unsettled, a one night hospital stay may be necessary. Most children have returned to normal activity within a few days.[63]

While the physical discomfort associated with harvesting bone marrow may appear to be minimal, there are also potential psychological implications arising from transplantation procedures[64] which may impact on the saviour child.

## The Psychological Implications of Being Conceived as a Donor

It has been noted that children born into a family health crisis (where the sibling is suffering from a life-threatening illness) are more likely to be exposed to higher levels of psychological stress.[65] A study conducted by researchers at the University of California revealed that a third of children who had siblings undergoing bone marrow transplantation procedures (irrespective of whether the child was a donor), showed signs of post-traumatic stress, with donor children experiencing a more negative impact.[66] A review of the literature in this field undertaken by Packman and others found that siblings of children undergoing HSCT procedures are at risk of developing psychosocial and behavioural problems, including 'post-traumatic stress reactions, anxiety, low self-esteem, feelings of guilt and school problems' and that further studies are needed to reduce the negative effect of the HSCT experience on siblings.[67] More recent research relating to the psychosocial impact on children who donate tissue to their siblings reveals that donors experience a range of psychosocial issues and that sibling donation 'is embedded within a familial network that has positive and negative consequences'.[68]

It has also been reported that children who act as tissue[69] donors may experience positive benefits. One study reported that children who acted

---

63  *Re Inaya (Special Medical Procedure)* [2007] FamCA 658 [40].

64  ibid.

65  Grace Chang and others, 'A Comparison of Related and Unrelated Marrow Donors' (1998) 60 Psychosomatic Medicine 163, cited in MacLeod and others (n 62) 224.

66  Philip Cohen, 'Donor's Dread: Why do Children Who Help a Sick Sibling End up Depressed?' (1997) 55 New Scientist 20.

67  W Packman and others, 'Psychological Effects of Hematopoietic SCT on Pediatric Patients, Siblings and Parents: A Review' (2010) 45 Bone Marrow Transplantation 1134, 1138.

68  B Pillay and others, 'The Psychosocial Impact of Haematopoietic SCT on Sibling Donors' (2012) 47 Bone Marrow Transplantation 1361, 1365.

69  Human tissue is often defined as either 'regenerative' or 'non-regenerative'. For example, in the Australian state of Queensland, 'regenerative' tissue is defined

as tissue donors in cases where the transplantation procedure to a sibling was successful, had a 'predominantly positive impact on many life domains, including relationships, view of world, feelings about self and decreased helplessness, and insight into their sibling's illness'.[70] Interestingly, it was also reported that many of the positive outcomes and findings concerning successful donation procedures were also present to some extent in cases where donation was unsuccessful.

Despite the positive implications of donation that have been reported in some studies, it appears to be more common for sibling donors to experience negative psychological consequences following an unsuccessful donation procedure.[71] Common emotions expressed by participants include anger, guilt and blame, and this is increased in cases where the donor feels that he or she was not provided with sufficient support following the death of a sibling.[72] It is also reported that donors also often feel a sense of responsibility for the death of their siblings following an unsuccessful donation procedure, and these feelings were more significant for donors who lacked adequate emotional support following the death of their sibling.[73]

As there is no published research that specifically examines the psychosocial impact on saviour children who are conceived specifically to donate tissue to relatives (particularly siblings), the research outlined above is useful in terms of highlighting the range of psychological risks that *might* occur in such circumstances (in addition to the speculative risk outlined above concerning the psychological impact of being selected as a saviour). Children born as saviour siblings who later act as tissue donors will be subjected to the same procedures as other sibling donors. The risk of harm in this regard is therefore similar.

Despite the research findings outlined above, other commentators have argued that children should not necessarily be precluded from acting as tissue donors for their relatives. Snelling comments:

> Whilst there is evidence that some children have suffered psychological distress after bone marrow donation, it is not apparent that this is limited to donors, nor has it been sufficient to preclude the practice of sibling bone marrow donation. None of the studies suggested that sibling bone marrow donation should not

---

as 'tissue that, after injury or removal, is replaced in the body of a living person by natural processes of growth or repair' and 'non-regenerative tissue is 'tissue other than regenerative tissue' (Transplantation and Anatomy Act 1979 (Qld), s 4).

70  MacLeod and others (n 62) 227–8.

71  ibid. 228.

72  ibid.

73  ibid.

occur: rather, appropriate support should be provided to the children and families involved, and continuing follow-up studies should be performed.[74]

It might also be argued that preventing a child from acting as a tissue donor may result in significant psychological distress should the intended tissue recipient subsequently die. This reasoning has been adopted in a number of legal cases involving minors who are called upon to act as tissue donors, as a basis for determining that donation is in their best interests thereby exposing them to tissue harvesting procedures.[75] This approach has even been adopted in cases where the donor child is very young and the recipient is not a sibling, based on the view that the child might benefit from a *future* relationship with his or her sibling or family member, as would the family as a whole.[76] For example, in the Australian Family Court decision of *Re Inaya (Special Medical Procedure)*, it was stated:

> … what also needs to be considered is how [the donor child] and the family would feel in the event that [his or] her non-involvement in the procedure was the '*cause*' of [the sick child's] death. In a family in which the connections are so intense and emotional and social reliance so great, the failure to act protectively and to make self sacrifice for the sake of another family member would be, potentially great.[77]

Importantly, although the literature in this field suggests that there are a number of physical implications and psychological harms and benefits that follow from acting as a child tissue donor, the key question that arises is whether the potential harms in this context justify imposing restrictions on access to ART services, thereby preventing the child from being conceived. As I explain below, for a number of important reasons the assessment of the risks and benefits inherent in tissue harvesting procedures should be undertaken at the time such procedures are contemplated. Other commentators have similarly noted that while it is appropriate to seek to protect the interests of prospective child donors, concern about harm in this context should be dealt with at the time that this becomes relevant (if at all).[78] Fundamentally, although we might reasonably conclude that tissue harvesting procedures performed on children are capable

---

74  Snelling (n 34) 23.

75  This approach will be considered below.

76  This reasoning is similar to Michelle Taylor-Sands' 'relational' approach to interpreting the 'welfare of the child' requirement imposed under ART law and policy: see (n 3) 71–95.

77  *Re Inaya (Special Medical Procedure)* [2007] FamCA 658 [88].

78  Strong and others (n 1) 21.

of falling within Feinberg's notion of harming, these harm-based concerns should not be relied upon to prevent the parents from carrying through their reproductive decision. If this were so, the result is that the prospective child will not be conceived and will therefore have no interests that are capable of being set back or furthered.

## Incomparable Alternatives for the Saviour?

As discussed in Chapter 5, the central aspect of Feinberg's approach to harming requires an application of the counterfactual baseline approach.[79] Accordingly, an individual, 'B', suffers a setback to her interest when that interest is left in a worse position than they would have been had the other person, 'A', not acted as he did.[80] As explained by Feinberg, '[t]he subjunctive phrase – "had *A* not acted as he did" – is the counterfactual clause'.[81] Essentially, the counterfactual baseline test requires a consideration of how the affected person's interest or interests have been impacted as a result of the alleged harm-doer's actions. One of the most frequently cited arguments against the proposition that children conceived using embryo selection technologies are harmed, is that there is no alternative for the particular child to be born into different or alternative circumstances. Instead, the *particular* child would never be born at all;[82] unless conception occurs the particular child in question will never have interests that are capable of being set back as a different child might be conceived if another form of conception takes place. This is an example of the non-identity problem.

When applying the counterfactual baseline test to determine the potential harm that might result from a specific reproductive decision, this will nearly always result in the conclusion that it is in the prospective child's interests to be born. As noted by John Harris, '[t]o give the "highest priority to the welfare of the child to be born" is always to let that child come into existence, unless

---

79 See Chapter 5. Stephen Wilkinson outlines three different forms of the counterfactual baseline approach, although his arguments are considered in the context of selecting embryos in favour of disability. Wilkinson notes that the definition of 'harm' depends on the type of baseline approach which is used in a particular case: Wilkinson (n 45) 74.

80 Joel Feinberg, 'Wrongful Life and the Counterfactual Element in Harming' (1987) 4 Social Philosophy and Policy 149; Nils Holtug 'The Harm Principle' (2002) 5 Ethical Theory and Moral Practice 357, 357, 369.

81 Feinberg (n 80).

82 This argument has been referred to as the 'non-identity problem': see Derek Parfit (n 27). See also Robert Boyle and Julian Savulescu, 'Ethics of Using Preimplantation Genetic Diagnosis to Select a Stem Cell Donor for an Existing Person' (2001) 323 British Medical Journal 1240, 1241, cited in Sheldon and Wilkinson (n 49) 152.

existence overall will be a burden rather than a benefit'.[83] Colin Gavaghan has made a direct link to the non-identity problem in the context of conceiving saviour children, observing that 'the alternative to being born as a tissue donor is not to be born into a more conventional family setting, but rather, *not to be born at all*'.[84] Frequently, however, this argument is used as a ground for dismissing the harm-based objections, without further analysis of how the saviour child might be subsequently 'harmed' after his or her conception. For example, Gavaghan observes that once this test is applied, 'it becomes difficult to conclude that the child created as a tissue donor is harmed by those decisions upon which its very existence is dependent'.[85]

Even though an argument such as the one outlined above by Gavaghan may help to explain why the child will not be harmed by being conceived (a point of view that I explore further below), the difficulty with this argument is that it enables commentators to *completely* disregard all of the harm-based objections. Thus, once the non-identity problem is used as a basis to object to the harm-based arguments, future risks of harm to the saviour child can be completely dismissed from the debate without further consideration, even though such risks might be foreseen at the pre-conception stage. In this sense, the application of the counterfactual test (resulting in a reference to the non-identity problem) has the *potential* to completely disregard any type of evaluation based on the notion of harm. As observed by Rosalind McDougall, this type of argument 'effectively precludes meaningful consideration under a harm-focused approach of the child produced by a particular reproductive decision'.[86]

As an example, let us consider a couple's decision to conceive a saviour child in circumstances where it is foreseen that the child will, most likely, be subjected to a donation procedure following birth. By applying the counterfactual baseline approach at the pre-conception stage, any harm-based objections that might be relevant to the harvesting of tissue from the prospective child might be dismissed on the view that the potential child has no interests until he or she is born and therefore cannot be harmed by the reproductive decisions that brought him or her into being. However, by contrast, if we accept the view that the child is *not harmed by being conceived*, but might later be subjected to a form of harm that is linked to the parents' intentions for conceiving the child, we can still assess the significance of this link (at least to some extent). Thus, some

---

83 John Harris, 'The Welfare of the Child' (2000) 8 Health Care Analysis 33.

84 Colin Gavaghan, 'Designing Donors? Tissue-Typing and the Regulation of Pre-Implantation Genetic Diagnosis' (2004) 3 Web Journal of Current Legal Issues 11 (emphasis in original text).

85 ibid. 12.

86 Rosalind McDougall, 'Acting Parentally: An Argument against Sex Selection' (2005) 31 Journal of Medical Ethics 601, 602.

commentators have argued that there are certain welfare interests relevant to all
children that should be protected, even if those children do not already exist.
Michelle Taylor-Sands comments that there are certain 'universal' interests
of future children that should be protected under a responsible framework
of regulation.[87]

As discussed above, it might be possible to argue that a child who is subjected
to a tissue harvesting procedure is harmed according to Feinberg's notion of
harming, if we assess the child's interests at the time the harvesting procedure
takes place (for example, once the child has interests). Thus, the procedure in
question carries no inherent benefit for the child and will set back the child's
interests at least to some extent, even though the setback may be regarded as
relatively minor in the grand scheme of things (particularly when balanced
against the benefit to the family as a whole and the child's future relationship
with the sibling or relative). If this action also amounts to a form of wrongdoing
against the child, this would fulfil Feinberg's definition of 'harming'.

Given that the prospective parents in such circumstances are likely to foresee
that a saviour child might be exposed to some of the risks of harm outlined
above once the child is born, there is at least some causal link between the parents'
reproductive decision and the infliction of the subsequent harm(s) that may occur
once the child is born. This causal link exists because it is foreseen – at the pre-
conception stage – that specific risks of harm might result from the motivations
underpinning the child's conception (for example, being purposely conceived as a
tissue donor). Views such as Gavaghan's might help to explain why the child's *life*
will not be a harmful one, but this does not necessarily explain why the causal link
between the intentions of the parents in conceiving the child and the risks of harm
that might follow from those intentions should be dismissed completely without
further exploration. An examination of this causal link provides an opportunity
to undertake a more meaningful analysis of the harm-based objections. And
in my view there are other compelling reasons to help explain why the harm-
based objections can be dismissed from the debate to preserve the notion of
reproductive liberty, without relying solely on the non-identity problem.

I should emphasise that I am not seeking to establish whether the
counterfactual baseline approach is or is not appropriate to existential questions
of this kind.[88] This would require a different focus, underpinned by an analysis
of the non-identity problem. The non-identity problem is incredibly contentious
and there is no consensus among commentators as to how the problem should
be resolved.[89] Stephen Wilkinson has considered its relevance in the context

---

87  Taylor-Sands (n 3) 52.

88  For an analysis of this particular issue, see Wilkinson (n 45) 68–77.

89  See Anna Smajdor, 'How Useful is the Concept of the "Harm Threshold" in
Reproductive Ethics and Law?' (2014) 35 Theoretical Medicine and Bioethics 321; see

of embryo selection technologies.[90] Proceeding on the basis that the existential arguments might provide one ground for rejecting the harm-based concerns, there is no reason why an alternative argument cannot also be made out to provide further justification for dismissing the link between the future harms that might be suffered by a saviour child and the actions and intentions of the parents in conceiving the child. As discussed below, this additional argument might also provide a basis to explain why limits on reproductive decision-making are unjustified, even in circumstances where alternative theories of harming relevant to reproductive decisions are accepted.[91] This additional argument might provide further support for the view that the harm-based objections should be dismissed from the debate, rather than relying on the existential argument alone. In this respect, as discussed below, the further guiding principles formulated by Feinberg[92] help to provide a more compelling basis for disregarding the harm-based objections. Prior to considering these principles, however, it is helpful to outline how other commentators have approached the applicability of the Harm Principle to reproductive decisions.

## Harming by Conceiving and the Harm Principle

Feinberg has acknowledged that there are problems with his original formulation of the Harm Principle when applied to reproductive matters. To account for this, he reconsiders his well-established definition of 'harm'.[93] His reformulated approach is applied in the context of wrongful life,[94] as is the majority of the literature that has considered the issue of harming by conceiving. This is a point of significance to which I shall return below.

---

also the commentary response to this paper, Nicola J Williams and John Harris, 'What is the Harm in Harmful Conception? On Threshold Harms in Non-Identity Cases' (2014) 35 Theoretical Medicine and Bioethics 337. See also, Melinda Roberts and David T Wasserman (eds) *Harming Future Persons: Ethics, Genetics and the Non-Identity Problem* (Springer 2009).

90  See Wilkinson (n 45) (68–98). See also, Roberts and Wasserman (n 89).

91  See text to n 102–106.

92  See Chapter 5, pp. 119–125.

93  Feinberg (n 80) 162.

94  Wrongful life cases involve children born with severe disabilities who bring actions in negligence against health care professionals who failed to advise the mother in relation to tests that could be conducted in order to determine whether, at the time of pregnancy, the foetus was likely to be born with a serious disability and/or fail to advise the mother to have an abortion. See E Haavi Morreim, 'The Concept of Harm Reconceived: A Different Look at Wrongful Life' (1988) 7 Law and Philosophy 3; Seana Valentine Shiffrin, 'Wrongful Life, Procreative Responsibility, and the Significance of Harm' (1999) 5 Legal Theory 117.

To determine whether an individual's conception constitutes a form of harm, Feinberg argues that it is more appropriate to consider whether a rational preference can be made between existing in the alleged harmful state and non-existence:

> When one party says that another would have been better off had he never been born, he is claiming that the preference for the one state of affairs over the other is a rational preference. Whether true or not, this is an intelligible claim without contradiction or paradox. ... If nonexistence in a given case would have been objectively preferable to existence, as judged for example by the law's convenient 'reasonable person', then any wrongful act or omission that caused (permitted) the child to be born can be judged to have harmed the child.[95]

As noted by Carson Strong, the implication of Feinberg's reformulated approach is that a child will be harmed as a result of his or her conception in only very rare cases:

> We might put it this way: the life would have to be so filled with pain or other forms of suffering that these negative experiences overshadow any pleasurable or other positive experiences the individual might have. Feinberg and a number of other commentators have referred to such extreme cases as lives 'not worth living'.[96]

The outcome of Feinberg's refined approach is that children born with less serious conditions are not harmed as a result of their conception: '[i]n Feinberg's terminology, an objective proxy would consider their lives to be rationally preferable to nonexistence'.[97]

John Robertson agrees with Feinberg's rational preference approach, but adds that conception does not constitute a form of harm where the resulting child receives a *net benefit* from existing.[98] Carson Strong is not convinced by this reformulated notion of harming by conceiving, as it requires an assessment of whether the individual's interests are advanced in some way. He argues that the difficulty with this approach is as follows:

---

95 Feinberg (n 80) 158–9.

96 Carson Strong, 'Harming By Conceiving: A Review of Misconceptions and a New Analysis' (2005) 30 Journal of Medicine and Philosophy 491, 495.

97 ibid.

98 John A Robertson, 'Procreative Liberty and the Control of Conception, Pregnancy and Childbirth' (1983) 69 Virginia Law Review 76.

As before, the problem is that this claim seems to be incoherent because it attempts to compare a person's state when she exists to her state if she does not exist ... [and] if she does not exist, there is no state of hers to be compared.[99]

Strong proposes that the appropriate test of harm should therefore focus on ascertaining the child's *overall* interests, which requires weighing the benefits associated with being alive against the harms that occur to the child *after* birth. According to Strong, when the child has a 'life worth living' the assessment would conclude that there is no *net harm* to the child.[100] But as with the other theories of harming by conceiving outlined above, this approach requires a balancing of harms and benefits. Again, this leaves the question: what level of benefit will be sufficient to outweigh the negative impacts on the child to conclude that there is no *net harm* to a child?

All of the approaches outlined above require some form of determination as to whether a child has a 'life worth living'.[101] Notably, however, John Harris has proposed an alternative account of harming, which is intended to overcome the issues highlighted above in relation to the application of the harm threshold to reproductive decision-making.[102] Harris refers to his 'harmed state account' as a basis for overcoming many of the problems encountered when applying the comparative account of harming (for example, the counterfactual baseline approach); his account relies on simply assessing whether a person has been placed in a position regarded as harmful.[103] As summarised by Harris:

A condition that is harmful ... is one in which the individual is disabled or suffering in some way or in which his interests or rights are frustrated. The disability or suffering may be slight, just as harms are trivial. ... I would want to claim that a harmed condition obtains wherever someone is in a disabling or hurtful condition, even [if] that condition is only marginally disabling and even [if] it is not possible for that particular individual to avoid the condition in question.[104]

This argument might provide a compelling basis to 'leave open the possibility of all sorts of harm befalling future and present individuals even if they cannot

---

99  Strong (n 96) 497.

100  ibid. 498.

101  The literature surrounding the question of what constitutes a 'life worth living' is considered by Wilkinson (n 45) 70.

102  John Harris, *Wonderwoman and Superman: The Ethics of Human Biotechnology* (OUP 1992).

103  Williams and Harris (n 89) 346.

104  Harris (n 102) 88, cited in Williams and Harris (n 89) 347.

be said to have been made worse off'.[105] And fundamentally, such an account of harming might add weight to the arguments that a saviour child can be harmed by being purposely conceived as a tissue donor. However, I do not seek to resolve the issue of which account of harming should be accepted in the sphere of harming by conceiving,[106] as my argument is far more modest. The purpose of outlining these redefined notions of harming, as applied to the issue of conception, is to enable me to draw some important distinctions that are relevant to conceiving a saviour child.

### Conceiving a saviour child: distinguishing this category of conception

The commentators referred to above have all addressed the notion of harming by conceiving in the context of the wrongful life issue, where the assessment of harm concerns some form of disability or impairment. In this context, the main purpose of the harm evaluation is to provide for the recovery of damages under the law of negligence for a child who already exists. Essentially, the assessment is concerned with establishing that the child's *existence* is itself harmful for the purpose of establishing the 'damage' element of this action. This is an issue that courts in Australia have refused to address.[107] In contrast to this position, the purpose of the harm evaluation in the saviour child context arises for a very different reason: the question is whether the particular risks of harm provide justification for the state to limit reproductive liberty. As the harm assessment in this latter context is undertaken at the pre-conception stage as a welfare assessment, it relates to the possible harm that may be suffered by a future person who has not yet been conceived. This is very different to assessing whether the life of an existing child born with a disability or impairment constitutes a form of harm (for the purpose of establishing the damage element of a negligence action).

David Benatar makes an important distinction between these two contexts. He notes that when judgments are made about 'lives worth living' (such as those outlined above by Feinberg, Robertson and Strong), it is analogous to a 'life worth continuing' and he refers to this type of judgment as the 'present-life sense'.[108] Thus, these judgments can *only* be made about a person who already exists. Distinguishing this category, he goes on to comment that a 'life worth

---

105  Williams and Harris (n 89) 347.

106  ibid.

107  *Harriton v Stephens* (2006) 226 CLR 52.

108  David Benatar, *Better Never to Have Been: The Harm of Coming Into Existence* (OUP 2006) 22.

starting' and a 'life not worth starting' are judgments that can only be made about a potential and non-existent being.[109] He comments:

> ... the problem is that a number of people have employed the present-life sense and applied it to future-life cases, which are quite different. When they distinguish between impairments that make a life not worth living and impairments that, though severe, are not so bad as to make life not worth living, they are making the judgements in the present-life cases. ... But the problem is that these notions are then applied to future-life cases. In this way, we are led to make judgements about future-life cases by the standards of present-life cases.[110]

Benatar further notes that the threshold for judging between present-life and future-life cases is therefore different. Judging whether a life is 'so bad' in the present-life context requires a much higher threshold of harm (such as that outlined above, which requires the conclusion that the individual's life is 'not worth living') compared to a consideration of whether a particular impairment is sufficiently bad to make life not worth beginning in the future-life context.[111] This is because in the former context the assessment relates to judging the circumstances of a *person* who already exists, but in the latter it requires consideration of a particular *condition* and how it would impact on a person who does not yet exist.[112]

---

109 ibid.

110 ibid. 22–3.

111 ibid. 23.

112 This of course depends on how one views the concept of personhood. If, for example, a number of embryos have already been created and a decision is made to implant one embryo over another, some may argue that both have potentiality as a person, and the 'future-life' distinction may be more difficult to justify. However, this would not necessarily be an issue when the preconception welfare principle is applied: at this initial stage, IVF and PGD have not commenced and the couple's gametes have not been combined. This means that there is no person in any sense at the time the assessment is made. Furthermore, interestingly, in the wider context of PGD, which involves screening out genetic conditions and disabilities (essentially, the majority of harming by conceiving literature is focused on disabilities), a similar distinction is made between 'people affecting' judgments (the expressivist argument), and judgments relating to potential people and the effect that reproductive decision-making has on their potential for flourishing. The former is concerned with an analysis of disability and how it impacts on people within society. The latter viewpoint is more concerned with considering the way in which the decision will promote the flourishing of the child who will be born without a disability (it is non-person associated). This distinction is somewhat similar to the one made by Benatar between present and future-life assessments. See Glover (n 2) 26–36.

Importantly, in the saviour child context, the relevant harm objections relate to a number of specific risks that *may* later (but not necessarily) eventuate following the child's birth.[113] Although these risks may, either individually or collectively, fall within the scope of the Harm Principle, if we assess the child's interests at the time the harmful conduct eventuates, this should not lead us to conclude that the child's *existence* will constitute a form of harm when undertaking the pre-conception welfare assessment. Overall, the child will, it is expected, be born free from disability and in good health. Even if the redefined theories of harming by conceiving are applied to the saviour child issue, it is difficult to assert that the child is likely to have a life that is either 'not worth living' or a life that is considered to be, 'on balance', a harm. For this reason it is not appropriate to apply the revised interpretation of the Harm Principle to the pre-conception harm assessment for creating saviour children. The child's *life* is not expected to be, all things considered, a harmful one.

As I argue above, despite the conclusion that the child's *life* is not likely to be regarded as a harmful one, the justification for considering the harm-based objections further is centred on the link between the parents' motivation for conceiving the saviour child and the foreseen 'harms' that might later occur as a result of this. Additionally, we might accept – based on Harris's 'harmed state account' – that some of the implications of acting as a tissue donor may well place the child in a disabling position or subject him or her to suffering, even if this is very slight, thus fulfilling Harris's account of harming.[114] On this basis, there is some merit to the view that the subsequent harms are indeed linked to the purpose behind the child's conception. And even if the parents do not *directly intend* to harm the child in some way once he or she is born, they are nevertheless likely to foresee these risks to some extent based on the fact that they might, for example, intend to harvest tissue from the child once born.

I should also acknowledge a potential objection to this line of reasoning. If the particular link between the parents' motivations and the potential subsequent

---

113 It is possible to state that any pregnancy may result in a child suffering harm as a result of being born. Importantly, however, it is argued that the 'harm' in the wrongful life context is causally linked to the negligence of the health professional in failing to conduct the relevant tests/negligently conducting the tests. This is very different from stating that the *reason(s)* for conceiving the child are what caused the harm(s). Thus, any child who is conceived may indeed be harmed either as a result of being born (in extreme cases) or following birth. Significantly, the harm in this context results from some other act or omission and is unrelated to the parents' motivation for having the child. In fact, the argument in such cases is that if they were aware of the harm in question, the child would not be born at all. The distinguishing factor in the saviour child context is that the harms raised within the literature are linked, at least in some way, to the reasons underpinning the child's conception.

114 See (n 104) and accompanying text.

harm to a saviour is accepted as requiring further evaluation, then this has important implications for reproductive decision-making more generally. Thus, it might be argued that parents (or prospective parents) should refrain from reproducing whenever they foresee – at the pre-conception stage – that a child might suffer various forms of harm during his or her life. As we are all likely to suffer some form of harm during our lives, an objection to my argument might be outlined in the following terms. Harm is likely to befall all children during their lives and if the foreseeability of this is of any relevance to determining the permissibility of a reproductive decision, then this link should be examined in all cases of reproduction.

A key distinguishing factor in the saviour child context is that although various harms such as illness or other traumatic life experiences await all children,[115] and while these harms may be foreseen (or in some cases, expected), parents do not generally intend to inflict such harms upon their children when they reproduce. These harms arise as an inevitable consequence of being human. Significantly, by contrast, some of the harms that might befall a saviour child are not only foreseen, but may also be *intended* (for example, the physical harm that results from subjecting a child to a bone marrow harvesting procedure). In my view, this is a distinguishing factor that justifies further exploration of the causal link. Prior to analysing this link further, I also want to first consider the other important element to Feinberg's notion of harming, by addressing the issue of wrongdoing in the saviour child context.

## Conceiving Saviour and the Notion of Wrongdoing

As outlined in Chapter 5, Feinberg defines a wrong as an unjustified or inexcusable interference with an interest that is ranked of higher priority when weighed against an interest that is conflicting.[116] When applied to the issue of conceiving a saviour child, a potential wrong against the child might be framed as the unjustified or inexcusable interference with the child's interests for the benefit of treating another person. The question of whether the child has been wronged is determined by considering whether the interference in question is justified or excusable. In the same way as before, however, it is difficult to argue that a child is wronged by the particular reproductive decision that ultimately

---

115 For a fascinating perspective of the harms of human existence, see Benatar (n 108).

116 Joel Feinberg, *The Moral Limits of the Criminal Law: Harm to Others* (OUP 1984) 35. This approach has been considered extensively and challenged by other commentators; see Hamish Stewart, 'Harms, Wrongs, and Set-Backs in Feinberg's *Moral Limits of the Criminal Law*' (2001) 5 Buffalo Criminal Law Review 47; Harris (n 102) 88–92; Gavaghan (n 4).

led to his or her existence, as the *particular* child's conception depends entirely
on the 'wrongful' conduct occurring. As with assessing potential setbacks to
interests, it is unlikely that the child is *wronged* by being conceived. Instead,
he or she may be wronged (just like any other individual) *following* birth. For
example, when considering the harvesting of human tissue, any assessment of
wrongdoing occurs at the time that the interference with the child's interests in
physical integrity and so forth takes place (for example, after the child's birth).
At best, we might accept that the circumstances surrounding a prospective
saviour child's conception place that child in a position of risk in terms of being
wronged by certain future unjustified invasions of interests, which are linked to
the intentions of the family in conceiving the child.

An opposing argument that might be put forward against my formulation of
potential wrongdoing in this context, is that the potential wrong arises from the
parents' motivation for conceiving the child and that the child is created solely as
a source of tissue for the existing sick child.[117] Although this may appear to be a
valid concern, the concept of wrongdoing under a harm-based framework centres
on the potential impact on the child's welfare and not the inherent morality of the
parents' decision to conceive the child. This argument must be distinguished from
the view that it is *inherently wrong* to create a saviour sibling. As I discuss further
in Chapter 7, this latter argument is underpinned by deontological reasoning and
assesses not just the impact on the child, but the motivation of the parents for
creating the child, including the morality of their decision.

Wrongdoing in the context of a harm analysis is therefore focused on the
contravention of the resulting child's *interests*, not the inherent morality of the
parents' reproductive decision. As with the issue of setting back another's interests,
the focus is concerned with the link between the motivation and intentions for
having the child and any wrongs that are linked to those intentions, which might
be inflicted upon the child once born (for example, as a result of being subjected
to a bone marrow harvesting procedure that contravenes the child's interests).
This raises the difficult question of whether it is justifiable to procreate in the
knowledge that a child conceived in particular circumstances might be wronged in
some way when the wrongdoing in question is foreseen by the parents in advance.

Other commentators have argued that conception is often morally
problematic, but that this does not necessarily provide a basis for saying that
conception should not occur. In the context of reproduction more generally,
Shiffrin observes that when conception occurs and this places the child at risk
of future harm, this is difficult in a moral sense:

> If our actions now set into motion causal chains that will result in a [child's
> rights] being violated in the future, this action is, at best, morally problematic.

---

117 See Ram (n 32) 280.

That the effect is not imminent and the future rights holder is not present at the time of our action matters little.[118]

However, Shiffrin qualifies her argument by stating that a reproductive decision may be morally permissible if the imposer of the harm may 'justifiably be held responsible for its harmful results'.[119] She further notes that:

Acknowledging such responsibility might help to explain why such action may be permissible. One might believe that imposing overall beneficial conditions that nonetheless involve significant burdens is permissible, when the beneficiary is unable to consent, if one attempts to alleviate or partially shoulder the burdens one imposes. Thus, one might hold that the unconsented-to burdens of life do not make it *wrong* to procreate per se, but rather *wrong* to procreate without undertaking a commitment to share or alleviate any burdens the future child endures (emphasis added).[120]

Applying this to the conception of a saviour child, it can be acknowledged that the creation of such children is indeed morally problematic. The child's conception sets into motion a chain of events that might lead to the infliction of the relevant 'harms'. However, for those families who are willing to accept responsibility, or as Shiffrin frames it, 'shoulder the burden' of their reproductive decision, it could be argued that the harm-based objections voiced in the debate become less persuasive. Where the family demonstrate a willingness and commitment to support the child as he or she encounters such burdens, this might provide a compelling basis to hold that the family's decision to conceive a saviour child is morally permissible; this argument may shield against the harm-based objections centred on the notion of wrongdoing. Other commentators have also noted the potential to minimise the risks of harm in this context, although such views are not framed from the perspective of shielding against the notion of wrongdoing. Stephen Bellamy notes that the risk of psychological harm to a saviour child may be minimised depending on how the family addresses the circumstances surrounding the child's conception:

… much depends on how the situation is handled within the family. Certainly, with love … there need be no major problem any more than there need be in the explanation of other less usual family circumstances such as adoption.[121]

---

118 Shiffrin (n 94) 138.
119 ibid. 139.
120 ibid. 139.
121 Bellamy (n 29) 7.

The family might adopt a variety of options to minimise the impact on the child, which may include family counselling or being open with the saviour child from an early age about his or her conception in preparation for when the child is old enough to question the circumstances surrounding his or her conception. In the context of donor-conceived children, it is recognised that there are potential psychological implications for the child in learning about the circumstances of his or her conception. To minimise the risk to the children conceived in such circumstances, openness in the family unit has been encouraged.[122] A similar approach can be adopted in the context of conceiving saviour children. In Chapter 8, I discuss the potential benefit of exploring – at the pre-conception stage – the potential issues relevant to possibly minimising the risks of harm. Importantly, in circumstances where a family is committed to supporting and enhancing the welfare of any future child, the family should not be prevented from carrying through a particular reproductive decision based on a speculative risk of harm. In cases where the family show a willingness and commitment to support a future child's development, the moral objections to that decision based on the notion of wrongdoing become less forceful.

## Shielding Against the Harm-Based Objections: The Guiding Principles and Causative Considerations

By acknowledging that there is at least some link between the motivation of the parents in conceiving a saviour child and the potential risks of harm that may follow once the child is born, the significance of the harm-based objections can be examined further. In this context it is the *link* between the family's decision to create a saviour child and the subsequent harms that might stem from that decision with which I am concerned.

### Guiding Principles and the Risks of Harm

It is important to note that even if some of the potential risks of harm to the saviour (as outlined above) are accepted as falling within the scope of the Harm Principle, this does not necessarily mean that complete restriction of individual liberty is justified. According to Feinberg, in cases where the harm threshold is, or will be triggered, there are a number of further principles that must be considered to determine whether intervention with liberty is justified.[123]

---

122 Glenn E McGee, Sarah V Brakman and Andrea D Gurmankin, 'Gamete Donation and Anonymity: Disclosure to Children Conceived With Donor Gametes Should not be Optional' (2001) 16 Human Reproduction 2033.

123 See Chapter 5.

As discussed in Chapter 5, Feinberg was of the view that the appropriateness of the regulatory response in circumstances where the harm threshold is engaged should be determined by first considering the *risk* of harm – which is calculated by considering the probability of the risk eventuating and gravity of that potential risk.[124] This should then be considered in comparison to the burden of taking steps to minimise or prevent the risk of the harm in question.[125] If the *risk* of harm is considered to be of a level that justifies restricting liberty, the state may justifiably intervene with liberty, so long as the burden of implementing measures to minimise the harm is proportionate to that risk.[126]

When undertaking a pre-conception harm assessment in the saviour child context, it can be argued that there is no justification for regulatory intervention that results in a complete restriction of reproductive decision-making. As highlighted above, the risk from the embryo biopsy procedure is unknown and although there is emerging research that suggests the risks relevant to the embryo biopsy must be monitored, there is no conclusive evidence to suggest that there are developmental risks to children born following PGD. Similarly, it is extremely difficult to try and predict the probability of any harm in terms of the child's future psychological development. Even if the probability of such harm occurring could be established, it would be very difficult to predict the seriousness of the harm should it result. There is no evidence currently available to suggest that children created as saviours are affected psychologically by learning of the reasons for their conception, and therefore, the risk of harm in this regard is speculative.[127]

An argument that may be more difficult to defend, however, even when relying upon these further guiding principles, is the objection concerning the potential harm that may result from harvesting tissue from a saviour child (either bone marrow or an organ). In some cases, the exact probability of this type of harm will be difficult to predict. For example, *perhaps* the harvesting of bone marrow would not be necessary if an umbilical cord blood stem cell transplantation procedure were successful in curing the sick child's condition (providing that the affected child were to remain in good health following the procedure). However, despite this, it could at least be argued that the *gravity* of the physical risk of harm from a donation procedure, should it be needed, is greater given that there are known physical risks inherent in donation

---

124 Feinberg (n 116) 190–1. John Harris has also made a similar observation: John Harris, 'Reproductive Liberty, Disease and Disability' (2005) 10 Reproductive BioMedicine Online 13.

125 Feinberg (n 116) 191.

126 ibid. 189.

127 This is a view that has been expressed by Wilkinson (n 45) 113.

procedures, which might be more easily ascertainable compared to the other risks outlined above.

In addition to these principles, I think there is, however, a more convincing principle that can be considered to support the preservation of reproductive liberty for parents seeking to create a saviour child. This additional principle is concerned with a closer analysis of the causal link between the child's conception and the alleged resulting harm (or harms), and focuses upon factors such as the proximity of the harm and other relevant normative considerations. Surprisingly, other commentators have not considered the issue of the proximity of harm in comparison to the act of conception within the literature relating to the creation of saviour children.

## Causal Links: Necessary Conditions and Proximity

In cases where the Harm Principle is, or might be, potentially engaged, Feinberg proposes that limiting liberty is justified when a connection can be made between the 'harmer' and the 'victim'.[128] For this purpose, it is necessary to determine a causal relationship between a particular action and the alleged harm. In the general context of conception, we might reasonably conclude that the parents should not be responsible for certain harms that the child experiences throughout his or her life, simply because they made the decision to bring that child into existence. In contrast, we might conclude that responsibility should be imposed for further harms that are directly inflicted upon a child by his or her parents, after conception. One clear reason for attributing responsibility in the latter context, but not the former, is the fact that there are different causal factors at play.

Feinberg notes that in the context of legal causation, a distinction has been made between factors that are considered to be 'necessary conditions' of a particular outcome and those that are considered to be 'proximate' causes of that outcome.[129] Proximity is often considered to be a concept of importance when determining whether blame or liability should be imposed for a particular form of harm.[130] Without this concept, an indeterminate number of causes may be considered as 'necessary conditions' and therefore relevant. Thus, Feinberg observes that 'there may be an infinite number of ways in which the world will be different because [one] act was done and not another'.[131] Significantly, the

128 Feinberg (n 116) 118.

129 ibid. 121–2.

130 Michael S Moore, 'Causation and Responsibility' (1999) 16 Social Philosophy and Policy 1.

131 Feinberg (n 116) 121.

notion of proximity has been relied upon to determine which factor(s) should be regarded as *the* relevant cause(s) of harm.[132]

From an analysis of jurisprudence and other scholarly work concerning the concept of proximity, Feinberg comments that '[o]ne cannot help but suspect that all the leading theories of proximate cause "pick out elements"' which are applicable to some cases but not others.[133] He goes on to observe that determining *the* cause of harm:

> ... involves us in such matters as (depending on one's theory) the justice or efficiency of public policies, the nature of the wrongdoer's fault, foreseeability, the scope of risks, normal patterns and abnormal deviations, the voluntariness of human interventions, and more.[134]

In concluding on the concept of proximity, Feinberg summarises that:

> ... the inquirer's purposes may well lead him to single out as *the* cause an event, a motion, an underlying condition, an omission, or an action, either just prior to the consequence, or substantially earlier.[135]

When applying this reasoning to the act of conceiving a saviour child, it can be observed that conception is a 'necessary condition' for all of the saviour's life experiences, whether harmful, beneficial or otherwise. Yet, in terms of the specific risks of harm that may emerge from being conceived as a saviour, the link between the child's conception and the infliction of the harm may be harder to draw. The fact that the act of conception is something that happens 'substantially earlier' in the chain of events prior to the infliction of any harm does not in itself provide a basis for dismissing the causal link between conception and the subsequent harm. The resulting harm, if any, is likely to *surface* either at the time of the donation procedure or in the case of psychological harm, once the child has developed the requisite understanding to consider the implications of his or her conception. Importantly, however, there are other causative factors that may be more significant when attributing responsibility for the infliction of the relevant harm(s), which deem the act of conception as causally insignificant.

This argument can be demonstrated by returning to the donation example outlined above, where it was established that the harvesting of tissue might set back the child's interests and if this action were to also constitute a wrong, the

---

132 Moore (n 130).
133 Feinberg (n 116) 123.
134 ibid. 124.
135 ibid.

Harm Principle would be engaged. Significantly, although it might be possible to argue that the motivation for conceiving the child set into motion the chain of events that led to the infliction of the particular harm, this seems to ignore the fact that there are other causal factors of greater significance that are relevant to the infliction of the harm(s).

A parent's ability to consent to medical procedures on behalf of a child is not unfettered; decision-making in respect of the child should be exercised in accordance with the child's best interests.[136] This is especially true in the context of donation procedures where there are often statutory safeguards in place to ensure that children are not unjustifiably subjected to such procedures.[137] These safeguards often involve the approval and/or endorsement of other professionals or public officials, suggesting that authorisation of a tissue harvesting procedure will only occur in circumstances where it is deemed to be in the child's best interests.[138] However, it should be acknowledged that some commentators have questioned the adequacy of existing safeguards concerning the donation of tissue by children created intentionally as donors.[139] Nevertheless, such a safeguard is important, as it effectively determines whether the interference with the child's interests is unjustified for the purpose of assessing whether the child is wronged. Thus, in cases where these safeguards are not complied with (or if the child's interests are not sufficiently assessed), the performance of a donation procedure may amount to a form of wrongdoing based on the fact that it would unjustifiably contravene the child's interests.

In circumstances where a tissue harvesting procedure is performed contrary to the child's best interests, it can be argued that this form of 'harm' is not *directly* linked to the decision to conceive the child, but is instead attributable to the actions of the parents and the medical team in physically subjecting the child to the procedure. Not only do these actions have consequences that are more significant in space and time, but they also *contravene* the child's interests. Thus, subjecting a child to a tissue harvesting procedure that is contrary to his or her best interests (for example, such as, potentially, removing an organ)

---

136 Sarah L Woolley, 'The Limits of Parental Responsibility Regarding Medical Treatment Decisions' (2011) 96 Archives of Disease in Childhood 1060. This is a principle that has also been emphasised in case law; see *Department of Health and Community Services (NT) v JWB (Marion's Case)* (1992) 175 CLR 218.

137 Shih-Ning Then, 'The Legality of Tissue Transplants for the Benefit of Family Members in the UK and Australia: Implications for Saviour Siblings' (2009) 10 Medical Law International 23.

138 See *Re GWW and CMW* (1997) FLC ¶92–748; *Re Inaya* (2007) 213 FLR 278.

139 See Then (n 137); Natalie Morrison and John Devereux, 'Child Saviours: Reconceiving the Legal Dimension' (2014) 22 Tort Law Review 9; Natalie Morrison and John Devereux, 'Child Saviours: Reconceiving the Ethical Dimension' (2014) 22 Tort Law Review 3.

should be regarded as the causally significant cause of harm, rather than relying upon these risks of harm to prevent families – at the pre-conception stage – from accessing ART services.

In contrast, the link between the act of conception and the risk of psychological harm is more difficult to separate. Thus, the very reason for the child's conception is to be *selected* as a source of tissue for another person, which is argued to be a potential cause of this risk of harm. However, as outlined above, there are also psychological risks associated with being born into a family setting with an existing health crisis and risks associated with acting as a donor. For this reason, it may be particularly difficult to link a specific form of 'harm' to the reproductive decision (and actions) of the prospective parents. The child's psychological development is likely to be impacted by a wide range of factors; attempting to single out the motivation for the child's conception as *the* relevant contributing factor ignores the range of other family circumstances that may affect the saviour child. Moreover, it is also very possible to argue that the motivation for conceiving the child might have a positive impact on the child. The child might feel comforted by the fact that his or her parents were willing to go to such extraordinary lengths to save his or her relative, suggesting that the parents may offer the same level of support, love and devotion to the saviour child.

In either case, without evidence to establish the psychological impact on the child in these circumstances, the view that the motivation for the child's conception *may* have a positive or negative effect on the child's psyche remains purely speculative. Therefore, in the context of a pre-conception harm analysis, this risk of harm cannot be established with any certainty. It is for this reason that the guiding principles provide a compelling basis to dislodge the harm-based objections from the debate, to justify the view that the state should not completely restrict reproductive decision-making in this context.

## Conclusion

The discussion in this chapter highlights the difficulty in applying a harm-based framework to reproductive decision-making. The majority of the literature relating to the issue of harming by conceiving relates to the wrongful life context. However, there are important distinctions that need to be drawn between different cases of conceiving. This includes distinguishing between the present-life and future-life contexts, as each will involve the application of differing value judgments. The application of the pre-conception welfare assessment represents a future-life assessment and effectively involves a determination of whether the child should not be conceived due to a number of prospective harms that may follow once the child is born. It was acknowledged that some regard the application of the counterfactual baseline approach as equivalent to the view that it is nearly always in the best interests of a child to be born. As explained, this provides a basis to dismiss many of the risks of harm that may be foreseeable at the pre-conception stage, but most importantly, this provides a justification for dismissing those harms that are linked to the intentions for conceiving the child.

Many of the specific risks of harm in the saviour child context might be regarded as harms within Feinberg's original formulation of harming, assuming that the assessment of harm takes place once the child has interests that are capable of being wrongfully set back. By acknowledging that there is a link between the parents' motivation for conceiving the child and the subsequent harms that might result from being conceived as a tissue donor, the harm-based objections can be analysed further.

Ultimately, my argument is that these particular risks of harm do not provide a sufficient basis for a restrictive regulatory approach on this issue, which I supported by reliance on Feinberg's guiding principles. Nevertheless, as I discuss in the following chapter, the restrictive approach adopted under the current regulatory landscape appears to be underpinned by wider ethical reasoning and arguments based on morality. It is therefore also necessary to consider the significance of these concerns further.

# Chapter 7
# Creating Saviour Children: The Wider Ethical and Moral Arguments

## Introduction

It has been stated that the notion of harm that dominates the bioethical debate concerning the creation of saviour children also encompasses 'concerns about moral hazards to society at large' and 'concerns about the destruction of embryos'.[1] On this view, there are clearly a number of wider concerns that have been outlined in the literature, which although might be framed from a harm-focused perspective can be more accurately described as objections based on other ethical and philosophical reasoning, or concerns about morality more generally. It is important to consider these wider objections as there are a number of restrictions imposed under the current regulatory frameworks, which arguably seek to address some of these wider ethical concerns. The significance of these concerns – in terms of their relevance to the regulatory response – is also explored further in Chapter 8.

Given that the decision to conceive a saviour child will impact directly on only a small number of people, reliance on the wider ethical concerns as a basis for restricting reproductive decision-making might be viewed as an encroachment on the liberty of families seeking to utilise assisted reproductive technology (ART) services for this purpose. Nevertheless, the media's portrayal of this issue together with political debate on the topic[2] has placed it within the public domain as a moral issue. Tom Beauchamp and LeRoy Walters note that public moral dilemmas do not have, and are unlikely to have, a single theory

---

1 Kimberly A Strong and others, 'It's Time to Reframe the Savior Sibling Debate' (2011) 2 AJOB Primary Research 13, 14.

2 In the UK, the amended Human Fertilisation and Embryology Act 1990 (UK) specifically addressed the issue of 'saviour siblings' and it was subject to a free vote in the House of Commons. See 'MPs Reject "Saviour Sibling" Ban' (BBC News, 19 May 2008) <http://news.bbc.co.uk/2/hi/uk_news/politics/7409264.stm> accessed 26 November 2014.

or method for resolution.[3] The difficulty of regulating issues such as pre-implantation genetic diagnosis (PGD) was noted in a report published by the Human Genome Research Project:

> Particular challenges are presented when regulating in this area where views may be polarised and morally or politically charged, and where the science is complex and rapidly evolving. In determining the parameters of legislation [or regulation], legislatures cannot solely rely on public consensus, as there may in fact never be one.[4]

The ethical and moral concerns raised in the literature relating to the creation of saviour children can be summarised as encompassing the following three arguments. First, concerns have been voiced in relation to the moral status of human embryos, as ART techniques for the creation of saviour children involve the creation of multiple embryos and the discarding of unwanted or unsuitable embryos. Second, it has been argued that purposely conceiving a child as a tissue donor signifies a commodification of children, or represents the view that such children are conceived merely as a means to an end. Third, it has been argued that the selection of prospective children on the basis of their tissue type is a step on a slippery slope towards allowing the use of ART services for the creation of 'designer babies'. These objections are considered below, but it is perhaps worth noting that the range of ethical and moral issues raised in the literature on this issue demonstrates the divergent viewpoints at stake. It is therefore unlikely that consensus will be reached on some, if not all, of these issues.

## The Moral Status of the Embryo

The use of in vitro fertilisation (IVF) and PGD inevitably requires the creation of multiple embryos. The PGD process usually involves an analysis of the genetics of a number of embryos. 'Suitable' embryos are then implanted for the purpose of establishing a pregnancy. This means that some embryos are not used, and more controversially, a number of the embryos created during the process are deemed unsuitable for implantation. When this process is utilised for the purpose of establishing tissue type, embryos that match the tissue type of the intended recipient will be deemed suitable for implantation, but where

---

3 Tom L Beauchamp and LeRoy Walters, *Contemporary Issues in Bioethics* (6th edn, Thomson/Wadsworth 2003) 5.

4 Human Genome Research Project, *Choosing Genes for Future Children: The Regulatory Implications of Preimplantation Genetic Diagnosis* (2006 Dunedin) 306.

relevant, those confirmed as carrying a genetic defect or condition will be discarded (or potentially donated for the purpose of scientific research, where permitted). This process therefore impacts on the views relating to prenatal life.

The issue of whether discarding embryos constitutes the destruction of human life depends on the values and beliefs of the individual making that assessment. For this reason, the question of whether PGD is ethically acceptable has many similarities with the debate relating to abortion, which also depends upon views concerning the point at which human life begins. In terms of social views, there is unlikely to be consensus on when human life begins.[5] Some may adopt a gradualist view, which means that a developing foetus is worthy of greater respect in comparison to an embryo.[6] It is for this reason that the use of PGD has been viewed as ethically less problematic compared to prenatal screening, as it avoids the need for a woman to undergo an abortion following prenatal diagnosis (by which stage the foetus is more developed).[7] However, other viewpoints, such as the Roman Catholic perspective, value prenatal life from the moment of conception and regard PGD as morally wrong because it involves the destruction of human life for those embryos that are left to perish.[8] On either view, PGD is made more controversial by the fact that it requires the creation of potential life purely for the sake of genetic analysis (or in the saviour child context, for the purpose of establishing tissue type).[9] Interestingly, however, it has been noted that secular scholars (and even some Christian scholars) view the use of embryo selection technologies for the purpose of establishing tissue type as acceptable, based on the view that the embryo does not have the full status of a human person.[10]

There is no doubt that the creation of embryos in vitro creates significant ethical and moral concerns in relation to the destruction of human or prenatal life.[11] However, the concern relating to spare embryos is not unique to the saviour child issue, as it is likely to be relevant in nearly all IVF procedures.[12]

---

5 See Alison Cranage, 'No Consensus on Where Human Life Begins' (*BioNews*, 3 November 2008) <http://www.bionews.org.uk/page_13559.asp> accessed 26 November 2014.

6 For an analysis of the moral status of the foetus, see Raanan Gillon, 'Is There a "New Ethics of Abortion"?' (2001) 27 Journal of Medical Ethics ii5–ii9; Mary Anne Warren, 'On the Moral and Legal Status of Abortion' (1973) 57 The Monist 43.

7 Human Genome Research Project (n 4) 162. Gillon (n 6).

8 Human Genome Research Project (n 4).

9 ibid.

10 Strong and others (n 1) 16.

11 See Colin Gavaghan, *Defending the Genetic Supermarket: Law and Ethics of Selecting the Next Generation* (Routledge-Cavendish 2007) 54–64.

12 Unless, of course, fertility clinics are restricted to the point that they are only allowed to create one embryo at a time for the purposes of implantation or are required

Irrespective of the perspective that one adopts when considering the status of the human embryo, it is important to note that the creation and destruction of multiple embryos is an inevitable consequence of most IVF procedures. The objections based on the moral status of the human embryo have not been afforded greater priority over the principle of reproductive liberty in the wider context of IVF. Between the years of 1991 and 2005, it was estimated that in the United Kingdom (UK) approximately 1.2 million embryos were not used in treatment procedures.[13] Michael Sandel similarly observes that according to 2003 study, some 400,000 embryos were 'languishing in American fertility clinics, with another 52,000 in the United Kingdom and 71,000 in Australia'.[14]

Importantly, by allowing prospective parents to utilise IVF services in the general context of ART, it can be stated that the potential 'harm' to those who view the destruction of embryos as the destruction of human life, is not given priority over the reproductive decision-making of those who seek access to such services. While many people may oppose reproductive techniques on the basis of the arguments just mentioned, the fact that ART techniques are permitted in the wider sense makes it difficult to assert that these objections are relevant to embryo selection technologies, particularly in relation to the selection of tissue type.[15] Thus, as noted by Strong and others, many commentators have highlighted the inconsistency of arguments that oppose PGD practices based on the loss of surplus embryos argument, when IVF is permitted generally and abortion practices are tolerated.[16] For this reason, the potential 'harm' that some members of society may suffer as a result of others who access this technology provides no basis for curtailing reproductive liberty in the saviour child context.

Furthermore, arguments concerning the status of the human embryo are essentially based on morality rather than being harm-focused in nature. As

---

to implant all embryos created in an IVF cycle. Italian fertility clinics have been severely limited in such a way when providing ART services: see Rachel Anne Fenton, 'Catholic Doctrine versus Women's Rights: The New Italian Law on Assisted Reproduction' (2006) 14 Medical Law Review 73.

13 MacKenna Roberts, 'UK Parliament Alarmed by 1.2 Million Leftover IVF embryos' (*BioNews*, 7 January 2008) <http://www.bionews.org.uk/page_13266.asp> accessed 26 November 2014.

14 Nicholas Wade, 'Clinics Hold More Embryos than Had Been Thought' *New York Times* (9 May 2003) 24, cited in Michael Sandel, *The Case against Perfection: Ethics in the Age of Genetic Engineering* (Belknap Press 2007) 110.

15 However, this does not mean that the moral status of the embryo or foetus is completely insignificant: respect for the embryo should be maintained throughout any ART regulatory policy, and many of the regulatory policies considered throughout this book make reference to the need to treat the embryo with dignity and respect.

16 Strong and others (n 1) 16.

established in Chapter 5, a harm-based perspective is focused on determining that the objectionable conduct in question has wrongfully set back the interests of another. It is difficult to establish exactly whose interests will be thwarted or set back by allowing other members of society to utilise embryo selection technologies for the creation of a saviour child. The assertion that people are harmed by the conduct of another based on the view that such practices are contrary to an individual's values or beliefs, does not provide a sufficient basis for justifying the imposition of restrictions on reproductive liberty. Something more than offence is required to justify a restrictive regulatory approach.

## Commodification and 'Means End' Objections

Arguments against the creation of saviour children often rely on the proposition that such decisions represent a 'commodification' of children (Strong and others argue that 'instrumentalization' is a more appropriate term)[17] or that the use of the technology for this purpose contradicts Kant's categorical imperative, as the child is conceived as a means to an end. These linked arguments are examined below. However, it is important to highlight the fact that the current regulatory landscape prioritises these ethical objections to some extent; the current regulatory approaches in Australia and the UK require parents to justify their motives for conceiving a saviour child by satisfying a clinician or an ethics committee that they had intended to conceive another child as an addition to their family and not merely as a source of tissue for an existing sick person.[18] Additionally, legislation in the UK limits the accessibility of ART services for the creation of saviour children to cases where the condition of the affected child (who must be a sibling) is treatable with umbilical cord blood stem cells, bone marrow or other tissue ('other tissue' excludes the harvesting of an organ under the legislation).[19] As I have argued elsewhere,[20] this restriction is underpinned, at least to some extent, by deontological reasoning. Thus, permitting parents to purposely conceive an organ donor has been argued as inherently wrong and a contradiction of Kantian reasoning.[21]

---

17 Strong and others (n 1) 14.

18 See Chapter 3.

19 Human Fertilisation and Embryology Act 1990 (UK), sch 2, paras 1ZA(1)(d), (4).

20 Malcolm K Smith, 'The Human Fertilisation and Embryology Act 2008: Restrictions on the Creation of "Saviour Siblings" and the Relevance of the Harm Principle' (2013) 32 New Genetics and Society 154.

21 ibid. 164.

## Saviour Children and the Commodification Concerns

Merle Spriggs observes that the commodification argument has been relied upon by prominent bodies such as the French National Consultative Ethics Committee for Health and Life Sciences (CCNE), which observed that one of the most important issues in this context is the need to ascertain the 'authenticity of the parental project' and the 'risk of the child becoming a commodity'.[22] The argument against the use of the technology in this context is fundamentally based on the view that such techniques will potentially change the way in which reproduction and parenthood are viewed within society.[23]

The commodification argument is underpinned by the view that the permissibility of utilising ART services to create a saviour child poses a threat to our understanding of how procreation is viewed within society more generally. This reasoning is not too dissimilar to some of the ethical objections that were voiced in response to the establishment of IVF techniques as a new technology; such techniques were seen as posing a threat to the special nature of procreation on the basis that children are a gift or a blessing, and medical means to assist this process was potentially damaging to this purpose.[24] As Michael Sandel notes, the threat posed by embryo screening technologies is the impact that such technologies might have on the natural order of procreation.[25] He therefore argues that conceiving a child on the basis of his or her genetic characteristics is inherently wrong;[26] the argument is thus a deontological one.

The view that the special nature of procreation is threatened by the use of embryo selection technologies for the creation of saviour children is questionable. Social views concerning reproduction and family structures have changed significantly in recent times. As outlined in the report of the Human Genome Research Project:

> ... dichotomy which contrasts natural reproduction (in which children are categorised as a 'blessing') with assisted reproduction (in which children are labelled more as products of their parents' desires) seems in some ways to be too simplistic to describe the complexities of reproduction in the 21st century.[27]

---

22 Merle Spriggs, 'Commodification of Children Again and Non-disclosure Preimplantation Genetic Diagnosis for Huntington's Disease' (2004) 30 Journal of Medical Ethics 538, 538.

23 Human Genome Research Project (n 4) 165.

24 See Sandel (n 14) 92–7.

25 ibid. 99–100.

26 ibid. 3.

27 Human Genome Research Project (n 4) 165.

It is difficult to accept that reproductive liberty should be limited to avoid the threat that these technologies pose to the 'natural order of procreation'. This argument does not succeed in the wider context of ART techniques, as IVF procedures are now generally accepted. As discussed below, this theoretical argument is also far removed from the views and values of parents who have purposely conceived children as tissue donors, or have considered this option.[28] Moreover, as with the arguments concerning the moral status of the embryo, from a harm-based perspective it is difficult to determine how this argument might impact on the interests of others. It is not possible to determine how another person's interests will be wrongfully set back by a family's decision to conceive a saviour child, based on the impact of the commodification objections. At most, the use of the technology in this regard might be seen as morally offensive, but there is no suggestion that health professionals should be forced to provide services that are contrary to their personal values and/or religious beliefs;[29] it is simply that families should have unrestricted access to ART services to fulfil their reproductive choices. Nevertheless, as discussed above,[30] the regulatory policies that address the creation of saviour children seek to mitigate these ethical concerns, albeit at the expense of the liberty of families seeking access to ART services for this purpose.

## The 'Means to an End' Objection

It is also frequently cited that allowing families to access ART services for the creation of a saviour child will result in such children being conceived merely as a means to an end. This assertion is based on Kant's categorical imperative, which holds that we have a duty to respect other people as individuals and not treat them simply as a means to an end.[31] Treating others as a means to furthering one's own objectives (or the interests of another) therefore appears to violate this rule.[32] As Ruth Deech and Anna Smajdor note:

> Unarguably, a child conceived in order to provide tissue for a sick sibling is conceived as a means to an end: the end of curing the sibling. For many people,

---

28  This view is based on the empirical research undertaken by Kimberly Strong and others (n 1), which is discussed further below.

29  Strong and others (n 1) 21.

30  See also Chapter 3.

31  Immanuel Kant, 'Fundamental Principles of the Metaphysic of Morals' in Allen W Wood (ed), *Basic Writings of Kant* (The Modern Library 2001).

32  Tom L Beauchamp and James F Childress, *Principles of Biomedical Ethics* (OUP 2001) 351, cited in Gavaghan (n 11) 156.

this seemed to be the end of the matter: the proposition was an unacceptable violation of the rule, and must not therefore be allowed.[33]

The Ethics Committee of the Human Fertilisation and Embryology Authority (HFEA) made reference to this argument by linking it to the welfare of the child principle:

> It could be suggested that positive consideration of the welfare of the child requires respect for beings as ends and that the putative child be treated not simply as a means to a further end but also always as an 'end in itself'.[34]

The means to an end objection has also been expressed in much stronger terms:

> ... there is a real problem. We are not treating this saviour sibling as a human being of equal worth to other humans. We are not creating this saviour sibling to be a child in its own right. We have created it – designed it – to be a source of spare parts for an existing child. If you start designing other human beings, you are putting them on a lower level than yourself.[35]

However, this comment is based on a number of unjustifiable assumptions about the intentions of the parents and the way that they will treat a saviour child once he or she is conceived. Moreover, the argument that the child is 'designed' is based on a misconceived understanding of PGD practices. As discussed below, the PGD process involves analysing the genetics of embryos for the purpose of *selecting* them for implantation in an IVF cycle. Thus, the process does not provide a means of 'designing' the genetics of future offspring.

One argument that weakens the 'means to an end' objection is that any transaction between two individuals is capable of being regarded as ethically problematic based on this reasoning. Colin Gavaghan notes that an application of this argument could result in the conclusion that any contract for services that uses human effort and labour would prima facie seem to violate the principle.[36] Gavaghan therefore argues that the rule should be formulated to mean that 'there is nothing objectionable per se in using someone as a means, provided

---

33 Ruth Deech and Anna Smajdor, *From IVF to Immortality: Controversy in the Era of Reproductive Technology* (OUP 2007) 69.

34 Ethics Committee of the Human Fertilisation and Embryology Authority, *Ethical Issues in the Creation and Selection of Preimplantation Embryos to Produce Tissue Donors* (2001) 5.

35 Richard Nicholson, 'Saviour Siblings: Is it Right to Create a Tissue-Donor Baby?' (Debate, Guardian Newsroom, 16 October 2003).

36 Gavaghan (n 11) 156.

[we] do not lose sight of the fact that s/he is also an end in him/herself'.[37] Sally Sheldon and Stephen Wilkinson argue that Kant's categorical imperative has been incorrectly applied to the saviour child context; Kant's dictum counselled not against using people as a means but against 'treating them *merely* or *solely* as means' to an end (emphasis added).[38] Other commentators have outlined similar criticisms, noting that Kant's categorical imperative is only violated if the child is treated *merely* or *solely* as a means to an end.[39]

The requirement for families to justify their reproductive decision, by convincing a clinician or an ethics committee that they intended to conceive another child as an addition to their family and not merely as a source of tissue, ignores the more important consideration of whether the parents will treat the child as an end in himself or herself. A family's ability to value a child as an individual, for his or her own worth, and not merely as a means to an end, is not necessarily lacking in circumstances where the family did not intend to conceive a child before a compatible tissue donor was needed. The motives underpinning a decision to conceive a child may not be directly relevant to the prospective child's 'capacity and opportunity to flourish'.[40] It is frequently the case that children are born in circumstances where there are no parental motivations for their conception, or where the child is wanted to satisfy the interests of the parents. As noted by Katrien Devolder, in the context of natural reproduction there are numerous reasons relevant to a family's decision to reproduce, including the strengthening of a relationship; continuity of the family name; and the economic and psychological benefits a child brings to parents when they age.[41] Importantly, parental motivation (or lack of reason in the case of unplanned pregnancies) for conceiving a child does not provide us with grounds to conclude that the parents will not fulfil their parental duties and act as good parents.[42]

Relying on a family's prior intentions – that were relevant before one of their family members required a transplantation of tissue – for the imposition of restrictions on their reproductive liberty is an unjustified regulatory response. It has

---

37  ibid.

38  Sally Sheldon and Stephen Wilkinson, 'Hashmi and Whitaker: An Unjustifiable and Misguided Distinction?' (2004) 12 Medical Law Review 137, 146.

39  Gavaghan (n 11) 156; Jeanne Snelling, 'Embryonic HLA Tissue Typing and Made-to-Match Siblings: The New Zealand Position' (2008) 9 Medical Law International 13, 22; Stephen Bellamy, 'Lives to Save Lives – the Ethics of Tissue Typing' (2005) 8 Human Fertility 5; Deech and Smajdor (n 33) 69–70; Katrien Devolder, 'Preimplantation HLA Typing: Having Children to Save Our Loved Ones' (2005) 31 Journal of Medical Ethics 582, 583–4. See also Strong and others (n 1) 14.

40  Strong and others (n 1) 15.

41  Devolder (n 39) 584.

42  Strong and others (n 1) 15.

been observed that parents have mixed intentions all of the time when it comes to reproductive decision-making.[43] Fundamentally, the factors motivating parents to conceive a child should not necessarily be determinative of whether a family is permitted to carry through their reproductive choices, as long as they demonstrate a willingness to support and care for the child once he or she is born.[44] As Katrien Devolder comments, 'we judge people on their attitudes toward children, rather than on their motives for having them'.[45] This argument can be strengthened further when viewed in the light of the potential benefits of allowing families to access ART services for this purpose. Thus, the potential end result is that the parents will end up with two healthy children, rather than losing one sick child.[46]

As I argued in Chapter 4, as it is generally accepted that there is a strong interest in reproductive freedom without state intervention, which can only be restricted in exceptional circumstances,[47] restrictions on the basis of these arguments seem precarious. These ethical arguments are quite distinct from the harm arguments outlined in Chapter 6. As Gavaghan notes, these arguments are:

> ... not merely a rephrasing of the principle of non-maleficence [or harm], but something quite distinct from it. Thus, even – as seems likely – if all parties involved are net beneficiaries in terms of harms and benefits, we may have done something ethically wrong if, in the process, we treated some of them as mere instruments.[48]

Ultimately, however, there is little evidence available to suggest that prospective or actual parents of saviour children will treat such children as 'mere instruments'. This objection is speculative and rests on the assumption that the welfare and interests of children will not be safeguarded by the parents, or cannot be adequately protected once they come into being; an argument that I explored and advocated against in Chapter 6. Moreover, as discussed below, empirical research examining the views of families who have conceived a saviour child (or are contemplating it), suggests that such views are erroneous from the perspective of these families.[49]

---

43 Bellamy (n 39) 7.

44 This would seem a more appropriate formulation of Kant's dictum. As Gavaghan notes, the duty seems to be focused on acting in a way that respects every other human being for himself or herself rather than solely as a means to one's own advances. Furthermore – citing another commentator – he states that '[i]n short, how one is treated by others over the course of one's life is more morally significant than the reasons for causing one to exist'; see (n 11) 157–9.

45 Devolder (n 39) 584.

46 Sheldon and Wilkinson (n 38) 146.

47 Strong and others (n 1) 15; see also Chapter 4.

48 Gavaghan (n 11) 157.

49 See n 74–77 and accompanying text.

## Slippery Slope to 'Designer Babies'?

The final ethical objection relevant to the wider ethical concerns is the argument that the use of ART services for the creation of saviour children will result in embryo selection technologies being used to select children on the basis of other, 'less desirable' characteristics. Liberal reproductive policies have been heavily criticised with opponents arguing that, in time, such policies may permit parents to select a varying range of genetic characteristics for their offspring. This argument is essentially based on the view that if we allow parents to use ART services to create saviour children, then this is the first step on a slippery slope towards the practice of so-called 'designer babies'.

At the outset, one key point that should be made concerning this argument – the potential threat of 'harm' in this context does not arise as a direct result of allowing families to conceive saviour children using ART services, but is instead levelled at the *potential* for the technology to be used for *other* purposes. There are two different types of argument put forward in relation to the slippery slope that will be briefly considered: the logical and the empirical arguments.[50]

The logical argument seeks to compare two similar courses of action. When one of the actions is morally acceptable, but the other is less desirable or morally problematic, but no conceptual distinction can be drawn between the two, neither or both of the actions should be permitted.[51] In the context of creating saviour children, the logical argument can only be effectively applied if there is no conceptual distinction that can be drawn between the use of embryo selection technologies for the purpose of establishing tissue type, and the use of these technologies for the selection of other genetic traits or characteristics. If this argument were to succeed, the result is that the two uses of the technology should either be permitted or prohibited, as there is no logical distinction to be drawn between them.

The empirical argument on the other hand involves a prediction that permitting one course of action now will lead to a different, less desirable course of conduct being permitted in the future.[52] As one commentator notes:

> What the empirical version boils down to is that once we have opened the door just a crack ... the floodgates will soon be flung wide – 'whether we like it or not, you'll soon see that the use of genetic technology to conceive designer babies will no longer be stoppable.[53]

---

50  Guido de Wert, 'Preimplantation Genetic Diagnosis: The Ethics of Intermediate Cases' (2005) 20 Human Reproduction 3261, 3263.

51  ibid.

52  ibid.

53  ibid.

Guido de Wert makes the important observation that the slippery slope arguments in this context rely upon the presumption that the use of embryo selection technologies for the creation of 'designer babies' is not ethically acceptable.[54] This is a view that has been challenged by some commentators.[55] The ethical acceptability of conceiving 'designer babies' more generally is beyond the focus of this book.[56] However, it is important to note that the use of the term 'designer babies' is somewhat misleading, as PGD techniques involve genetic analysis of embryos that are created during an IVF cycle so that prospective parents can choose to implant suitable embryo(s) for the purpose of achieving a pregnancy, based on the embryo's genetic characteristics. Essentially, the issue is one of selection, rather than design. Parents will not be able to choose characteristics for which their genetics do not permit.[57]

When applying the logical slippery slope argument, a clear distinction can be drawn between the use of embryo selection technologies for the creation of saviour children and other potential uses of the technology. Fundamentally, in the context of conceiving a saviour child, the baby is not being 'genetically moulded to fit the parental picture of the perfect child'[58] and the decision is not motivated by 'parental whim'.[59] The strength of the logical argument therefore appears weak,[60] as regulatory policy relating to the use of PGD services is capable of differentiating between the different purposes behind embryo screening.

The empirical slippery slope argument is also difficult to accept. The concern that allowing families to use ART services to conceive saviour children will, over time, lead to an acceptance that PGD services can be used for the conception of designer babies, is problematic.[61] It has been noted that just because 'a new technology could be used for morally objectionable purposes, it is by no means inevitable that it will be used in this way'.[62] As highlighted above, it is possible to restrict the use of PGD services for certain purposes, while at the same time allowing such technologies to be used for other purposes. Regulatory policy can effectively draw distinctions between the different uses of the technology (as

---

54  ibid.

55  See Julian Savulescu, 'Procreative Beneficence: Why We Should Select the Best Children' (2001) 15 Bioethics 413.

56  For a wider analysis of the ethics of embryo selection technologies, see Stephen Wilkinson, *Choosing Tomorrow's Children: The Ethics of Selective Reproduction* (OUP 2010).

57  See Bellamy (n 39) 6.

58  de Wert (n 50) 3263.

59  Bellamy (n 39) 6.

60  de Wert (n 50) 3263.

61  ibid.

62  Strong and others (n 1) 14.

is demonstrated particularly well by the HFEA Code of Practice in the UK).[63] In summary, adopting a more liberal regulatory approach in relation to the use of ART services for the creation of saviour children does not mean that all potential uses of embryo selection technologies will eventually be permitted. As Sheldon and Wilkinson comment:

> Merely stating that saviour siblings are the first steps toward allowing parents to use embryo testing to choose other characteristics remains nothing more than unsubstantiated assertion.[64]

In this book I have argued that the use of ART services for the creation of saviour children is generally ethically acceptable and that the arguments based on the risks of harm in this context do not provide sufficient grounds for restricting reproductive choice. Given that regulatory policy is capable of restricting 'less desirable' uses of PGD techniques, the slippery slope argument provides no basis for limiting the accessibility of ART services for the creation of saviour children. Furthermore, from a harm-based perspective, as with the other arguments considered in this chapter, it is extremely difficult to ascertain the interests of those who object to the creation of saviour children on the basis of the slippery slope arguments. Even if it were possible to ascertain such interests, it is difficult to establish the extent to which the interests of such people would be thwarted or set back by allowing access to the technology for this purpose. Additionally, it is difficult to argue that other members of society will be 'wronged' by a family's decision to conceive a saviour child, as the concept of wrongdoing also requires some engagement of the interests of others.

## The Ethical Objections and Their Relevance to Parental Decision-Making

Although empirical research is lacking in relation to the potential harms that may befall saviour children conceived by way of ART, important research is emerging in relation to the views of clinicians and families concerning the ethical reasoning in this field. Kimberly Strong and others have undertaken an empirical research study that examines the attitudes of health professionals towards the creation of saviour children and contrasts this against the ethical objections

---

63 This is something that is also noted by de Wert (n 50). See Chapters 2 and 3 concerning the UK regulatory approach relevant to PGD and pre-implantation tissue-typing.

64 Sheldon and Wilkinson (n 38) 148.

outlined in the literature.[65] In this research study, health professionals caring for children who might benefit from haematopoietic stem cell transplant (HSCT) procedures, such as a bone marrow, peripheral blood or umbilical cord blood transplantations, were interviewed. Additionally, the researchers interviewed a number of families who have been faced with decisions about pursuing HSCT procedures for their sick children, to obtain their views on using ART services to conceive a saviour child. What is particularly interesting about this study is that the views of health professionals on the topic are very strongly linked to the ethical and theoretical arguments outlined in the bioethical literature, but that there is a strong disconnect between the bioethical reasoning and the views of families who might be faced with this issue.[66]

The study reveals that the health professionals interviewed focused predominantly on the harm-based arguments, in terms of the risks to the donor (particularly the psychological harms).[67] The health professionals also couched the risks of harm in terms of the commodification and 'means end' objections, or the slippery slope arguments.[68] This led the researchers to conclude that many of the views voiced by health professionals concerning the saviour child issue were gleaned from the literature on this topic.[69] Health professionals also frequently expressed the view that they were more comfortable with the practice of families using ART services to conceive saviour children in circumstances where they had not 'finished their family'.[70] However, in contrast to this, some of the health professionals interviewed in the study also acknowledged that a couple's decision about whether to extend their family is capable of change, particularly when faced with significant life events (such as a child's illness).[71] Some positive aspects of the process were also identified, such as the prospect that the creation of a saviour child might result in a strong bond between the two children.[72]

The views of the families who took part in the study were different to those expressed by the health professionals. Of the 10 parents interviewed in the study, none expressed concern about the risk that the saviour child might be treated as a commodity or that he or she might potentially suffer psychological harm.[73] Instead, parents focused on the utility of their decision, which is an aim

---

65 Strong and others (n 1).
66 ibid. 20.
67 ibid. 18.
68 ibid. 17.
69 ibid. 17.
70 ibid.
71 ibid. 18.
72 ibid. 18–19.
73 ibid. 19.

of achieving the best outcome for their children.[74] Interviews with the parents also revealed that they are often reluctant to judge other families facing the same issues, and instead empathise with such families rather than rely on moral and ethical reasoning to cast judgment.[75] The researchers also note that the parents interviewed in the study formed the view that 'outsiders' could not judge their circumstances, as they lack the experience to fully understand their situation; thus, parents considering other families in the same circumstances suggest that there is a sense of immunity from moral judgment.[76] Interestingly, some parents expressed the view that it is more important to judge parents on how they care for their children, rather than on their motivations for having them.[77]

There are a number of interesting points that can be taken from this research study for the purpose of evaluating the significance of the ethical and theoretical arguments and how these should guide the regulatory position. Notably, the research study is limited in terms of its implications, based on the small size of the study. Nevertheless, it is the first empirical study of its kind and therefore provides a valuable insight on how the arguments outlined in the bioethical literature are relevant to those faced with such decisions.

Fundamentally, the ethical concerns outlined in the literature appear to be influencing (or even perhaps determining) the views of health professionals who work in the field of HSCT procedures. This is significant, as professionals in this field have a role to play in advising families about their treatment options, which might include the legitimate decision to conceive a saviour child.[78] Consequently, the authors of the study assert that the arguments pursued in the bioethical literature impact negatively on the views of health professionals.[79] Thus, it is stated that the 'ethical debates … have fostered a level of controversy that functions to keep [the option of conceiving a saviour child] on the fringes of "established" medical practice', and therefore these arguments 'are used (illegitimately) to assert that PGD for HLA [human leukocyte antigen] typing is either not clinically indicated or that the harms of this practice outweigh its benefits'.[80] Strong and others therefore argue that health professionals are reluctant to advise families of the option of conceiving a saviour child, which means that this legitimate information about this option is being withheld.[81]

---

74  ibid. 19.

75  ibid.

76  ibid. 20.

77  ibid. 20. Interestingly, this perspective is similar to the view put forward by Devolder; see n 45 and accompanying text.

78  ibid.

79  ibid. 20.

80  ibid.

81  ibid.

## Conclusion

It is interesting to observe that the majority of the bioethical literature relevant to the issue of conceiving a saviour child has sought to argue *against* the ethical and philosophical objections outlined above. None of the arguments examined in this chapter provide convincing reasons to justify the imposition of restrictions on reproductive liberty. The arguments explored above are focused on issues of morality or objections based on how the conduct of some members of society might be morally offensive. Importantly, as outlined in Chapter 4, given that the notion of reproductive liberty is afforded protection as an interest in its own right, interference with that interest requires strong justification. In Chapter 5, it was further explained that a justificatory basis for interfering with this interest might be established where harm to others is likely to ensue without regulatory intervention, subject to a number of guiding principles. Therefore, what might be a less problematic proposition to accept in relation to the arguments explored in this chapter, is that they provide us with a strong basis for explaining why a particular reproductive decision in a given case is, or is not, ethically sound, or at least, might help explain why such conduct is morally problematic. These arguments, however, do not help to establish that reproductive liberty can be legitimately restricted in circumstances where a family is seeking to utilise ART services to conceive a saviour child.

Finally, it is important to note that although the theoretical and moral issues have been explored extensively in the bioethical literature, this body of literature has also arguably swayed the outlook of some health professionals (and perhaps regulators) towards viewing the creation of saviour children as an illegitimate option for the treatment of a child in need of a HSCT procedure.[82] It cannot be denied that this body of moral and ethical reasoning has played a role in shaping the debate since the first reported saviour child was purposely conceived using ART services in October 2000. However, while the bioethical literature might provide a valuable reflective tool for exploring the ethical boundaries of reproductive decision-making, it does not assist us in a regulatory sense, where there is a need to justify coercive or prohibitive regulatory policies. As I explain in the following chapter, the regulatory approaches in Australia and the UK are in need of review and reform, based on the fact that some of the ethical principles outlined in this chapter are unjustifiably prioritised at the expense of the liberty of families seeking to create a tissue-matched donor child using ART services.

---

82 ibid.

Chapter 8

# Regulating Assisted Reproductive Technology Services for the Creation of Saviour Children: A Way Forward

## Introduction

Throughout this book I have argued that the accessibility of assisted reproductive technology (ART) services for the purpose of conceiving a saviour child should not be subject to restrictive policies which are underpinned by illegitimate moral, ethical and harm-based objections. Nevertheless, as outlined in Chapters 2 and 3, the regulatory frameworks in place in Australia and the United Kingdom (UK) are unjustifiably restrictive. Thus, legislation in a number of Australian jurisdictions limits access to ART services. Additionally, even where there are no statutory restrictions imposed upon access to services, guidelines on the topic arguably provide clinicians and ART centres with the discretion to refuse services based on moral and ethical grounds, or because they disagree with the motivation that is driving parents to conceive a saviour child. This final chapter of the book draws together the arguments developed in the previous chapters to evaluate the current regulatory frameworks in place in Australia and the UK. After analysing these frameworks, I will conclude by suggesting a way forward in terms of regulation on this issue.

## Evaluating the UK Position: An Overly Restrictive Approach?

A useful starting point for drawing together the regulatory and normative issues outlined in this book is to evaluate the UK position.[1] As discussed in Chapter 3, statutory provisions were enacted in 2008 that limit the use of ART services

---

1 The arguments outlined in this section of the chapter have been published elsewhere: see Malcolm K Smith, 'The Human Fertilisation and Embryology Act 2008: Restrictions on the Creation of "Saviour Siblings" and the Relevance of the Harm Principle' (2013) 32 New Genetics and Society 154–70.

for the creation of a saviour child in the UK. Additionally, it was established that the Code of Practice issued by the Human Fertilisation and Embryology Authority (HFEA) contains detailed provisions relevant to the creation of saviour children. Notably, the guidance in the Code of Practice is more flexible in comparison to the statutory requirements, as the latter will require legislative reform should it be accepted that it is in need of reform. Schedule 2, para 1ZA(1)(d) of the Human Fertilisation and Embryology Act (1990) states that a licence to authorise embryo testing can be issued:

> In a case where a person ('the sibling') who is the child of the persons whose gametes are used to bring about the creation of the embryo (or of either of those persons) suffers from a serious medical condition which could be treated by umbilical cord blood stem cells, bone marrow or other tissue of any resulting child, establishing whether the tissue of any resulting child would be compatible with that of the sibling.

This effectively means that there are a number of statutory requirements that must be satisfied before a family will be permitted to use in vitro fertilisation (IVF) and pre-implantation genetic diagnosis (PGD) services to create a saviour child. Essentially, ART services for this purpose can only be provided where:

1. the condition of the existing sick child is treatable with umbilical cord blood stem cells, bone marrow or other tissue (excluding organs);
2. the existing sick child is suffering with a 'serious' condition;
3. the intended recipient of the tissue is a sibling.

These requirements are now analysed in turn.

### Requirement 1: Condition Must Be Treatable with Umbilical Cord Blood Stem Cells, Bone Marrow or 'Other Tissue'

In this context, reference to 'other tissue' of the resulting child does not include any whole organ of the child.[2] Although this first limitation might appear to exclude the possibility that a saviour child might act as an organ donor, it does not explicitly prohibit organ donation per se, as this is a matter that would have to be decided by considering the law of consent at the time of the proposed donation. For this reason, it can be said that the legislation prohibits the provision of ART services for the creation of a saviour child, if the parents demonstrate an intention – at the pre-conception stage – to harvest an organ from the prospective child once he or she is born. Essentially, the provision is

---

2 Human Fertilisation and Embryology Act 1990, sch 2, para 1ZA (4).

about determining the motives of the parents at the pre-conception stage in terms of their intentions for tissue harvesting.

Families intending only to harvest umbilical cord blood stem cells and/or blood products, will be largely unaffected by this aspect of the legislation (as long as the affected relative does not require an organ transplant). In such a case, as the family is not intending to harvest an organ from the saviour child, they satisfy this part of the legislation. Once a child is conceived, this provision has no bearing upon the legality of a proposed transplantation procedure; such an issue is governed by the human tissue legislation.

Nevertheless, there may be an extreme case where a family, prior to accessing ART services, intends to create a saviour child as a potential organ donor. In such a case, the family's intention would prevent them from accessing the technology in the UK. As discussed in Chapter 6, the state has a legitimate interest in protecting the welfare of children. This interest is likely to extend to protecting children from the harm that may result from the harvesting of organs (such as the harvesting of a kidney), as this would cause a child physical harm (and also potentially psychological harm). However, Stephen Wilkinson observes that while there may be certain circumstances – such as forced tissue removal or the harvesting of non-regenerative organs – that are regarded as clearly wrong, this does not necessarily mean that it makes it wrong to conceive a saviour child.[3] In Chapter 6, I argued that even if this potential harm can be linked to the parents' motives for conceiving the child, there are reasons of proximity that determine this link as causally insignificant. Importantly, concerns about risks of harm that might befall the child once born should be dealt with at the time that they arise. This means that the appropriate regulatory response to this specific risk of harm is the implementation of adequate safeguards to prevent children from being subjected to unjustifiable tissue harvesting procedures.[4] Consequently, the effect of this statutory restriction is disproportionate to its aim – it goes beyond the scope of merely protecting the future interests of prospective saviour children; if relied upon for the purpose of restricting liberty, this principle will prevent such children from ever gaining interests, as they will not be conceived.

---

3 Stephen Wilkinson, *Choosing Tomorrow's Children: The Ethics of Selective Reproduction* (OUP 2010) 116.

4 See Shih-Ning Then, 'The Legality of Tissue Transplants for the Benefit of Family Members in the UK and Australia: Implications for Saviour Siblings' (2009) 10 Medical Law International 23; Natalie Morrison and John Devereux, 'Child Saviours: Reconceiving the Legal Dimension' (2014) 22 Tort Law Review 9; Natalie Morrison and John Devereux, 'Child Saviours: Reconceiving the Ethical Dimension' (2014) 22 Tort Law Review 3.

In Chapter 6, I also argued that irrespective of how a child is conceived (whether naturally or as a result of ART services), all children are at risk of suffering harm in their lives.[5] Given that there is no general requirement to refrain from reproducing naturally – on the basis that any resulting child may suffer harm in the future – future risks of harm that can be prevented, or at least minimised by existing safeguards, should not be relied upon as a basis for restricting reproductive liberty. In the UK context, the Human Tissue Authority's (HTA) Code of Practice concerning donation of solid organs for transplantation states that:

> Children can be considered as living organ donors only in extremely rare circumstances. In accordance with common law and the Children Act 1989 … before the removal of a solid organ or part organ from a child for donation, court approval should be obtained.[6]

The implication of this approach is that a child would not be subjected to such an invasive medical procedure unless a court has deemed that it is in that child's best interests. Importantly, therefore, the potential harm from the harvesting of organs should be addressed by the law governing consent at the *time that donation becomes relevant*.

It is more likely, however, that this particular statutory restriction is also a response to some of the deontological objections (outlined in Chapter 7) which view the decision to select a child on the basis of his or her tissue type as inherently wrong, based on the parents' motivations.[7] Furthermore, in such circumstances, the family's decision appears to contradict the Kantian principle that we should not treat others as a means to an end. As noted in Chapter 7, the strength of these arguments is questionable, particularly when used as a basis for restricting reproductive liberty. Nevertheless, some commentators may argue that in cases where the parents intend to create a child as an organ donor (compared to cases where the parents intend to harvest only blood products or tissue), the ethical force of the deontological objections is worthy of greater recognition. However, these restrictions cannot be justified from a harm-based perspective, given that the law is capable of protecting children from serious harm that might result from organ donation.

---

5 David Benatar, *Better Never to Have Been: The Harm of Coming into Existence* (OUP 2006) 29.

6 Human Tissue Authority, *Code of Practice 2: Donation of Solid Organs for Transplantation* (2014) 11. See also, Human Tissue Authority, *Code of Practice 6: Donation of Allogeneic Bone Marrow and Peripheral Blood Stem Cells for Transplantation* (2014) 14–15.

7 See Chapter 7, pp. 171–176.

*Requirement 2: Reference to the Existing Child's Illness*

Following the 2008 statutory reforms to the UK legislation, there is also now a requirement that the intended recipient of tissue is suffering from a 'serious' condition. The term 'serious' is not defined in the legislation, nor is it defined in the HFEA's Code of Practice.[8] It is interesting to observe that at the beginning of the UK legislative reform process, it was intended that the use of the technology be limited to those cases where the child is suffering from a 'life-threatening' condition.[9] During the extensive reform process, the Joint Committee on the Human Tissue and Embryos (Draft) Bill advocated for the use of the term 'serious' instead, noting:

> [w]e recognise that this is a delicate area. However, given the Government's apparent acceptance of the principle of selecting for 'saviour siblings' we do not understand why the practice is limited to 'life-threatening' conditions capable of treatment using umbilical cord blood stem cells. We recommend that the draft Bill be amended to substitute 'serious' for 'life-threatening'.[10]

This change was intended to avoid a position that was viewed as too restrictive,[11] but there were no clear reasons put forward to justify why such a condition was required, except that it was a 'necessary safeguard'.[12] In one sense it could be argued that the terminology adopted is irrelevant; any legislative condition of this kind, which completely restricts access for those who do not fulfil the requirement, is unjustified. As I have argued in this book, it is the harm-based reasoning that provides us with a more compelling basis for restricting liberty. The requirement that the existing sick child is suffering from a 'serious' condition does not appear to be relevant to the potential harm that may ensue in the absence of such a restriction – an argument that I explore below.

It is also important to note that in the absence of clear definitions for the terms adopted in this provision, the use of the term 'serious' may pose

---

8 However, there are a number of factors stipulated within the Code of Practice that will be relevant to considering the 'seriousness' of the existing child's condition: Human Fertilisation and Embryology Authority, *Code of Practice* (8th edn, 2009) guidance note 10.23.

9 United Kingdom, House of Lords, Parliamentary Debates 21 January 2008, 11–12 (Lord Lloyd of Berwick).

10 House of Lords, Joint Committee on the Human Tissue and Embryos (Draft) Bill, *Human Tissue and Embryos (Draft) Bill – Volume I: Report* (2007) [199].

11 United Kingdom, House of Lords, *Parliamentary Debates* 21 January 2008, 26 (Baroness Finlay of Llandaff).

12 United Kingdom, House of Lords, *Parliamentary Debates* 21 January 2008, 13–14 (Baroness O'Cathain of the Barbican).

difficulties. In some cases the affected child may not be severely ill but may nevertheless have a 'serious' illness. In other cases, the affected child might have a 'serious' condition and also be very ill. What is particularly interesting to note is that it is possible to argue that in cases where the affected child is diagnosed with a less than serious condition, the risk of harm to the saviour child is potentially *less* severe (although this will not always be the case). For example, in cases where the sick child has a less than 'serious' condition, the saviour child might be less likely to suffer harm. In such circumstances, he or she is *less* likely to be subjected to repeated donation procedures due to the fact that the affected child's condition might be more easily treated. This leaves the question: why should a couple be prevented from utilising the technology in circumstances where their child is suffering from a condition that is regarded as less than 'serious'?

The statutory requirement that the sick child be suffering with a serious condition is likely to reflect the view that the creation of a saviour child is justifiable in circumstances where there is an overall *benefit* for the existing sibling or the family; in cases where there are 'more convincing' reasons underpinning the decision to conceive a saviour child (based on the seriousness of the affected child's condition), there appears to be greater utility to support the decision. This implies that a family's decision to conceive a saviour child cannot be justified in cases where the affected child is suffering with a less than serious condition. However, this alone does not justify *prohibiting* access to the technology altogether. Essentially, although the concept of utility might provide further *support* for a particular reproductive decision, it does not help to provide a basis upon which we should feel justified in placing complete restrictions on the accessibility of the technology.

According to the pre-conception welfare assessment imposed under s 13(5) of the Human Fertilisation and Embryology Act 1990 (UK), the key factor of relevance is whether the welfare of the potential child (or another child of the family) will be adversely affected (that is, *harmed*). This assessment does not require an ART centre to determine that the existing sick child is suffering from a 'serious' condition. And if we consider the fact that an existing child of the family might suffer greatly if the parents' reproductive liberty is curtailed, then this adds further weight to their case for accessing the technology.[13] This does not necessarily depend upon the condition of the existing sick child being classed as 'serious'. Moreover, there is a key distinction to be made between a line of reasoning that *supports* or *adds weight to* a particular family's case to access ART services for the creation of a saviour child (for example, based

---

13 This view accords with the relational approach put forward by Michelle Taylor-Sands, *Saviour Siblings: A Relational Approach to the Welfare of the Child in Selective Reproduction* (Routledge 2013).

on the concept of utility), and arguments that provide a compelling basis upon which we are justified in *prohibiting* a particular family from accessing the technology altogether. Perhaps ethical reasoning such as this might be relevant to determining the extent to which a family should receive financial support from the state for carrying through their reproductive decision when there are limited state resources available (if at all).[14] However, it should not be used to justify prohibiting access to such services. The requirement to consider the condition of the affected child amounts to the implication that one child's existence is contingent upon the extent of another child's suffering, or at least in cases where the child is not yet severely ill, the potential suffering of a child.

One view that might be relied upon to object to my line of reasoning above is that, from a harm-based perspective, children created for the purpose of curing a sick child with a less than 'serious' condition may be at a greater risk of psychological harm.[15] This argument rests on the view that a saviour child might be adversely affected if there are 'less compelling' reasons to justify the motives for his or her conception, particularly when compared to another set of circumstances where a more 'compelling' reason for the child's existence is present (for example, the sibling had a life-threatening or serious condition). However, as I discussed in Chapter 6, this type of argument is based on a speculative risk of harm and has been described by other commentators as unconvincing, thus requiring more weighty evidence in this regard to justify a restriction on reproductive choice.[16]

The condition of the existing child is not a factor that should be relied upon by regulators to limit the accessibility of ART services, irrespective of whether the existing child's condition is not serious or life threatening. Where regulatory policy prioritises the welfare of prospective children who are conceived by way of ART services, the harm posed by conceiving a child to treat a person who has a less than 'serious' condition, or an illness that is not life threatening, is not necessarily increased compared to those cases where this requirement is fulfilled.

---

14 There may be merit in the view that state funding of ART services for families seeking to create a saviour child might provide greater value for money in terms of publicly funded health care services, compared to the ongoing cost of treating a seriously ill child who requires, for example, regular blood transfusions and/or bone marrow or other tissue transplantation procedures (assuming, of course, that a saviour child is successfully conceived and that a subsequent transplant to the sick child is successful). This argument is purely speculative as I am not aware of any published research that confirms this view.

15 See Chapter 6, pp. 145–148.

16 Sally Sheldon and Stephen Wilkinson, 'Hashmi and Whitaker: An Unjustifiable and Misguided Distinction?' (2004) 12 Medical Law Review 137, 155; see also, Stephen Wilkinson (n 3) 113.

*Requirement 3: The Relationship between the Saviour Child and
the Recipient*

The third limitation imposed under the UK legislation is that the intended recipient of blood or tissue products must be a sibling of the saviour child. Arguably, this restriction has been adopted from the policy developed by the HFEA prior to the statutory reforms in 2008, which determined that it was not permissible to use IVF and PGD services to create a saviour child where the intended recipient of tissue is a parent.[17] The Ethics Committee of the HFEA had observed that in cases where the intended recipient of tissue is a parent, the purpose 'appears *prima facie* to be morally less acceptable than selecting an embryo to provide tissue to treat a sibling, as it seems to replace concern for another with concern for oneself'.[18]

There is no evidence to suggest that children created for the benefit of other family members are at risk of being subjected to a *greater* level of harm than in cases where the recipient of tissue is a sibling. And the assertion that such conduct might be morally objectionable does not necessarily provide a sound basis for restricting the liberty of families seeking to conceive a saviour child for someone other than a sibling of the prospective child. Colin Gavaghan notes that the HFEA's Ethics Committee seemed to conflate conduct that was morally questionable with conduct that was morally condemnable.[19] As before, the objections raised against the creation of saviour children for relatives other than siblings, are based on speculation and are therefore difficult to address.

One reason that might be put forward to justify the imposition of such a restriction is that the clinical justification for conceiving a tissue donor for a relative other than a sibling is not compelling. The probability of success for haematopoietic stem cell transplantation (HSCT) procedures varies depending on the relationship between the donor and recipient. Thus, the success rate of HSCT procedures is far higher for HLA-identical *sibling* donations.[20] As human leukocyte antigen (HLA) type is inherited from both parents, it is not possible for a child to be an *identical* HLA match to one parent (or other relative). Therefore,

---

17 Colin Gavaghan, *Defending the Genetic Supermarket: Law and Ethics of Selecting the Next Generation* (Routledge-Cavendish 2007) 160–1; see Human Fertilisation and Embryology Authority Ethics Committee, *Ethical Issues in the Creation and Selection of Preimplantation Embryos to Produce Tissue Donors* (2001) <http://www.hfea.gov.uk/docs/ELC_5_july03.pdf> accessed 29 November 2014.

18 ibid. [2.21].

19 Gavaghan (n 17) 160–1.

20 Claudio Anasetti, 'What Are the Most Important Donor and Recipient Factors Affecting the Outcome of Related and Unrelated Allogeneic Transplantation?' (2008) 21 Best Practice & Research Clinical Haematology 691, 694–5.

creating a child for the purpose of treating a parent or other relative does not necessarily provide a significant medical benefit that could not be achieved from searching other existing family members (or beyond), as the HLA type of the child will never be an identical match to a non-sibling relative. On this basis, it *might* be possible for a parent or other relative to undergo a HSCT procedure with tissue from a related or non-related donor with an equal chance of the transplantation procedure succeeding (depending on the availability of blood and tissue products and whether there is a suitable donor available). The medical reasons therefore have the potential to weaken the arguments in favour of allowing access to IVF and PGD for tissue typing in cases where the intended recipient is not a sibling. However, even in light of the medical factors outlined above, permitting families access to ART services for the creation of a saviour child in circumstances where the intended recipient is someone other than a sibling does not necessarily increase the risk of harm to the prospective child. This is an overly restrictive limitation.

## Australian Assisted Reproductive Technology Regulatory Policy Concerning the Creation of Saviour Children: Further Factors of Concern

The criticisms outlined above concerning the UK legislative restrictions are equally applicable to the Australian regulatory framework, although the approach in Australia is arguably more flexible based on the fact that the requirements are set out in guidelines rather than legislation. As established in Chapter 3,[21] the National Health and Medical Research Council's *Ethical Guidelines on the Use of Assisted Reproductive Technology in Clinical Practice and Research* (2007) impose similar restrictions in the Australian context to those outlined above. For example, the requirement that the intended recipient of tissue is a sibling and that the medical condition of the sibling must be 'life-threatening' is very similar to the position under the UK legislation.[22] Therefore, my arguments against these restrictive conditions (outlined above in the context of the UK approach) are equally relevant here.[23] However, under the Australian framework there are a number of further limitations imposed, which also require analysis.

---

21 See Chapter 3, pp. 67–68.

22 National Health and Medical Research Council, *Ethical Guidelines on the Use of Assisted Reproductive Technology in Clinical Practice and Research* (2007) [12.3].

23 I acknowledge that the term 'life-threatening' under the Australian approach is likely to be more restrictive than the term 'serious' which is adopted in the UK legislation. However, as argued above, either term is unjustifiable.

## The Motives of the Couple Seeking Access to Assisted Reproductive Technology Services to Conceive a Saviour Child

In the Australian context, an ethics committee must be satisfied that those seeking to conceive a saviour child want to have another child as an addition to their family and not merely as a source of tissue for the existing child.[24] As discussed in Chapter 7, the obligation to consider the parents' motives in conceiving a saviour child appears to be aimed at addressing some of the deontological objections. It was established that the motives of parents in conceiving children are not necessarily relevant to assessing whether a prospective child will be at risk of harm once he or she is born. It was also acknowledged that parental motivation for conceiving children is often mixed and in some cases non-existent. Importantly, parents are normally judged on their attitudes towards children and not necessarily on their motives for conceiving them.[25] Given that all individuals or couples seeking access to ART services are required to satisfy the pre-conception welfare assessment, as discussed below, this should be the only relevant consideration when determining whether ART services should be provided for the purpose of conceiving a saviour child.

Some commentators have taken this principle a step further, by suggesting that couples seeking to conceive a saviour child should undergo psychological evaluation.[26] The reasoning behind this proposition is that such a requirement is necessary for establishing that the child is not at risk of exploitation. Wolf and others argue that:

> The donor child is at lifelong risk of exploitation, of being told that he or she exists as an insurance policy and tissue source for the sibling, of being repeatedly subjected to testing and harvesting procedures, of being used this way no matter how severe the psychological and physical burden, and of being pressure, manipulated, or even forced over protest.[27]

The conclusions drawn in the above extract are not proportionate to the risks of harm in this context,[28] which are regarded as speculative and uncertain.

---

24 National Health and Medical Research Council (n 22) [12.3.1].

25 See Katrien Devolder, 'Preimplantation HLA Typing: Having Children to Save Our Loved Ones' (2005) 31 Journal of Medical Ethics 582, 583–4.

26 Susan M Wolf, Jeffrey P Kahn, and John E Wagner, 'Using Preimplantation Genetic Diagnosis to Create a Stem Cell Donor: Issues, Guidelines & Limits' (2003) 31 Journal of Law, Medicine & Ethics 327, 333.

27 ibid.

28 Arguably, the imposition of such a requirement would also be an unjustified imposition on a couple's reproductive privacy: it would be unquestionable to subject

Furthermore, parents' authority to make decisions on behalf of their children extend only as far as is necessary to promote the child's best interests.[29] Additionally, the possibility of 'exploitation' in this context is discordant with the views of families faced with a decision about whether to conceive a saviour child.[30] Even if this concern is accepted as legitimate, it is a matter that should be safeguarded under the law of consent, so that children's interests are protected from exploitation in the context of tissue donation. Perhaps a compromise on this aspect of regulation is to expect that parents demonstrate a willingness to support and safeguard the interests of any children who may be born following the provision of ART services. Such an approach is a matter that can be determined within the boundaries of the pre-conception welfare assessment more generally.

The requirement for ART centres and/or ethics committees to screen the motives of parents is not justified from a harm-based perspective. This process is not necessarily a predictor of harm to the child. Moreover, as noted by Strong and others, 'parents' motives for having children are largely irrelevant to public policy debates'.[31] Interestingly, the former Infertility Treatment Authority (ITA) in Victoria sought legal advice concerning this requirement, which stipulated that it is likely to be difficult to accurately determine the motivation of parents 'faced with a terminally ill child, and a desire to complete their family'.[32] Thus, such requirement is arguably disingenuous and should not be considered as a relevant requirement within the regulatory landscape.[33]

---

those who procreate naturally to such assessment in order to ascertain their motives. See Emily Jackson, 'Conception and the Irrelevance of the Welfare Principle' (2002) 177 Modern Law Review 176–203; Emily Jackson, 'Rethinking the Pre-conception Welfare Principle' in Kirsty Horsey and Hazel Biggs (eds), *Human Fertilisation and Embryology: Reproducing Regulation* (Routledge-Cavendish 2006) 47.

29 *Secretary, Department of Health and Community Services (NT) v JWB and SMB (Marion's Case)* (1992) 175 CLR 218.

30 Kimberly A Strong and others, 'It's Time to Reframe the Savior Sibling Debate' (2011) 2 AJOB Primary Research 13. See also Chapter 7, pp. 182–183.

31 ibid. 22.

32 Infertility Treatment Authority, *Tissue Typing in Conjunction with Preimplantation Genetic Diagnosis: Interim Guidelines* (2007) 3.

33 Emily Jackson has evaluated the general pre-conception welfare principle and has also argued that the principle is disingenuous – similar reasoning can be applied in relation to the requirement to analyse the parents' motivation in the tissue-typing context. See n 28.

*Conceiving a Saviour Child: An Option of Last Resort?*

The final requirement outlined under the Australian framework that should be removed from regulatory policy is the need for ethics committees to establish that there are no other means available for treating the condition of the sick child. This approach appears to be aimed at concerns that the saviour child will be conceived merely as a means to an end – reasoning that was examined in Chapter 7 and dismissed as largely unjustified for the purpose of adopting prohibitive regulation. As noted by Strong and others, the option to conceive a saviour child is one that can be considered where a transplant procedure is not needed urgently and no suitable donor can be found.[34] This suggests that not all treatment options for the sick child would have been explored at the time a decision is made to purposely conceive a saviour child. Furthermore, these researchers argue that the ethical debate relevant to the creation of saviour children needs to be reframed so that the option of conceiving a saviour child using ART services is viewed by health professionals and regulators as a legitimate treatment option for children in need of a transplantation procedure.[35] This is a view that should also be adopted in regulatory policy relevant to the topic.

It could also be argued that the 'option of last resort' requirement may encourage 'gatekeepers' of ART services to assume that parents have not taken legitimate steps in attempting to do the best by their sick children, perhaps implying that they have not sought out suitable options for treatment before embarking upon the costly and highly stressful path of IVF. Such an assumption might be extremely damaging for families who are dealing with the treatment of a relative who has a potentially fatal condition. This requirement might also be viewed as an implication that families are willing to embark upon the IVF process frivolously, without giving sufficient thought to implications of their decision. In contrast to this view, it might be argued that parents who are willing to go to such lengths to help their existing child are demonstrating a significant commitment to furthering the welfare of their child(ren) and their family more generally.

One further objection against this restrictive requirement is that if families are obliged to wait until the creation of a saviour child (as a source of tissue) becomes an option of last resort, the prognosis and overall benefit for the existing sick child might be drastically impaired by this stage. Thus, transplantation of tissue – such as umbilical cord blood stem cells or bone marrow – at an earlier stage of the child's illness, or at least prior to a significant deterioration in the child's condition, might potentially avoid a more bleak prognosis for the sick child. Early treatment might not be an option if families are required to explore

---

34 Strong and others (n 30) 13.
35 ibid.

all other treatment options before conceiving a saviour child. Moreover, as discussed above concerning the 'seriousness' of the affected child's condition in the context of the UK position, conceiving a saviour child in circumstances where the existing sick child's condition is not 'serious' does not necessarily suggest that the saviour child is at an increased risk of harm. To the contrary, it might be possible to argue that the risk of harm to a prospective saviour child is decreased if he or she is conceived before all other means of treatment have been explored. A transplantation procedure from an identically matched sibling donor at an early stage of the child's illness – if successful – might potentially avoid the need for more invasive tissue harvesting procedures in the long run.

## Accessibility of Assisted Reproductive Technology Services

One of the most important aspects of the regulatory landscape that is in urgent need of reform is the imposition of statutory eligibility criteria in some Australian jurisdictions. In Chapters 2 and 3, it was established that in Victoria, South Australia and Western Australia, participants are not eligible for treatment procedures unless they are either medically infertile or at risk of transmitting a genetic disease or disorder when conceiving naturally. The result is that some families seeking to create a saviour chid are precluded from accessing services. Thus, families who require access to create a saviour child but who are not at risk of transmitting a genetic condition when conceiving naturally, are unable to access IVF and PGD in those jurisdictions. Notably, Victoria took steps to reform the restrictions on access by implementing new eligibility criteria under the 2008 legislative framework.[36] Although the reformed legislation does not explicitly permit access to ART services for the purpose of conceiving a saviour child, the legislation does provide for the Patient Review Panel to grant access to services in certain circumstances where prospective participants do not meet the statutory eligibility criteria as set out on the face of the legislation.[37] As discussed in Chapter 3, this could potentially encompass a determination of whether a family should be given access to ART services for the creation of a saviour child.[38] Although this is a move in the right direction, this approach is still nevertheless extremely restrictive. It requires those families who do not meet the statutory eligibility criteria to jump through extra hurdles in circumstances where different families – who possess similar motives for conceiving a saviour child – are able to access ART services without impediment.[39]

---

36 See Assisted Reproductive Treatment Act 2008 (Vic), s 10(2). See also Chapter 3, pp. 55–58.

37 Assisted Reproductive Treatment Act 2008 (Vic), s 85(e).

38 See Chapter 3, pp. 55–58.

39 See Chapter 3, p. 58.

It was also determined that the imposition of statutory eligibility criteria effectively precludes certain classes of people from gaining access to services and that some commentators have argued the state has no legitimate interest in restricting the accessibility of ART services by imposing requirements that amount to 'parental suitability' testing.[40] Commentators have argued that such restrictions are unjustified based on the view that prospective parents are not generally required to fulfil parental suitability assessments or required to justify their reproductive decisions when conceiving naturally. Interestingly, this line of reasoning was also adopted in a consultation document published by the New South Wales Health Department during its review of ART regulation. It was stated that a restrictive approach to the issue of access is not justifiable because:

> ... it is not the role of legislation to screen out 'good' prospective parents from 'bad' prospective parents. The law does not impose any restrictions upon individuals in the general community who wish to become parents. Indeed, it is generally considered a fundamental right of individuals to be able to have children and form families as they choose.

> ... The role of the legislature has not been to make rules regarding classes of persons who may or may not become parents (as this is not necessarily a predictor of harm) but to make rules to safeguard the rights of individual children whose welfare has been compromised.[41]

Similarly, the report of the HFEA's consultation on the pre-conception welfare principle emphasised that 'there is now a presumption to provide treatment, unless there is evidence that any child born to an individual or couple, or any existing child of their family, would face a risk of serious harm'.[42] I have argued in this book that the interest in liberty leans towards a presumption in favour of unrestricted reproductive decision-making for those seeking access to ART services. This reasoning should apply equally in the context of utilising ART services for the creation of saviour children. This inevitably

---

40 See Emily Jackson 'Conception and the Irrelevance of the Welfare Principle' (n 28); Emily Jackson, 'Rethinking the Pre-conception Welfare Principle' (n 28). This argument excludes considerations relating to how resources funded by the state should be distributed between members of society.

41 New South Wales Department of Health, *Consultation Draft, Assisted Reproductive Technology Bill 2003, Information Guide* (November 2003) 4.3.

42 Human Fertilisation and Embryology Authority, *Tomorrow's Children: Report of the Policy Review of Welfare of the Child Assessments in Licensed Assisted Conception Clinics* (2005) 1.

also requires some jurisdictions that adopt a system of licensing concerning this specific use of PGD services, to remove this unnecessary hurdle so that licensed centres are permitted to screen embryos for the purpose of establishing tissue type without having to gain case-by-case approval from the statutory regulatory body.

As a starting point, regulatory policy on this topic should prioritise the interest in reproductive liberty. Legislation should not impose a criterion that precludes access to ART services for the creation of saviour children. Furthermore, given that the accessibility of ART services can be restricted even where there are no statutory eligibility criteria imposed, policy should explicitly prioritise this presumptive position so that 'gatekeepers' do not unjustifiably restrict their services and that families are not required to convince clinicians or ethics committees that they possess legitimate motives for utilising the technology. This presumption is rebuttable only in cases where there is *evidence* to suggest that a risk of serious harm will result to the prospective child or to other members of the family. The relevant harm arguments are summarised below.

## A Way Forward for Regulating Assisted Reproductive Technology Services for the Creation of Saviour Children

What can essentially be taken from the arguments outlined so far in this chapter, is that the prescriptive and prohibitive regulatory approaches currently in place in Australia and the UK concerning the use of ART services for the creation of saviour children should be revoked (or repealed in the context of legislation). Essentially, the only aspect of the current regulatory framework – specific to the creation of saviour children – that should be retained, is the need to consider whether the provision of ART services is contrary to the welfare of the prospective child or existing children of the family. This effectively means that the assessment in relation to the prospective child's interests (and any other relevant interests) falls under the general pre-conception welfare assessment. Although there is a growing body of literature on the issue of whether there is any place for the pre-conception welfare principle in the general sphere of ART regulation, it is unlikely that the principle will be abandoned at any point in the foreseeable future. A pragmatic response is to therefore acknowledge that this principle will continue to play a key role in the sphere of ART regulation. This general principle is capable of encompassing the welfare concerns relevant to the conception of saviour children, while facilitating a more liberal approach to parental decision-making in this context.

## A Case-by-Case Welfare Assessment

Given that the focus of the pre-conception welfare assessment is to determine the potential harm when it is contemplated that ART services will be provided, the risk can be ascertained by reference to the individual circumstances of the family, as outlined below. Importantly, the application of the welfare principle in the saviour child context should be supplemented by policy guidance so that ART centres are able to establish genuine factors of concern relating to the prospective child's welfare. In other words, this will seek to prevent clinicians or other 'gatekeepers' from relying on illegitimate ethical reasoning to prevent families from accessing ART services for this purpose. Without such guidance, there is room for significant inconsistency between 'gatekeepers' when determining whether there are genuine grounds to invoke the welfare principle for the purpose of denying access to services.[43]

Fundamentally, the purpose of the case-by-case welfare assessment is to identify whether there are any particular factors that increase the risk of harm to a particular child in a given case. At the pre-conception stage, there is also an opportunity to establish measures that might assist the family in terms of potentially minimising any risk from occurring. This approach can be supported based on the following reasoning, which was outlined in Chapters 5 and 6:

1. Given that the *risk* of harm to a saviour child cannot be completely dismissed (even if the risk is low) *some* regulatory response appears to be justified, particularly as the risk of harm concerns the prospective child's welfare interests. However, this regulatory response should not be restrictive.

2. A presumption in favour of liberty should be the starting point for determining the question of access to ART services for the creation of a saviour child. If there are concerns in relation to the welfare of the prospective child, it should be made clear to 'gatekeepers' that this does not justify denying access to services – there may be other means available for attempting to minimise any risk of harm.

3. The risks of harm outlined in the debate generally are speculative, as there is no evidence to substantiate them. Therefore, such risks cannot be regarded as serious enough to justify a complete prohibition on access

---

43 This view can be supported by empirical research concerning the inconsistencies discovered between ART services providers, in terms of how law and policy is applied 'in the best interests of the child': Rachel Thorpe and others, 'In the Best Interests of the Child? Regulating Assisted Reproductive Technologies and the Well-being of Offspring in Three Australian States' 26 International Journal of Law, Policy and the Family 259.

to ART services for the creation of saviour children (for example, by way of statutory eligibility criteria that preclude access for some families).

4. Although the risks of harm to a prospective saviour child are small, it is possible that the risks might increase or decrease, depending on the individual circumstances of the family. A case-by-case welfare assessment takes account of this, so that the circumstances of each individual family can be considered to determine whether there are factors that pose a risk of harm, rather than relying on general ethical arguments that have no application to individual cases (although it should acknowledged that this assessment can never predict the risks of harm with certainty).

5. ART centres should also ensure that they provide families with sufficient information and appropriate counselling alongside the pre-conception welfare assessment, so that the risks can be explored with families and strategies can be suggested in an attempt to *minimise* any risks of harm (this is explained further below). This takes account of the further guiding principles relevant to the regulatory response under the Harm Principle.[44]

6. Importantly, the case-by-case approach does not require regulators to implement burdensome measures to evaluate the risk(s) of harm for each request to access pre-implantation tissue-typing services, as ART service providers are already required to assess the welfare of prospective children before providing ART services.

As there are significant burdens involved for families who embark upon this process, it is also important that health professionals and ART service providers adopt a fair and consistent approach when determining whether access to services should be provided or denied. There may be a range of individual circumstances that contribute towards an assessment of whether the risks of harm to a child conceived as a tissue donor are sufficient to justify restricting access to services. A family seeking access to ART services with the aim of conceiving a saviour child will have to consider and deal with many of the following factors:

- the illness of the existing sick child;
- the likely success of detecting a tissue-matched embryo in the IVF cycle (and where relevant, the likelihood of identifying an embryo for implantation that is of the correct tissue type and free from genetic disease);
- the likelihood of being able to use the blood stem cells from the umbilical cord (or bone marrow from the child) if a tissue-matched embryo is detected and a successful pregnancy established;

---

44 See Chapter 5, pp. 119–125.

- the success of the transplantation procedure in curing the sick child;
- the possibility of later remission for the sick child and the impact this may have on the family;
- the emotional and psychological implications in the event that the initial transplantation procedure is not successful, or in the event of a later remission;
- the health of the tissue-matched child if he or she acts as a donor;
- the emotional and psychological impact on the tissue-matched child when acting as a donor;
- the psychological impact on the donor child in discovering that he or she was (among other reasons) selected, conceived and born on the basis of his or her tissue type.

These factors will vary between families seeking to access tissue-typing services (and in some cases may vary significantly depending upon the medical condition of the affected child). Some of the above factors will be ascertainable at the pre-conception stage, even if it is not possible to predict such factors precisely. Importantly, although the circumstances facing the family may be relevant – at least to some extent – in determining the risk(s) of harm to a prospective saviour child, these factors should not be used as a 'checklist' for the purpose of conducting the welfare assessment. Instead, these factors should be used to explore the issues facing the family at the pre-conception stage – so that this can inform the relevant information that should be given to the family and the issues to be explored during counselling – so that this process might provide the family with strategies to help minimise the risks in question (even if this simply involves drawing attention to the fact that there are certain risks associated with their decision – such as the implications arising from subjecting children to tissue harvesting procedures – so that they are prepared to manage these risks if they arise at some point in the future).

### The Welfare Principle and its Application in the Saviour Child Context

As outlined above, the risks relevant to the creation of saviour children are not extraordinary and are therefore not worthy of a restrictive regulatory approach. The risk assessment in this context should simply fall within the scope of the welfare principle, as currently applied in the general sphere of ART services. This is not a radical suggestion for reform of the current framework, especially when considered in the light of recent trends concerning PGD regulation. Thus, most Australian jurisdictions have determined that PGD practices should be self-regulated by health professionals in accordance with ethical guidelines.[45]

---

45 See Chapter 2, pp. 33–36.

In terms of moving forward with regulation on this topic, the imposition of a welfare assessment in the saviour child context is not intended to give health professionals a discretionary power to make decisions about whether a family should or should not be granted access to services, based upon the health professional's own beliefs and values (although, as noted by Strong and others, health professionals could conscientiously object to providing services if this would be contrary to their own values or beliefs).[46] The role of the welfare assessment is to identify legitimate concerns that pose a risk of serious harm to the prospective child, while recognising that the notion of reproductive liberty is prioritised. Given the conclusions drawn in Chapters 6 and 7, a finding of a serious risk of harm is likely to be rare. Nevertheless, the guidance that is provided to ART centres and health professionals entrusted with this responsibility should outline a range of factors and principles to assist with the risk assessment – these factors should relate specifically to the risks associated with being conceived as a tissue donor. This policy approach is important, as it will provide a basis for consistency between decision-makers. It is fundamental that the decision to create a saviour child is presumed to rest with the couple.

The main purpose of the following section of this chapter is to establish the factors that should be regarded as relevant to the welfare assessment. The case-by-case approach proposed here is not significantly different to that outlined by the HFEA's Code of Practice in the UK, which similarly adopts the position that participants are *presumed* to be eligible to access ART services unless there is a 'serious' or 'significant' risk of harm to the child who will be born.[47] Importantly, however, it was established above that some of the requirements under the UK framework are overly restrictive and require reform.

## Assessing the Risk of Harm

In Chapter 5, it was established that determining the risk of harm requires a consideration of the probability of the harm occurring together with an assessment of the severity of the harm if it were to eventuate. As the circumstances of families who seek to conceive a saviour child by way of ART services are likely to vary to some degree, their differing circumstances might impact upon this harm assessment. The first stage is to therefore determine the factors that are relevant in terms of assessing the risk of harm in the saviour child context. The specific risks of harm – as outlined in Chapter 6 – are summarised below to clarify the extent to which they are relevant to the assessment.

---

46  Strong and others (n 30) 21.
47  See Human Fertilisation and Embryology Authority (n 8), guidance note 8.

*The physical risk of harm from the biopsy procedure*

As established in Chapter 6, the risk of physical harm from the embryo biopsy procedure is considered to be minimal, although recent evidence suggests that there is a need to monitor the long-term effects of PGD practices on children.[48] This risk factor is unlikely to vary between families seeking to access the technology for the purpose of determining the tissue type of embryos. Fundamentally, the same biopsy process is undertaken irrespective of the purpose of embryo testing. There appears to be no means of minimising this very small risk of harm occurring unless access to PGD services for this purpose is completely prohibited. As already established, such a response is disproportionate and would require a prohibitive approach in all cases where PGD is contemplated.[49] For these reasons, the physical risk of harm from the embryo biopsy procedure is not a factor that should be considered as relevant to the harm assessment undertaken as part of the welfare assessment.

*The risk of psychological harm to the child from being purposely selected as a tissue donor*

The probability and severity of psychological harm arising to the child will be difficult to clearly establish, but in some respects it could be argued that it might be commensurate with the seriousness of the family situation. For example, where a family health crisis is significantly serious (that is, the child is suffering from a very serious condition which has a major impact on the family unit), the probability of the child experiencing adverse psychological implications is likely to be increased. However, the severity of the psychological harm (if it were to eventuate) is far more difficult to predict. As discussed in Chapter 6, the psychological harm in this context is speculative and further research is needed to determine whether purposely conceiving a saviour child might result in psychological consequences for such children.

Although the speculative risk of psychological harm should not be relied upon to restrict access to ART services for the creation of a saviour child, it might be possible to suggest a number of strategies for the family to adopt, to potentially minimise the risk of such harm arising. This would ensure that reproductive liberty is left unrestricted, while also ensuring that steps are taken to prevent or minimise the risk of harm in question.

The potential psychological impact of acting as a tissue donor has been investigated by a number of researchers.[50] Given that there are often negative

---

48  See Chapter 6, pp. 136–140.

49  See Chapter 6, pp. 136–140.

50  Philip Cohen, 'Donor's Dread: Why do Children Who Help a Sick Sibling End up Depressed?' (1997) 55 New Scientist 20; Grace Chang and others, 'A Comparison

implications of such practices, this risk could be explored with the family at the pre-conception stage. A requirement could be imposed that compels service providers to provide information to families about such risks and to offer counselling for the purpose of exploring these potential risks. Raising these factors for consideration at the pre-conception stage may give the family an opportunity to fully consider the implications of their decision. It also gives families an opportunity to explore certain risk factors that they may not have contemplated prior to the counselling process. Fundamentally, early exploration of these issues might help to raise awareness of future risks so that the family can attempt to minimise the impact their decision has on the child once he or she is born and as he or she develops.

### The risk of physical harm from tissue harvesting procedures

As established in Chapter 6, it is possible to argue that the physical effects of tissue harvesting procedures performed on saviour children are capable of falling within Feinberg's definition of 'harming'.[51] However, for a number of reasons, I argued that even if this form of harm can be linked to the parents' motives for conceiving the child, there are reasons to conclude that the harmful consequences of such procedures are not causally linked to the reproductive decision that led to the child's conception.[52] For this reason, it is not a factor that should be considered as relevant to the pre-conception welfare assessment.

### The Relevance of the Further Guiding Principles

As established in Chapter 5, Feinberg argued that it is necessary to consider how any proposed regulatory response will impact on liberty and that measures intended to minimise or eliminate a risk of harm, should seek to preserve liberty where possible.[53] The number of people who are likely to utilise ART services for the purpose of conceiving a saviour child will be small. Nevertheless, a regulatory approach that imposes a blanket prohibition on

---

of Related and Unrelated Marrow Donors' (1998) 60 Psychosomatic Medicine 163; Kendra D MacLeod and others, 'Pediatric Sibling Donors of Successful and Unsuccessful Hematopoietic Stem Cell Transplants (HSCT): A Qualitative Study of Their Psychosocial Experience' (2003) 28 Journal of Pediatric Psychology 223; W Packman and others, 'Psychological Effects of Hematopoietic SCT on Pediatric Patients, Siblings and Parents: A Review' (2010) 45 Bone Marrow Transplantation 1134; B Pillay and others, 'The Psychosocial Impact of Haematopoietic SCT on Sibling Donors' (2012) 47 Bone Marrow Transplantation 1361.

51 See Chapter 6, pp. 144–145.

52 See Chapter 6, pp. 163–165.

53 Joel Feinberg, *The Moral Limits of the Criminal Law: Harm to Others* (OUP 1984) 193–8.

accessing ART services for this specific purpose will impact on *all* families who wish to conceive a saviour child. For this reason, restrictive statutory eligibility criteria should be removed so that access to ART services in this context is not overly restrictive. Similar reasoning can also be applied to justify the removal of the further restrictive conditions and requirements contained within the UK legislative framework and the Australian guidelines (outlined at the beginning of this chapter).

It can also be argued that my proposal to address the welfare concerns under the general scope of the pre-conception welfare principle is aimed at preserving reproductive liberty as much as possible. Intervention with reproductive decision-making would occur in only rare cases, and would require strong justification based on a risk of serious harm to the prospective child. As noted in the report of the Human Genome Research Project:

> The regulatory framework must be proportionate to the perceived harms or risks posed to justify the imposition of regulatory limits. When it is determined that regulation is necessary, regulatory measures should be kept to the minimum required in order to achieve the regulatory objective.[54]

The burden placed on regulators in terms of developing and maintaining policy for this specific use of PGD services might initially appear to be a burdensome measure, given that it will impact on only a very small number of people. However, regulatory policy in Australia and the UK already exists to address this specific use of PGD services. Updating these policies is a relatively straightforward task. Furthermore, the proposal to assess the welfare concerns relevant to the saviour child issue under the scope of the general welfare principle is not problematic or burdensome. Such an approach is a current feature of the regulatory frameworks in Australia and the UK. Therefore, the additional considerations relevant to the creation of saviour children can be easily integrated within the current regulatory approaches.

## Summarising the Proposed Approach

The proposal to consider the specific welfare concerns relevant to the creation of saviour children within the scope of the general pre-conception welfare principle is a proportionate regulatory response and is not overly burdensome. This approach prioritises the notion of reproductive liberty and aims to prevent unjustified limitation of reproductive liberty. To summarise, as part of the

---

54 Human Genome Research Project, *Choosing Genes for Future Children: The Regulatory Implications of Preimplantation Genetic Diagnosis* (2006 Dunedin) 306.

review process and in response to each request for tissue-typing services, the clinician or ART centre should consider:

- the individual circumstances of the family, including:
    - how the family circumstances might impact on the psychological development (if at all) of any child who is conceived as a source of tissue for an existing sick person;
    - the family's understanding of the risk of psychological harm in this context;
- that there may be strategies that can be adopted to minimise the risk of such harm occurring, and that in cases where the family is willing to adopt measures to learn about such risks and minimise them, then this might also decrease the risk in question (the appropriateness of measures such as the provision of adequate information and counselling to address this specific issue should be determined by the regulator);
- whether there is *evidence* to suggest that a child who will be born into a particular family as a tissue donor, is likely to suffer harm over and above that which can be reasonably expected (for example, there is evidence that the parents intend to exploit the child once born).

## Conclusion

In this book, I have outlined the current regulatory frameworks relevant to the delivery of ART services in Australia and the UK, with a particular focus on establishing how these frameworks impact on a family's decision to create a saviour child. The restrictions and limitations relevant to the use of this technology have been evaluated against the backdrop of a harm-focused approach, which is a central aspect of liberalism and an underlying theme in relation to many aspects of ART regulatory policy. I have also argued that the concept of reproductive liberty is worthy of respect and should be afforded presumptive priority under the regulatory framework. The harm-based objections relevant to the creation of saviour children have been described as the most influential in the debate and are often relied upon to justify a restrictive regulatory approach. However, I have challenged these harm-based objections and have argued that the interest in reproductive liberty should be prioritised. Moreover, I have also considered the wider ethical and moral concerns of relevance to the debate. Some of these wider concerns are clearly influential in terms of the regulatory landscape, as they underpin regulatory policy in this field. However, I have also argued against reliance upon the wider ethical reasoning as a basis for justifying restrictive policies in this field.

Based on the arguments developed in Chapters 6 and 7, I have evaluated the current regulatory approaches in Australia and the UK in this chapter. Ultimately, I have argued that it is necessary to revoke the specific aspects of current regulatory policy that address the use of ART services for the creation of saviour children and that the restrictive legislative provisions in place in the UK should be repealed. Additionally, I have proposed that the welfare assessment concerning prospective saviour children be undertaken as part of the pre-conception welfare principle more generally, and have outlined a number of key factors that should be used to guide 'gatekeepers' in this context. It has been argued that it is the role of responsible regulation to ensure that there are adequate safeguards in place to minimise harm to future children, where possible.[55] The regulatory response that I have proposed is intended to safeguard the interests of prospective saviour children, while ultimately preserving the interest in reproductive liberty.

Although the regulatory objective in each jurisdiction is likely to vary, my proposals for moving forward with regulation in this field can be incorporated relatively easily within each of the relevant frameworks. It is of fundamental importance that we acknowledge that in circumstances where reproductive choice reflects a decision of such significance and meaning for the family concerned, restrictions on liberty should only occur in very rare circumstances and must be based on a genuine need to safeguard the interests of others.

---

55 Taylor-Sands (n 13) 52.

# Bibliography

## Articles/Books/Reports

Alghrani A and Harris J, 'Reproductive Liberty: Should the Foundation of Families be Regulated?' (2006) 18 Child and Family Law Quarterly 191

Anasseti C, 'What Are the Most Important Donor and Recipient Factors Affecting the Outcome of Related and Unrelated Allogeneic Transplantation?' (2008) 21 Best Practice & Research Clinical Haematology 691

Baker DJ, 'The Harm Principle vs Kantian Criteria for Ensuring Fair, Principled and Just Criminalisation' (2008) 33 Australian Journal of Legal Philosophy 77

Beauchamp TL and Childress JF, *Principles of Biomedical Ethics* (5th edn, OUP 2001)

Beauchamp TL and Walters L, *Contemporary Issues in Bioethics* (6th edn, Wadsworth 2003)

Bellamy S, 'Lives to Save lives – The Ethics of Tissue Typing' (2005) 8 Human Fertility 5

Benatar D, *Better to Never Have Been: The Harm of Coming Into Existence* (OUP 2006)

Bennett B, 'Symbiotic Relationships: Saviour Siblings, Family Rights and Biomedicine' (2005) 19 Australian Journal of Family Law 195

Berlin I, *Two Concepts of Liberty* (Clarendon Press 1958)

Black J, 'Regulation as Facilitation: Negotiating the Genetic Revolution' 61 (1998) Modern Law Review 621

Boyle R and Savulescu J, 'Ethics of Using Preimplantation Genetic Diagnosis to Select a Stem Cell Donor for an Existing Person' (2001) 32 British Medical Journal 1240

Brazier M, *Medicine, Patients and the Law* (3rd edn, Penguin 2003)

Cairo MS and Wagner JE, 'Placental and/or Umbilical Cord Blood: An Alternative Source of Hematopoietic Stem Cells for Transplantation' (1997) 90 Blood 4673

Chalmers D, 'Professional Self-regulation and Guidelines in Assisted Reproduction' (2002) 9 Journal of Law and Medicine 414

Chang G and others, 'A Comparison of Related and Unrelated Marrow Donors' (1998) 60 Psychosomatic Medicine 163

Charlesworth M, *Bioethics in a Liberal Society* (CUP 1993)

Cohen P, 'Donor's Dread: Why do Children Who Help a Sick Sibling End up Depressed?' (1997) 55 New Scientist 20

Committee on Homosexual Offences and Prostitution, *Report of the Committee on Homosexual Offences and Prositution* (1957)

Cooper D, 'The Lockhart Review: Where Now for Australia?' (2006) 14 Journal of Law and Medicine 27

Deech R and Smajdor A, *From IVF to Immortality: Controversy in the Era of Reproductive Technology* (OUP 2007)

Demack A, *Report of the Special Committee Appointed by the Queensland Government to Enquire into the Laws Relating to Artificial Insemination, In Vitro Fertilisation and Other Related Matters* (Queensland Parliament 1984)

Department of Health (UK), *Reconfiguring the Department of Health's Arm's Length Bodies* (2004)

——, *Government Response to the Report from the House of Commons Science and Technology Committee: Human Reproductive Technologies and the Law* (2005)

——, *Review of the Human Fertilisation and Embryology Act: Proposals for Revised Legislation (Including Establishment of the Regulatory Authority for Tissue and Embryos)* (2006)

Devolder K, 'Preimplantation HLA Typing: Having Children to Save Our Loved Ones' (2005) 31 Journal of Medical Ethics 583

Diekema DS, 'Parental Refusals of Medical Treatment: The Harm Principle as Threshold for State Intervention' (2004) 25 Theoretical Medicine 243

Editorial, 'Preimplantation Donor Selection' (2004) 358 The Lancet

Epstein RA, 'The Harm Principle – And How it Grew' (1995) 45 University of Toronto Law Journal 369

European Society of Human Reproduction and Embryology Ethics Task Force, Françoise Shenfield and others, (2003) 'Taskforce 5: Preimplantation Genetic Diagnosis' 18 Human Reproduction 649

Family Law Council of Australia, *Creating Children: A Uniform Approach to the Law and Practice of Reproductive Technology in Australia* (AGPS 1985)

Feinberg J, *Social Philosphy* (Prentice-Hall 1973)

——, *The Moral Limits of the Criminal Law: Harm to Others*, vol 1 (OUP 1984)

——, *The Moral Limits of the Criminal Law: Offense to Others*, vol 2 (Oxford University Press 1984)

——, 'Wrongful Life and the Counterfactual Element in Harming' (1987) 4 Social Philosophy and Policy

——, *The Moral Limits of the Criminal Law: Harm to Self*, vol 3 (Oxford University Press 1989)

——, *The Moral Limits of the Criminal Law: Harmless Wrongdoing*, vol 4 (Oxford University Press 1990)

Fenton RA, 'Catholic Doctrine versus Women's Rights: The New Italian Law on Assisted Reproduction' (2006) 14 Medical Law Review 73

Fenton RA and Dabell F, 'Time for change (1)' (2007) 157 New Law Journal 848

Fox M, 'The Human Fertilisation and Embryology Act 2008: Tinkering at the Margins' (2009) 17 Feminist Legal Studies 333

Gavaghan C, 'Deregulating the Genetic Supermarket: Preimplantation Screening, Future People, and the Harm Principle' (2000) 9 Cambridge Quarterly of Healthcare Ethics 244

——, 'Designing Donors? Tissue-Typing and the Regulation of Pre-Implantation Genetic Diagnosis' (2004) 3 Web Journal of Current Legal Issues 11

——, *Defending the Genetic Supermarket: The Law and Ethics of Selecting the Next Generation* (Routledge-Cavendish 2007)

Gillon R, 'Is There a "New Ethics of Abortion"?' (2001) 27 Journal of Medical Ethics ii5

Glover J, *Choosing Children: Genes, Disability and Design* (OUP 2006)

Gray J, *Mill on Liberty: A Defence* (2nd edn, Routledge 1996)

Gray J (ed) *John Stuart Mill, On Liberty and Other Essays* (OUP 1991)

Grundell E, 'Tissue Typing for Bone Marrow Transplantation: An Ethical Examination of Some Arguments Concerning Harm to the Child' (2003) 22 Monash Bioethics Review 45

Harris J, *Wonderwoman and Superman: The Ethics of Human Biotechnology* (OUP 1992)

——, 'The Welfare of the Child' (2000) 8 Health Care Analysis 33

——, 'Reproductive Liberty, Disease and Disability ' (2005) 10 Reproductive BioMedicine Online 13

Hart H, *Law, Liberty and Morality* (Stanford University Press 1963)

Holtug N, 'The Harm Principle' (2002) 5 Ethical Theory and Moral Practice 357

House of Commons Science and Technology Committee, *Human Reproductive Technologies and the Law* (2005)

Human Fertilisation and Embryology Authority, *Sex Selection: Options for Regulation* (HFEA 2003)

——, *Tomorrow's Children, Report of the Policy Review of the Welfare of the Child Assessments in Licensed Assisted Conception Clinics* (HFEA 2005)

Human Genome Research Project, *Choosing Genes for Future Children: The Regulatory Implications of Preimplantation Genetic Diagnosis* (Dunedin 2006)

Jackson E, *Regulating Reproduction: Law, Technology and Autonomy* (Hart Publishing 2001)

——, 'Conception and the Irrelevance of the Welfare Principle ' (2002) 177 Modern Law Review

——, *Medical Law: Text, Cases and Materials* (OUP 2006)

——, *Medical Law: Text, Cases and Materials* (3rd edn, OUP 2013)

Kerridge I, Lowe M and Stewart C, *Ethics and Law for the Health Professions* (4th edn, The Federation Press 2013)

King D, 'Preimplantation Genetic Diagnosis and the "New" Eugenics' (1999) 25 Journal of Medical Ethics 176

Knight C and Smith M, 'Editorial: The Human Fertilisation and Embryology Act 2008' (2013) 32 New Genetics and Society 107

Laing JA and Oderberg DS, 'Artificial Reproduction, the "Welfare Principle" and the Common Good' (2005) 13 Medical Law Review 328

Lloyd D and Freeman MDA, *Lloyd's Introduction to Jurisprudence* (5th edn, Stevens & Sons 1990)

Ludlow K, 'What About me? How Far Do We Go in the Interests of the Child in Assisted Reproductive Technology?' (2006) 6 Queensland University of Technology Law and Justice Journal 214

MacLeod KD and others, 'Pediatric Sibling Donors of Successful and Unsuccessful Hematopoietic Stem Cell Transplants (HSCT): A Qualitative Study of Their Psychosocial Experience' (2003) 28 Journal of Pediatric Psychology 223

Madanamoothoo A, 'Saviour Siblings and the Psychological, Ethical and Judicial Issues that It Creates: Should English and French Legislators Close the Pandora's Box?' (2011) 18 European Journal of Health Law 293

Mason JK and Laurie GT, *Mason & McCall Smith's Law and Medical Ethics* (8th edn, OUP 2011)

McCandless J, 'Cinderella and Her Cruel Sisters: Parenthood, Welfare and Gender in the Human Fertilisation and Embryology Act 2008' (2013) 32 New Genetics and Society 135

McDougall R, 'Acting Parentally: An Argument against Sex Selection' (2005) 31 Journal of Medical Ethics 601

McGee GE, Brakman SV and Gurmankin AD, 'Gamete Donation and Anonymity: Disclosure to Children Conceived with Donor Gametes Should Not be Optional' (2001) 16 Human Reproduction 2033

McLean S, *Modern Dilemmas: Choosing Children* (Capercaillie Books 2006)

McLean S, '"The Fertilising Conflict of Individualities": HG Well's *A Modern Utopia*, John Stuart Mill's *On Liberty* and the Victorian Tradition of Liberalism' in *Papers on Language and Literatutre* (Southern Illinois University 2007)

Moore MS, 'Causation and Responsibility' (1999) 16 Social Philosophy and Policy 1

Morreim EH, 'The Concept of Harm Reconceived: A Different Look at Wrongful Life' (1988) 7 Law and Philosophy 3

Morrison N and Devereux J, 'Child Saviours: Reconceiving the Ethical Dimension' (2014) 22 Tort Law Review 3

——, 'Child Saviours: Reconceiving the Legal Dimension' (2014) 22 Tort Law Review 9

Nelson E, *Law, Policy and Reproductive Autonomy* (Hart Publishing 2013)

Nys T, 'The Tacit of Competence in J. S. Mill's *On Liberty* ' (2006) 25 South African Journal of Philosophy 313

Packman W and others, 'Psychological Effects of Hematopoietic SCT on Pediatric Patients, Siblings and Parents: A Review' (2010) 45 Bone Marrow Transplantation 1134

Parfit D, *Reasons and Persons* (OUP 1984)

Patrizio P and others, 'High Rate of Biological Loss in Assisted Reproduction: It is in the Seed, Not in the Soil' (2007) 14 Reproductive BioMedicine Online 92

Petersen K, 'The Regulation of Assisted Reproductive Technology: A Comparative Study of Permissive and Prescriptive Laws and Policies' (2002) 9 Journal of Law and Medicine 483

Petersen K and Johnson MH, 'SmARTest Regulation? Comparing the Regulatory Structures for ART in the UK and Australia' (2007) 15 Reproductive BioMedicine Online 236

Picoult J, *My Sister's Keeper* (Allen & Unwin 2005)

Pillay B and others, 'The Psychosocial Impact of Hematopoietic SCT on Sibling Donors' (2012) 47 Bone Marrow Transplantation 1361

Porter G and Smith M, 'Preventing the Selection of "Deaf Embryos" under the Human Fertilisation and Embryology Act 2008: Problematizing Disability?' (2013) 32 New Genetics and Society 171

Priaulx N, 'Rethinking Progenitive Conflict: Why Reproductive Autonomy Matters' (2008) 16 Medical Law Review 169

Ram NR, 'Britain's New Preimplantation Tissue Typing Policy: An Ethical Defence' (2006) 32 Journal of Medical Ethics 279

Report of the Joint Committee of the House of Lords and House of Commons on the Human Tissue and Embryos (Draft) Bill, 2007: Vol I: Report (Session 2006–2007, HL Paper 169-I, HC Paper 630-II)

Resnick D, 'The Moral Significance of the Therapy-Enhancement Distinction in Human Genetics' (2000) 9 Cambridge Quarterly of Healthcare Ethics 365

Riley J, *Mill on Liberty* (Routledge 1998)

Ringen S, 'Liberty, Freedom and Real Freedom' (2005) 42 Society 36

Roberts M and Wasserman DT (eds), *Harming Future Persons: Ethics, Genetics and the Non-Identity Problem* (Springer 2009)

Robertson JA, 'Procreative Liberty and the Control of Conception, Pregnancy and Childbirth' (1983) 69 Virginia Law Review 76

——, *Children of Choice: Freedom and the New Reproductive Technologies* (Princeton University Press 1994)

Ryan A, *The Philosophy of John Stuart Mill* (2nd edn, Palgrave Macmillan 1987)

Sampino S and others, 'Effects of Blastomere Biopsy on Post-natal Growth and Behaviour in Mice' (2014) 29 Human Reproduction 1875

Sandel M, *The Case against Perfection: Ethics in the Age of Genetic Engineering* (Belknap Press 2007)

Savulescu J, 'Procreative Beneficence: Why We Should Select the Best Children' (2001) 15 Bioethics 413

SACRT, 'Eligibility for Assisted Reproductive Technology' Memorandum 1, reported in South Australian Council on Reproductive Technology, *Annual Report* (2004) 21).Scott R, 'Choosing between Possible Lives: Legal and Ethical Issues in Preimplantation Genetic Diagnosis' (2006) 26 Oxford Journal of Legal Studies 153

Scott KL, Long KH and Scott RT, 'Selecting the Optimal Time to Perform Biopsy for Preimplantation Genetic Testing' (2013) 100 Fertility and Sterility 608

Sheldon S and Wilkinson S, 'Hashmi and Whitaker: An Unjustifiable and Misguided Distinction?' (2004) 12 Medical Law Review 137

——, 'Should Selecting Saviour Siblings be Banned?' (2004) 30 Journal of Medical Ethics 535

Shiffrin SV, 'Wrongful Life, Procreative Responsibility, and the Significance of Harm' (1999) 5 Legal Theory 117

Skene L and Thomson J (eds), *The Sorting Society: The Ethics of Genetic Screening and Therapy* (CUP 2008)

Smajdor A, 'How Useful is the Concept of the "Harm Threshold" in Reproductive Ethics and Law?' (2014) 35 Theoretical Medicine and Bioethics 321

Smith MK, 'Reviewing Regulation of Assisted Reproductive Technology in New South Wales: The Assisted Reproductive Technology Act 2007 (NSW)' (2008) 16 Journal of Law and Medicine 120

——, 'Regulating Assisted Reproductive Technologies in Victoria: The Impact of Changing Policy Concerning the Accessibility of In Vitro Fertilisation for Preimplantation Tissue-typing' (2012) 19 Journal of Law and Medicine 820

——, 'The Human Fertilisation and Embryology Act 2008: Restrictions on the Creation of "Saviour Siblings" and the Relevance of the Harm Principle' (2013) 32 New Genetics and Society 154

Smith SD, 'Is the Harm Principle Illiberal?' (2006) 51 The American Journal of Jurisprudence 1

Snelling J, 'Embryonic HLA Tissue Typing and Made-to-Match Siblings: The New Zealand Position' (2008) 9 Medical Law International 13

Spriggs M, 'Commodification of Children Again and Non-disclosure Preimplantation Genetic Diagnosis for Huntington's Disease' (2004) 30 Journal of Medical Ethics 538

Stewart H, 'Harms, Wrongs, and Set-Backs in Feinberg's *Moral Limits of the Criminal Law*' (2001) 5 Buffalo Criminal Law Review 49

Strong C, 'Harming by Conceiving: A review of Misconceptions and a New Analysis' (2005) 30 Journal of Medicine and Philosophy 491

Strong KA and others, 'It's Time to Reframe the Saviour Sibling Debate' (2011) 2 AJOB Primary Research 13

Taylor-Sands M, 'Selecting "Saviour Siblings": Reconsidering the Regulation in Australia of Pre-implantation Genetic Diagnosis in Conjunction with Tissue-typing' (2007) 14 Journal of Law and Medicine 551

——, *Saviour Siblings: A Relational Approach to the Welfare of the Child in Selective Reproduction* (Routledge 2013)

Ten CL, *Mill on Liberty* (Clarendon Press 1980)

Then S-N, 'The Legality of Tissue Transplants for the Benefit of Family Members in the UK and Australia: Implications for Saviour Siblings' (2009) 10 Medical Law International 23

Thorpe R and others, 'In the Best Interests of the Child? Regulating Assisted Reproductive Technologies and the Well-being of Offspring in Three Australian States' (2012) 26 International Journal of Law, Policy and the Family 259

Tsitas E, 'The Role of the Creative Arts in Bioethical Debates' (2006) 6 Queensland University of Technology Law and Justice Journal 255

Verlinsky Y and others, 'Over a Decade of Experience With Preimplantation Genetic Diagnosis: a Multicenter Report' (2004) 82 Fertility and Sterility 292

Victorian Law Reform Commission, *Assisted Reproductive Technology & Adoption: Final Report* (2007)

Warburton N, *Philosophy: The Classics* (3rd edn, Routledge 2006)

Warnock M, *Report of the Committee of Inquiry into Human Fertilisation and Embryology* (The Warnock Report, 1984)

——, *Making Babies: Is There a Right to Have Children?* (OUP 2002)

Warren MA, 'On the Moral and Legal Status of Abortion' (1973) 57 The Monist 43

Wert Gd, 'Preimplantation Genetic Diagnosis: The Ethics of Intermediate Cases' (2005) 20 Human Reproduction 3263

Wilkinson S, *Choosing Tomorrow's Children: The Ethics of Selective Reproduction* (OUP 2010)

Williams NJ and Harris J, 'What is the Harm in Harmful Conception? On Threshold Harms in Non-Identity Cases' (2014) 35 Theoretical Medicine and Bioethics 337

Wolf S, Kahn J and Wagner J, 'Using Preimplantation Genetic Diagnosis to Create a Stem Cell Donor: Issues, Guidelines & Limits' (2003) 31 Journal of Law, Medicine & Ethics 327

Woolley SL, 'The Limits of Parental Responsibility Regarding Medical Treatment Decisions' (2011) 96 Archives of Disease in Childhood 1060

United Kingdom, *Government Response to the Report from the Joint Committee on the Human Tissue and Embryos (Draft) Bill* (Cm 7209 2007)

## Book Chapters

Bennett B and Smith M, 'Assisted Reproductive Technology' in White B, McDonald F and Willmott L (eds), *Health Law in Australia* (2nd edn, Thomson Reuters 2014)

Berlin I, 'John Stuart Mill and the Ends of Life' in Gray J and Smith GW (eds), *J S Mill On Liberty in Focus* (Routledge 1991)

Brazier M, 'Reproductive Rights: Feminism or Patriarchy' in Harris J and Holm S (eds), *The Future of Human Reproduction: Ethics, Choice and Regulation* (OUP 1998)

Dworkin G, 'Challenges to Self-Determination: Paternalism' in Feinberg J and Coleman J (eds), *Philosophy of Law* (6th edn, Wadsworth 2000)

Feinberg J, 'The Child's Right to an Open Future' in Aiken W and LaFollette H (eds), *Whose Child? Children's Rights, Parental Authority, and State Power* (Rowman and Littlefield 1980)

Gray J, 'Mill's Conception of Happiness and the Theory of Individuality ' in Gray J and Smith GW (eds), *J S Mill On Liberty in Focus* (Routledge 1991)

Jackson E, 'Rethinking the Pre-conception Welfare Principle' in Horsey K and Biggs H (eds), *Human Fertilisation and Embryology: Reproducing Regulation* (Routledge Cavendish 2007)

Kant I, 'Fundamental Principles of the Metaphysic of Morals' in Wood AW (ed), *Basic Writings of Kant* (The Modern Library 2001)

Petersen K, 'Genetic Technologies and ART: Ethical Values, Legal Regulation and Informal Regulation' in Freckelton I and Petersen K (eds), *Disputes and Dilemmas in Health Law* (Federation Press 2006)

Riley L, 'Equality of Access to NHS-Funded IVF treatment in England and Wales' in Horsey K and Biggs H (eds), *Human Fertilisation and Enbryology: Reproducing Regulation* (Routledge-Cavendish 2007)

Ryan A, 'John Stuart Mill's Art of Living' in Gray J and Smith GW (eds), *J S Mill On Liberty in Focus* (Routledge 1991)

Szoke H, 'Australia – A Federated Structure of Statutory Regulation of ART' in Gunning J and Szoke H (eds), *The Regulation of Assisted Reproductive Technology* (Ashgate 2003)

Szoke H, Neame L and Johnson L, 'Old Technologies and New Challenges: Assisted Reproduction and its Regulation' in Freckelton I and Petersen K (eds), *Disputes and Dilemmas in Health Law* (Federation Press 2006)

## Cases

*Australia*

*ABY & ABZ v Patient Review Panel (Health & Privacy)* [2011] VCAT 1382

*ABY & ABZ v Secretary to the Department of Health (Human Rights)* [2013] VCAT 625

*Department of Health and Community Services (NT) v JWB (Marion's case)* (1992) 175 CLR 218

*Harriton v Stephens* (2006) 226 CLR 52

*In the Marriage of GWW and CMW* (1997) 136 FLR 421

*JM v QFG & GK* [2000] 1 Qd R 373

*McBain v The State of Victoria* [2000] FCA 1009

*Morgan v GK* [2001] QADT 10

*Patient Review Panel v ABY & ABZ* [2012] VSCA 264

*Pearce v South Australian Health Commission* (1996) 66 SASR 486

*PQ v Patient Review Panel (Health & Privacy)* [2012] VCAT 291

*Re Inaya (Special Medical Procedure)* [2007] FamCA 658

*Rogers v Whitaker* (1992) 175 CLR 479

*Rosenberg v Percival* (2001) 205 CLR 434


Europe

Cases C-6/90 and C-9/90 *Francovich and Bonafaci v Italy* [1992] IRLR 84

*Evans v United Kingdom* (European Court of Human Rights, Grand Chamber, Application No 6339/05, 10 April 2007)

*Francovich v Republic of Italy* [1995] ICR 722 ECJ Cases C-6 and 9/90

ICR 722 ECJ Cases C-6 and 9/90


UK

*Evans v Amicus Healthcare* [2003] EWHC 2161

*Leeds Teaching Hospitals NHS trust v A and others* [2003] EWHC 259 (QB)

*Montgomery v Lanarkshire Health Board* [2015] UKSC 11

*Pearce v United Bristol Healthcare NHS Trust* [1999] 48 BMLR 118

*R v Human Fertilisation and Embryology Authority ex parte Blood* [1999] Fam. 151

*R (on the application of Assisted Reproduction and Gynaecology Centre) v Human Fertilisation and Embryology Authority* [2002] EWCA Civ 20

*R (on the application of Quintavalle) v Human Fertilisation and Embryology Authority* [2005] 2 All ER 555

*R (on the application of Rose) v Secretary of State for Health and the HFEA* [2002] EWHC 1593 (Admin)

*R v Secretary of State for Health, ex parte Bruno Quintavalle (on behalf of Pro-Life Alliance)* [2001] EWHC Admin 918

*Sidaway v Board of Governers of the Bethlem Royal Hospital and the Maudsley Hospital* [1985] AC 871

## Legislation

*Australia*

Acts Amendment (Prohibition of Human cloning and Other Practices) Act 2004 (WA)

Anti-Discrimination Act 1991 (Qld)Assisted Reproductive Treatment Act 1988 (SA)

Assisted Reproductive Technology Act 2007 (NSW)

Assisted Reproductive Treatment Act 2008 (Vic)

Civil Liability Act 2002 (Tas)

Civil Liability Act 2003 (Qld)

Commonwealth of Australia Constitution Act

Family Law Act 1975 (Cth)

Family Relationships Act 1975 (SA)

Human Reproductive Technology Act 1991 (WA)

Human Reproductive Technology Amendment Act 2004 (WA)

Infertility Treatment Act 1995 (Vic)

National Health and Medical Research Council Act 1992 (Cth)

Parentage Act 2004 (ACT)

Prohibition of Human Cloning Act 2002 (Cth)

Prohibition of Human Cloning for Reproduction and the Regulation of Human Embryo Research Amendment Act 2006 (Cth)

Reproductive Technology (Clinical Practices) Act 1998 (SA)

Reproductive Technology (Clinical Practices) (Miscellaneous) Amendment Act 2009 (SA)

Research Involving Human Embryos Act 2002 (Cth)

Surrogacy Act 2008 (WA)

Surrogacy Act 2010 (NSW)

Surrogacy Act 2010 (Qld)

Surrogacy Act 2012 (Tas)

Transplantation and Anatomy Act 1979 (Qld)

*Western Australian Government Gazette, 30 November 2004* (201 edn, 2004)

Wrongs Act 1958 (Vic)

*Europe*

Council Directive 2004/23/EC of 31 March 2004 on setting standards of quality and safety for the donation, procurement, testing, processing, preservation, storage and distribution of human tissues and cells [2004] OJ L102/48

*UK*

Children Act 1989 (UK)
Human Fertilisation and Embryology Act 1990 (UK)
Human Fertilisation and Embryology Act 2008 (UK)
Human Rights Act 1998 (UK)


## Other Sources

*Reference*

*The Australian Oxford Paperback Dictionary* (4th edn, OUP 2006)
*Macquarie Concise Dictionary* (4th edn, Macquarie Library 2006)


*Australia*

*Code of practice/guidelines/schemes*
National Health and Medical Research Council, *Ethical Guidelines on Assisted Reproductive Technology* (NHMRC 1996)
——, 'Ethical Guidelines on the Use of Assisted Reproductive Technology in Clinical Practice and Research' (NHMRC 2007)
Reproductive Technology Accreditation Committee, *Code of Practice for Assisted Reproductive Technology Units 2005* (4th revision, Fertility Society of Australia 2005, February)
——, *Code of Practice for Assisted Reproductive Technology Units* (Fertility Society of Australia 2008, May)


*Legislative materials and government documents*
Australian Government, *Legislation Review: Prohibition of Human Cloning Act 2002 and the Research Involving Human Embryos Act 2002* (Lockhart Review 2005)
Chalmers D, *Committee to Investigate Artificial Conception and Related Matters* (Tasmania Parliament 1985)
Infertility Treatment Authority, *Tissue Typing in Conjunction with the Preimplantation Genetic Diagnosis: Interim Guidelines* (Victoria Parliament 2007)
——, *Conditions for Licence: Clinics, Hospitals and Day Procedure Centres* (8th edn, Victoria Parliament 2008)
——, *Genetic Testing and the Requirements of the Infertility Treatment Act 1995: Policy in Relation to the Use of Pre-implantation Genetic Diagnosis (PGD)* (Victoria Parliament 2008)

New South Wales, Legislative Council, *Parliamentary Debates* 27 November 2007, 4382 (Tony Kelly)

——, Legislative Assembly, *Parliamentary Debates* 7 November 2007, 1 (Reba Meagher)

New South Wales Law Reform Commission, *Artificial Conception – Surrogate Motherhood* (1985)

——, *Artificial Conception – Human Artificial Insemination* (1986)

——, *Artificial Conception – In Vitro Fertilisation* (1988)

Victoria, Legislative Assembly, Legislative Assembly, *Parliamentary Debates* 10 September 2008, 3442 (Rob Hulls)

——, Legislative Assembly, *Parliamentary Debates* 7 October 2008, 3759 (Robert William Clark)

——,Legislative Assembly, *Parliamentary Debates* 7 October 2008, 3783 (David Morris)

Parliament of Western Australia Legislative Assembly, *Select Committee on the Human Reproductive Technology Act 1991* (1999)

Reproductive Technology Council, *Western Australia's Human Reproductive Technology Act 1991 and Human Reproductive Technology Amendment Act 1996: Summary (April 1996)* (1996)

——, *Acts Amendment (Lesbian and Gay Law Reform) Act 2002 – Amendment of the Human Reproductive Technology Act 1991 and the Artificial Conception Act 1985* (2002)

——, *Approval for Diagnostic Testing of Embryos: Advice to Clinics* (2004)

South Australian Council on Reproductive Technology, (Regulations under the Reproductive Technology Act 1988 – Reproductive Technology (Code of Ethical Clinical Practice) 1995, reg 11(1))

——, *Eligibility for Assisted Reproductive Technology* (Memorandum 1, 2004)

Victorian Assisted Reproductive Treatment Authority, *Conditions for Use of Tissue Typing in Conjunction with Preimplantation Genetic Diagnosis (PGD)* (Victoria Parliament 2010)

## Presentations

Kirby M, 'The Fundamental Problem of Regulating Technology' (Conference on the Ethical Governance of Information & Communications Technology and the Role of Professional Bodies, Australian National University, 1 May 2008) <http://www.hcourt.gov.au/assets/publications/speeches/former-justices/kirbyj/kirbyj_1may08.pdf> accessed 25 November 2014

## Written correspondence

Email from Tracey Petrillo (Senior Policy and Education Officer, Victorian Assisted Reproductive Treatment Authority) to Malcolm Smith, February 2011

## UK

### Code of practice/guidelines/schemes

Human Fertilisation and Embryology Authority, *Code of Practice* (8th edn, HFEA 2009)

Human Tissue Authority, *Code of Practice 6: Donation of Allogeneic Bone Marrow and Peripheral Blood Stem Cells for Transplantation* (2014)

### Legislative materials and government documents

Department of Health (NSW), *Review of the Human Tissue Act 1983* (1997)

——, *Consultation Draft, Assisted Reproductive Technology Bill 2003, Information Guide* (2003)

——, *Assisted Reproductive Technology Act 2007: Statutory Review* (2013)

Department of Health (UK), *Review of the Human Fertilisation and Embryology Act* (2005)

——, *Human Tissue and Embryos (Draft) Bill (2007)* (2007)

Ethics Committee of the Human Fertilisation and Embryology Authority, *Ethical Issues in the Creation and Selection of Preimplantation Embryos to Produce Tissue Donors* (2001)

United Kingdom, House of Lords, *Parliamentary Debates* 10 December 2007

——, House of Lords, *Parliamentary Debates* 19 November 2007

——, House of Lords, *Parliamentary Debates* 19 November 2007

——, House of Lords, *Parliamentary Debates* 21 January 2008

——, New South Wales Department of Health, *Parliamentary Debates* 21 January 2008

### Consultation documents

Department of Health (UK), *Review of the Human Fertilisation and Embryology Act: A Public Consultation* (2005)

——, *Consultation on Proposals to Transfer Functions from the Human Fertilisation and Embryology Authority and the Human Tissue Authority*, Consultation Paper (June 2012)

### Theses

Szoke H, 'Social Regulation, Reproductive Technology and the Social Interest: Policy and Process in Pioneering Jurisdictions' (PhD thesis, University of Melbourne 2004)

### Websites

Cranage A, 'No Consensus on Where Human Life Begins' (*BioNews*, 2008) <http://www.bionews.org.uk/page_13559.asp> accessed 26 November 2014

Human Fertilisation and Embryology Authority, *HFEA to Allow Tissue Typing in Conjunction with Preimplantation Genetic Diagnosis* (2001) <http://www.hfea.gov.uk/961.html> accessed 10 August 2014

——, 'HFEA Confirms That HLA Tissue Typing May Only Take Place When PGD is Required to Avoid a Serious Genetic Disorder' (2002) <http://www.hfea.gov.uk/935.html> accessed 14 November 2014

——, *HFEA Agrees to Extend Policy on Tissue Typing* (2004) <http://www.hfea.gov.uk/763.html> accessed 10 August 2014

——, 'FAQ's on EU Standards' (*HFEA*, 2012) <http://www.hfea.gov.uk/fertility-clinic-questions-eu-standards.html> accessed 26 July 2014

MacKenna Roberts, 'UK Parliament Alarmed by 1.2 Million Leftover IVF embryos' (7 January 2008) <http://www.bionews.org.uk/page_13266.asp> accessed 26 November 2014

'MPs Reject "Saviour Sibling" Ban' *BBC News* (19 May 2008) <http://news.bbc.co.uk/2/hi/uk_news/politics/7409264.stm> accessed 26 November 2014

The Open University, 'The Right to Have Babies' (2008) <http://open2.net/ethicsbites/right-have-babies.html> accessed 31 August 2014

Wade N, 'Clinics Hold More Embryos than Had Been Thought' *New York Times* (9 May 2003)

# Index